PUNCHLINES

PUNCHLINES

The Case for Racial, Ethnic, and Gender Humor

Leon Rappoport

PRAEGER

Westport, Connecticut
London

Library of Congress Cataloging in Publication Data

Rappoport, Leon.
    Punchlines : the case for racial, ethnic, and gender humor / Leon Rappoport.
      p. cm.
    Includes bibliographical references and index.
    ISBN 0–275–98764–7 (alk. paper)
    1. Ethnic wit and humor—History and criticism.   2. Wit and humor—Social
aspects. I. Title.
    PN6149.E83R37   2005
    817.009'3552—dc22   2005019267

British Library Cataloguing in Publication Data is available.

Library of Congress Catalog Card Number: 2005019267

ISBN: 0–275–98764–7

First published in 2005

Praeger Publishers, 88 Post Road West, Westport, CT 06881
An imprint of Greenwood Publishing Group, Inc.
www.praeger.com

Printed in the United States of America

The paper used in this book complies with the
Permanent Paper Standard issued by the National
Information Standards Organization (Z39.48–1984).

10 9 8 7 6 5 4 3 2 1

To the comedians
who run all the risks of trying to be funny;
To the scholars of humor
who try to explain why it is so important;
and
to whoever sketched the face of a Zen monk
all aglow with pleasure as he exclaimed
"Oh joy! To know at last there is no perfect
happiness in this life."

Contents

Acknowledgments

The origins of this book go back to the time when Kansas State University introduced an undergraduate program of courses in American Ethnic Studies, and I decided to try teaching a class on the psychology of ethnic humor. It became very successful, attracting large numbers of students, and so my primary debt is to them; their enthusiastic participation showed me that one could open the Pandora's Box of racial, ethnic, and gender comedy, and not only get away clean, but also gain important perspectives on our remarkably diverse society. I am also grateful to my social science colleagues, some of whom were understandably dubious about the scholarly value of the topic yet were willing to trust me with it. There were others, however, such as the culture historians Joseph Amato and George Kren, the sociologist George Peters, and psychologists Ron Downey and David Summers, who provided immediate encouragement and helpful suggestions as this book began taking shape.

The International Society for Humor Studies and its publications have been an invaluable resource for my research and writing. Special thanks are therefore due to Don and Alleen Nilsen who founded the society, who have nurtured it for the past quarter century, and who themselves have contributed significant research on ethnic humor.

Finally, as can be seen in the following pages, although I have drawn upon the work of many other humor scholars and am duly grateful to all of them, it was mainly the pathbreaking writings of Christie Davies that first inscribed ethnic humor on my cognitive map.

Introduction: The Hazards and Joys of Racial, Ethnic, and Gender Humor

Humor based on racial, ethnic, and gender stereotypes has always been a touchy subject, particularly in our current era of political correctness when even hinting at it can be the kiss of death for any public figure. In colleges and universities, faculty tempted to crack wise at the expense of any national, religious, sexual, or handicapped group risk the loss of their jobs and reputations. As a social psychologist who was first attracted to the field in order to investigate the apparent irrationality of prejudice, I am fully aware of all the good reasons for our present sensitivity to such jokes. Some of my own research on attitudes and social conflict even might have contributed to this sensitivity.

On the other hand, at no time in the past have we ever had so much down-and-dirty racial and ethnic humor circulating throughout our society via films, TV comedy concerts, the Internet, and stand-up performers in comedy clubs. Even more prevalent are the softer forms on display in popular TV sitcoms, where the presence of one or more Jewish, black, Asian, Hispanic, or gay characters seems to have become mandatory. Although most of these sitcom characters are presented in a sympathetic fashion—perhaps a bit screwy but usually lovable—the humor they contribute is mainly based on how they either directly represent or contradict familiar stereotypes. So despite concerns about political correctness, it is no exaggeration to suggest that our society is awash in racial, ethnic, and gender humor as never before.

How did this happen? Is it, as so many ultraconservative commentators seem to enjoy suggesting, simply one more sign, along with sexual promiscuity, gay liberation parades, and low math scores in our public schools, that our society as a whole is going to hell? Or is the increasing prevalence of such humor a reaction against our efforts to achieve a politically correct, multi-

Tie into biological article *Comedic stereotype* *ethnic Humor*

cultural environment? Sigmund Freud would not be surprised by such a reaction. His main thesis in *Civilization and Its Discontents* was that the more
we try to repress our primitive impulses, the more likely they are to break out
in unexpected ways. Freud's theory of personality relates directly to the childish pleasure many of us get from dirty jokes and insulting comedy routines.
But the explanations suggested in this book would not satisfy either conser-
vatives like Rush Limbaugh or theorists like Sigmund Freud. Although my
perspective is closer to that of Freud, it draws a good deal from the work of
the philosophers who at least since Plato and Aristotle have been struggling
to figure out what makes a good joke and why we laugh. It appeals almost as
much to sociology, history, and anthropology as to psychology. This ecu-
menical approach probably follows from the fact that I fell into work on
stereotype humor by accident.

is that the politically correct term?

Unlike some scholars who have spent their careers studying humor, I
enjoy it but do not have a deep passion for it. In fact, it has been my impression—with apologies to Kingsley Amis who first turned the phrase—that inside many humor scholars there is a stand-up comedian struggling to get out.
I am not one of them. I generally do not remember many jokes and hardly
ever tell any, and when I do tell them I usually mess up the punch lines (which
I personally find quite amusing). So how did I come to write this book?

It began when the faculty at my university decided to offer a set of
classes under the heading of American Ethnic Studies. My part in this was
due to the prominence of social psychology in research on prejudice, and, to
the consternation of some of my colleagues, I volunteered to develop a course
on ethnic humor. My first class included a diverse group of mainstream
whites, several Hispanics, African Americans, and I believe a few Jews and gays
(they did not say and I did not ask). They all seemed to enjoy exploring the
origins and psychology of humor, particularly when discussion focused on
classic stand-up comedy videos by Richard Pryor, Robin Williams, Whoopi
Goldberg, and several others. While the assortment of stereotypes, slurs, and
obscenities in these videos provided momentary *frissons* for the students, the
material also had a surprising didactic value. A good deal of serious social
psychology can be piggy-backed onto the analysis of dirty words.

or ... vly is

I learned that most people can appreciate the universality of disparaging humor—that it is found in all human groups—as well as the creativity of
those who produce and perform it. To see the likes of Richard Pryor, Billy
Crystal, or George Carlin singlehandedly confront and master diverse audiences with routines ridiculing many of their values and attitudes is to see the
power of art in action. Like all successful art, such humor allows us to suspend or rise above reality. This is no small thing, since social and emotional
group differences are largely unmentionable, locked out of polite society.

Humor opens them up. There is an undeniable sense of relief associated with our reflexive delight in a good joke or parody that skewers some of our conceits or prejudices, including "correct" liberal ideals. Such humor frees us, however momentarily, from the weight of our efforts to be properly respectable and good. It gives us license to be spontaneously bad, to violate the rules of conventional morality.

This, in a way, is like the feeling of joyous abandon one may have when jumping fully clothed into a mud bath. Call it the "joy of transgression," yet combined with a more subtle joy of transcendence. If we can suspend reality in order to enjoy the guilt-free fantasy worlds of a Harry Potter or Peter Pan, we are already prepared to enter the comedic world where Jackie Mason can make us laugh by describing the differences between Jews and gentiles, George Carlin can ridicule the American military for its apparent tradition of bombing "brown people," or Chris Rock can blame Hillary Clinton for not offering to perform her husband's preferred sexual acts. Like Pan, the comedians are not just inviting us to transgress the conventional boundaries of reality, good taste, patriotism, and so forth; they are also inviting us to join them in a cognitive playground where anything goes.

The important point, however, is that they are not inviting us to *abandon* our moral values, only to rise above them for a moment, take a breather from being good and from the serious work of trying to make a better world. We are not talking here of decadent Roman orgies. Rather, there seems to be nothing wrong with playing in the muddy pools of human folly for a little while—mud baths, after all, can have medicinal properties—as long as we can rinse off before going back to work. Indeed, we may then even carry our burden of goodness a little more lightly, and with the broader perspective that can follow from having had a good laugh at our sacred cows.

I thought this was a rather original, bold way of speaking in defense of racial, ethnic, and gender humor until I discovered that the philosopher Erasmus had preceded me by about five centuries. His sixteenth-century book *In Praise of Folly* essentially makes the same general argument: that in many ways, impulsive, foolish, irresponsible thoughts and behaviors are what make the practical realities of life bearable.

Although much of this book discusses the nature of stereotype humor and provides quite a few examples, it is not all simply focused on jokes and their implications. An important general theme is that in contemporary American society, such humor is well on its way to being transformed from an expression of prejudice to an assertion of pride. No viewer of popular films or TV sitcoms can fail to see this concrete reality shown by countless "in your face" assertions of racial, ethnic, and gender identity that accompany routines ridiculing middle-aged white males, which is the only group that remains a safe, all-purpose target. There are several reasons why this has happened, but the primary psychological factor can be specified in one word: irony. This book will have achieved its major purpose if readers come to appreciate the insight that dawned on me only after years of immersion in the subject matter, namely, that prejudice has no greater enemy than irony and satire. It is this increasingly prevalent ironic worldview, much of it due to the influence of Jewish and African American comedians, that has shifted the weight of most racial, ethnic, and gender comedy in our society from prejudice toward pride. When held up to ridicule in the context of irony, slurs and stereotypes testify to the strength of those who defy them.

It may be helpful, too, for me to say something about how I intend to justify this sweeping claim in the following ten chapters. Although each chapter can be read as a stand-alone essay, all the chapters are arranged in a commonsense progression, starting in Chapter 1 with a general overview of the inherent ambiguities of stereotype humor and a discussion about why it should not simply be dismissed as a matter of prejudice. Because all humor trades on ambiguity, Chapter 2 offers a summary walk through the various ways scholars and philosophers from the classical Greeks to the present have been trying to understand the mechanics of comedy and why we laugh. Chapter 3 reviews modern social science theories and research findings about racial, ethnic, and gender humor, emphasizing its surprisingly wide range of uses within minority groups. Chapter 4 examines the origins and implications of the stereotypes, slurs, and obscenities that serve as fundamental components of ethnic humor.

Citations of theory and research findings in these initial chapters occasionally make for some heavy conceptual lifting, but I have tried to lighten the load by including examples of relevant jokes. Be that as it may, this section of the text provides the foundation for discussions of contemporary stereotype humor, beginning in Chapter 5 with the remarkable story of how Jews and African Americans have moved from being the primary targets of ridicule to become the major creators of ironic humor in our society. Chapter 6 describes the historical development of Jewish and African American folk humor that ethnic comedians, especially Lenny Bruce and Richard Pryor, brought into the American mainstream. Gender humor, including the difficulties and breakthrough achievements by women comedians, gays, and lesbians, is taken up in Chapter 7. Further discussion in Chapter 8 focuses on how stand-up comedians have detoxified much of racial and ethnic humor today by showing that exaggerated stereotypes can be funny, even to groups being ridiculed. Chapter 9 is devoted to the childhood experiences, developmental trajectories, and hardships faced by professional comedians as they master their art. Chapter 10 concludes the book by summarizing the research evidence and philosophical arguments supporting the funny-serious benefits of racial, ethnic, and gender humor in our diverse society. Throughout all of this book, I have tried to give readers a fair measure of entertainment by salting the narrative with a mixed bag of illustrative jokes and comedy lines. I am sure that at least some of them are pretty good, because I have been able to shock a few of my politically correct colleagues into gales of laughter.

haha.

1

The Sword and Shield Metaphor and Other Perspectives

At its best, humor simultaneously hurts and heals, makes one larger from a willingness to make oneself less.

—*Louis Kronenberger*

The sword and shield metaphor has been used by more than one writer on stereotype humor because people typically think of stereotype humor as a weapon designed to ridicule and insult minority groups. All too often this has been true, but it is also true that such humor can be a shield serving the interests of minority groups. Most of us, scholars included, are not aware of this. Lois Leveen, for example, claimed that when doing research for an article on multiethnic literature, it came to her as a "shocking discovery" that jokes may be an effective way for people to demonstrate pride in their group identity. In short, depending on its context, such humor can be offensive, aimed at ridicule of a stereotyped group; defensive, aimed at protecting the group from ridicule; or both. Consider this not-very-funny joke: "Why are Jews not concerned about the abortion controversy? Because they don't consider a fetus to be viable until after it graduates from medical or dental school." If the teller and the audience are gentiles, it could be taken as anti-Semitic, a criticism of Jews for their arrogance and excessive ambition. But if the teller and audience are Jewish, it could be taken as an amusing expression of Jewish pride in the high standards they set for their children.

Lois Leveen cites another relevant joke concerning the civil rights struggle of the 1960s, when African Americans in the South were prevented from voting because registration required them to pass a difficult literacy test. After a highly educated black man manages to satisfy all the requirements, the registrars come up with an additional test. They show him the headline in a Chinese newspaper and ask if he can explain what it means. He immediately says, "Yes, it means niggers don't vote in Mississippi again this year." Leveen points out that blacks would see the joke as an ironic expression of pride and self-assertion in the face of oppression. Racist whites, on the other hand, might see the joke as demonstrating how an uppity Negro could be put in his place.

The ambiguity here illustrates a fundamental perspective on humor that will show up throughout this text: depending on their context, jokes and comedy routines involving minorities can have different meanings at different times for different audiences. At the negative extreme, they may be taken as expressions of prejudice encouraging people to accept dehumanizing stereotypes. Yet in contemporary society, one is equally or more likely to encounter various forms of humor that ridicule abusive stereotypes. As will be shown in later chapters, most if not all minority groups also enjoy a great deal of protective self-critical humor, as well as jokes aimed at the mainstream majority. Furthermore, and to make matters more complex, such humor is not restricted to minority versus majority situations; it is also frequently seen in majority versus majority cases. So males tell disparaging jokes about females and vice versa, Europeans about Americans, rural people about city people, soldiers about sailors, and so on. The study of stereotype humor, therefore, is not merely about jokes targeting minorities, or minorities responding with jokes of their own about majorities. It extends to the ridicule humor aimed at different national, regional, cultural, and occupational or professional groups—think of all the lawyer jokes—and has a great deal to do with the ways people in these groups adapt to their environments, cope with stress, and seek to define themselves by derogating others.

But while the majority of humor scholars and comedians tend to agree with the sword and shield perspective, many well-intentioned people believe that the shield is a false rationalization. Their commonsense view is that whatever benefits may be associated with disparaging humor are outweighed by the suffering it imposes on targeted minorities. This was clearly true in the nineteenth century, and a good part of the twentieth as well, when virtually all immigrants, Jews, African Americans, and Native Americans, suffered from serious discrimination and even violent prejudice. But is it true today, and is it possible to prove one way or the other? A reflection of the potential for violence in ethnic humor is clear in the old joke about a southern sheriff who interrupts a mob about to lynch a black man: "Stop! We are a civilized community. Let's give this boy a fair trial before we lynch him." Although it is meant to ridicule prejudice in the Old South, it is surely not very funny to African Americans, and might even be cynically amusing to white racists. The same issue comes up in a joke relevant to the Holocaust: "How do you fit a hundred Jews into a Volkswagon? Four go in the seats, one in the trunk, and ninety-five in the ashtray." It is not very funny for Jews to be reminded of the Nazi death camps or for Germans who regret the Nazi period, but it might well be amusing to anti-Semites.

A more elaborate example of the problem here is what may be called the "Archie Bunker Question." When humor is used in a context of parody designed to show that stereotypes about minorities are essentially narrow minded and stupid, does it really reduce prejudice, or does it make prejudice seem more acceptable? There is no clear answer to this question. As the central character in a popular TV show of the 1970s, *All in the Family*, Archie was shown expressing all of the stereotypes about the groups he called "hebes," "jungle bunnies," "spics," and "gooks." At the time, audience reaction surveys indicated that people got the point, since most viewers said they enjoyed the humor and saw Archie so far removed from mainstream attitudes as to be a relatively harmless fool. Some critics suggested, however, that people would simply not admit that they liked the show because it gave them a socially acceptable excuse to indulge their prejudices about minorities and immigrants, including the liberal Democrats that Archie complained were supporting them. Worse yet, according to these critics, by simply dismissing Archie as an entertaining fool, viewers were ignoring the serious implications of his prejudices. Other commentators defended the show, pointing out that it always portrayed minority characters in a very positive way and that Archie himself was shown to be a social "loser," clinging to insulting stereotypes in order to prop up his ego. Arguments about the show were never settled one way or the other. In retrospect, the popularity of the show and others of the same type that soon followed with black characters who ridiculed whites might best be understood as demonstrating that people enjoy the forbidden pleasures of ethnic comedy even if they are not willing to admit it. Of course if this is true, then we have all the more reason to study the problem.

Unfortunately, study of such humor is difficult because of its ambiguity. Humor and ethnicity are each in themselves fairly slippery concepts. Dictionary definitions are no help. They describe humor as either (1) "that quality in a happening, an action, a situation, or an expression of ideas which appeals to a sense of the ludicrous or absurdly incongruous," or (2) "the mental faculty for discovering, expressing or appreciating ludicrous or absurdly incongruous elements in ideas, situations, happenings, or acts." These formal definitions clearly leave plenty of room for interpretation: is the humor out there, in the happenings and situations we observe? Is it something we ourselves create and impose on situations out there? Or is it some combination of both the situation and the observer? About the only thing we know for sure is that common experience, as well as some of the formal theories to be discussed later, support all of these interpretations.

The difficulty of settling on any straightforward definition of humor seems pale, however, compared with finding a straightforward meaning for ethnicity and race. One common dictionary entry is: "Having or originating from racial, linguistic and cultural ties with a specific group." But since many of us, especially in North America, have racial, linguistic, or cultural ties with two or more groups, this is not very helpful. Another, more elaborate entry suffers from the same ambiguity when it describes ethnicity as "relating to the community of physical and mental traits possessed by the members of a group as a product of their common heredity and cultural tradition." In this case, there is also a scientific problem, because we do not have any foolproof ways of identifying "the community of physical and mental traits possessed by the members of a group." When you look carefully at these entries, it would seem that one's ethnicity can be rooted almost anywhere in biology, culture, or psychology. True enough, perhaps, but obviously hard to pin down for practical purposes, so Irving Lewis Allen suggested a much handier definition of ethnicity in his 1983 book about ethnic slurs and stereotypes. Allen's one-line description specified an ethnic group as "any racial, religious, national origin or regional category of sub-culturally distinct persons." This has the virtue of getting us closer to the everyday, commonsense understanding of ethnicity, even if it leaves out people who do not appear to be "sub-culturally distinct." Some of the further uncertainties associated with the concept can easily be seen in the question of how a group should be named.

Groups have to be called something: Jew, Armenian, Native American, African American or Negro, or some other name, but it is not always clear who should be included under a given group name. Orthodox rabbis in Israel, for example, maintain that only individuals born to a Jewish mother can be considered Jewish, whereas reform rabbis accept anyone who converts regardless of their birth mother's background. If Jews convert to Christianity, are they still Jews? The Spanish Inquisition and the Nazis both ruled that they were, and carried out their persecutions accordingly, but imagine the dilemma of the Nazis who had to figure out a way to classify the children of converted Jews who had married gentiles. In the United States today, Native Americans are required to present complex legal documentation of their tribal lineage before they can receive official government recognition, and many Americans have mixed white, black, Native American, or Hispanic backgrounds that allow them to claim more than one type of ethnic identity. An interesting example involves recently discovered evidence showing that many Mexican Americans in New Mexico are descended from Spanish (Sephardic) Jews who had converted to Christianity and later migrated to Mexico in order to escape the Spanish Inquisition. It has also been estimated that a majority of African Americans have one or more white ancestors. The exemplary story here concerns Thomas Jefferson's relationship with his slave mistress Sally Hemmings. For more than a hundred years it was rumored that she bore him a child, and her descendants were accordingly entitled to claim a place in celebrations of Jefferson's historical heritage. The "legitimate" Jefferson heirs denied this until DNA analyses finally confirmed the Jefferson-Hemmings connection a few years ago.

Thus, it should be plain enough that simply at the level of what you may call yourself, let alone what others may call you, ethnicity can be quite problematic. It is said that Chaim Weizmann, the first president of the state of Israel, offered a simple solution: "Anyone who calls himself a Jew is a Jew." But this was not taken seriously, and the ambiguities associated with identity clearly remain a problem for others with more diverse historical backgrounds than the Jews.

The main point here is that when these two slippery concepts, ethnicity and humor, are combined, this only increases the ambiguity associated with each of them. Furthermore, when African Americans tell jokes about whites, and vice versa, we call it racial or ethnic humor; when African Americans tell each other jokes about other African Americans, we still call it racial or ethnic, but when whites tell each other jokes about whites, we do not call it ethnic unless the jokes involve stereotypes about particular white groups such as Jews, Poles, Italians, and so forth. The intrinsic difficulty of the whole affair is acknowledged by nearly all scholars of humor, and especially by professional comedians who must, of necessity, take humor very seriously, yet cover their uncertainties by—what else?—making jokes about it. This can be seen in a rare discussion of humor by five well-known comedians who appeared together at Harvard University in 1997. Hosted by Alan King and filmed for presentation on PBS as *The College of Comedy*, the show included Buddy Hackett, Tim Conway, Judy Gold, and Paul Rodriguez. Apart from their funny arguments about what makes something funny, which covered a broad variety of themes ranging from aggression to sex and simple incongruities, for the most part they skirted the issue of stereotype humor. When asked point blank about jokes concerning Hispanics, Rodriguez claimed that he was never offended so long as the joke was funny, and the others all agreed that anyone should be able to enjoy jokes about their own group in the spirit of good fun, without being offended, and if they cannot, then too bad for them. There was no consensus about the nature of racial or ethnic humor except for the implication that "you will know it when you see it."

The wonderful irony is that because humor—ethnic or otherwise—is so hard to pin down may be precisely why it has been a perennial challenge to scholars and philosophers. As far back as the ancient Greeks, there have been efforts to comprehend its meaning, including our persistent tendency to disparage and make up jokes at the expense of any group that does not share the same customs and values as ourselves. The earliest documented comedy by Aristophanes dates back to about 430 B.C.E. In at least one of his plays, *The Clouds*, Aristophanes created a thinly disguised parody of Socrates, the philosopher whose teachings ridiculed the conventional wisdom in his community.

Aristotle offered a more abstract view of humor, asserting that we are moved to laughter when we encounter any creature, human or otherwise, that appears malformed or acts in a deranged fashion. This idea seems confirmed by the costumes, makeup, and absurd or "deranged" routines employed by court jesters, clowns, and baggy-pants burlesque comedians. Another illustration of Aristotle's point can be seen in accounts of how eighteenth- and nineteenth-century "swells" would visit asylums in order to be entertained by the antics of the insane. Push this line of thought a bit further, and it can help explain why nineteenth-century white Americans enjoyed minstrel shows portraying the apparently absurd behaviors of blacks. One of the more bizarre and most extreme examples of the fact that people can be amused by observing the unusual behaviors of injured or impaired individuals has been described in a 1972 book by the anthropologist Colin Turnbull. During his study of the Ik, a remote African tribe, Turnbull noted that they typically laughed at anyone struggling after having been hurt in an accident. Such sadistic humor is not limited to an obscure African tribe. Holocaust survivors have described the same sort of behavior by their Nazi guards, who would occasionally entertain themselves by humiliating their prisoners. Sadly, we now have current examples of similar behaviors among some Americans guarding prisoners in Iraq.

The origins of our human preoccupation with various kinds of humor are thought to predate the ancient civilizations. Writing on the psychology of humor, Norman Holland maintained that its rudimentary sources were in primitive religious rituals concerning universal human fears about birth, death, warfare, and sex, most of which are still with us. Our current views of humor may seem far removed from such rituals, but a central point of similarity is the release of emotional tension. Holland cites archeological evidence showing that specially costumed priests and shamans presided over all important communal occasions, including certain feasts and festivals where people were encouraged to drop their inhibitions and more or less run riot. Among the ancient Greeks, arranging such moments of ecstatic revelry was a priority for the cult of Dionysus, the mythic god ruling over human passions.

Our word "comedy" is based on the Greek *komoidia*, a term referring to a major element of the Dionysian revels.

Further evidence for the primal origins of humor can be found in the traditions of Native Americans. Among the Sioux, certain individuals called *heyoka* served as tribal clowns, and the Zunis had priests who doubled as fun makers under the title of *koyemci*. One of their standard acts involved pretending to be foolish, irresponsible children. Variations on this particular theme have occasionally been used by modern comedians like Red Skelton and Jerry Lewis, who would assume a child's voice and body gestures. It is also still possible to see the release of inhibitions occurring at quasi-religious festivals such as Mardi Gras, where people dress in bizarre costumes and assume false identities. Rock concerts with their light shows, mosh pits, and easy availability of ecstasy in the form of a pill may not approximate Dionysian orgies but clearly serve similar functions.

Ritualized "roasts" of celebrities and powerful political leaders are yet another contemporary example harking back to the traditions of shamanistic humor. On these occasions, the respect usually given to the targets of the roast, and the aura of power surrounding them, is cast aside for a limited time as he or she undergoes a kind of ordeal of ridicule. We commonly see this as a test of character: are the victims of a roast worthy of their high status? Can they "take it" like a regular guy or gal despite the high position that ordinarily shields them from ribald criticism? In other, more serious psychological respects, the victim of the roast becomes a sacrifice object or scapegoat for the group, providing the group with the opportunity to release many of their emotions—envy, contempt, anger, or anxiety—that can only be expressed under the cover of humor. Also noteworthy is that the victims of modern roasts are always, in the end, given the opportunity to restore their dignity and reestablish their connection with the group by making funny responses to their critics.

Why do we seem to need such humor, particularly when dealing with people who differ from ourselves because of either their strangeness or their social status? Some philosophers have suggested the same general answer emphasized by modern psychologists. It is that humor, especially ethnic ridicule humor, helps us to cope with the risky or fearful nature of interpersonal relationships. This idea follows from the fact that anyone who seems clearly different from or alien to us because of their appearance, language, or behavior is almost always perceived as an immediate or potential threat. A classic example is the way Socrates got into trouble because of his teaching method. According to Plato's account, Socrates delighted his students by his clever ways of criticizing established community values and attitudes and making fools of local authorities who tried to argue with him. The authorities eventually got fed up with this irritating smart aleck, accused him of undermining the morals of their children, and sentenced him to exile which the Greeks considered equivalent to death, whereupon he chose to commit suicide by drinking poison.

A more common example is how ordinary people, even those we know very well, may sometimes say or do things that appear suddenly strange to us, and then we turn on them with aggressive ridicule aimed at reducing the threat posed by their behavior. Is there any family that has not occasionally seen ugly sarcastic remarks exchanged between teenagers and their parents, or husbands and wives? Such reactions are likely to be more serious when people encounter a genuine stranger, and can be understood as a "hardwired" reflex that probably first evolved among our hunter-gatherer ancestors. It shows up clearly among all groups of social mammals. If a strange wolf, chimp, or lion enters the territory of an established group, the newcomer will almost always be attacked and driven away. We, of course, do not do that anymore (well, sometimes we do: gangs like the Crips and Bloods still jealously guard their territories). Nevertheless, and even among the most civilized, the appearance of a stranger still creates anxieties that are often relieved by demeaning the stranger, making fun of him or her in a more or less ritualized fashion, and thus reducing the stranger to a nonthreatening status.

In general, modern scholars suggest several reasons why the study of humor is important. The first and most familiar is that the capacity for humor is a uniquely human quality. There is no substantial evidence indicating that anything like "our" humor exists among the other higher mammals, although there are anecdotal reports of playful behaviors among dolphins, chimps, and elephants, as well as studies showing that chimps and gorillas vocalize laughter in ways quite similar to humans. At least one investigator claims to have observed chimps laughing when they try to throw things at people or pee on them. But even if taken at their face value, these reports do not indicate much more than a primitive type of slapstick playfulness. Accordingly, the philosophical argument is that insofar as we can better understand all forms of our humor, we can better understand one of the unique features of our human condition.

A more practical argument for the study of humor is that it facilitates relationships between people throughout society. Like casual comments about sports, funny remarks provide a convenient way for strangers in public places to begin conversations with each other. When people are delayed on the ground in an airliner, for example, they usually start chatting with each other after someone loudly wisecracks about the speed and convenience of air travel. A time-honored method of ingratiation known to all salespeople involves telling a few jokes to potential customers. Jokes and wisecracks are also a familiar way for men and women to flirt with each other.

Another reason for the study of humor particularly relevant to psychology is that it still remains a relatively mysterious form of human behavior. We do not know why humor can break out in all sorts of unpredictable ways, or why a joke that works in one venue may not work in another, or why many women say they are attracted to men who can make them laugh. Nor is there any general agreement about even the most basic of commonsense issues, such as whether or not people have a measurable sense of humor, and if they do, whether it should be understood as a personality trait, an attitude, or a culturally conditioned behavior norm. There are "humor quotient" tests and questionnaires designed to measure an individual's sense of humor, but the results of such tests are questionable because virtually all humor except for physical slapstick depends on cultural knowledge and language skills. No test can assess all the different types of humor that exist in any society. Yet the fact remains that individuals vary in their appreciation of humor, in their willingness to go out of their way to experience it, in their ability to make up jokes or wisecracks on their own, and in their tendencies to use humor as a defense mechanism. The latter can be a serious issue for psychotherapists and counselors when dealing with clients who persistently try to joke about their problems.

A number of other questions remain debatable. Is humor primarily learned or instinctive? Most of us think it is both, although there is stronger evidence for the instinct position, mainly because infants and young children show spontaneous humor reactions in various situations. Can people be taught to appreciate humor? Maybe to some extent they can, but all we really know is that events triggering humor and laughter are different in different cultures and subcultures. An additional mystery is one that we all experience on occasions when humor evades or escapes from our conscious control. We laugh at things, and in situations, when we think we should not, and when we try not to. As will presently be discussed, Sigmund Freud had a good deal to say about this matter.

Humor is also studied by sociologists and anthropologists because it is a fundamental culture value. Perhaps more in North America than elsewhere, humor is seen as a desirable personal and social quality. We admire and reward those who can make us laugh, and go out of our way and pay admission fees to experience humor. But the experience depends on what we bring to it. In order to understand and appreciate most forms of humor, it is necessary to understand the norms, roles, and status patterns governing social activities in the culture. In order to understand the point of ethnic humor it is necessary to understand the stereotypes commonly applied to ethnic, racial, or national groups. For example, an obscure ethnic joke during World War II was, "Why do Italian tanks have four speeds in reverse and one in forward? In case they are attacked from the rear." There is no point to this joke unless one knows that during World War II the Italian army was stereotyped as performing badly in combat, frequently retreating and surrendering at the first opportunity, because Italian soldiers were reluctant to fight for their Fascist government.

All social scientists generally agree that proper understanding of any culture benefits from examination of its characteristic forms of humor. This is why anthropologists often struggle to "decode" the jokes circulating in the groups they study. It is not an easy task, because occasions for widely shared laughter in a group or society are usually based on a deep structure of cultural values and social norms that may appear irrational or inconsistent to a stranger. Consider what happens in our own society when we are in a group and someone lets go a loud fart. Sometimes we laugh, and at other times we pretend not to notice. It depends on circumstances that we all seem to intuitively understand but could not easily explain to a stranger from another culture. Furthermore, we can all be strangers to historical changes in our own culture. An instructive example appears in Judith Lee's 2000 book, *Defining New Yorker Humor*. She reports that in a "Notes and Comment" item by E. B. White printed in the March 9, 1929 issue, he ironically lamented that three of the most prominent, eligible young men of the period, Charles Lindbergh, Gene Tunney, and John Coolidge, had recently chosen to marry rich, upperclass Christian women. He then suggested, in a way that anticipated current concerns with diversity, that it might have been better for the country if they had instead married someone more ordinary, like "somebody's stenographer, or somebody's second wife, or a Jew." As a result, *The New Yorker* was promptly criticized by some readers for its anti-Semitism. There was certainly a great deal of prejudice against Jews circulating through our society in 1929. But few people today, including Jews, are likely to be upset by such an obviously tongue-in-cheek item. Instead, they are more likely to throw in some Jewish American Princess jokes, or a few references to Monica Lewinsky. Although changing historical conditions and social attitudes clearly influence the nature of humor—the things most people will laugh at in a given historical period—this issue has not received much attention from humor scholars because it is difficult to pin down.

An important exception is a 1999 study by Christie Davies, who analyzed historical changes in the jokes told by the English about the Welsh. During the sixteenth and seventeenth centuries, these jokes made fun of what the English believed to be the excessive pride and aggressive self-importance of the Welsh. Davies traced this belief to the behavior of Welsh smallholder gentry who were notoriously persistent about asserting their rights and traditions of independence. He noted several examples of jokes along this line in various plays by Shakespeare. By the late eighteenth century, however, there were major changes in Welsh society. The smallholders had largely disappeared, and the Welsh had been converted to Nonconformist Protestantism. This denomination was associated with piety, but many of its followers were also considered to be tricky and devious in their dealings with outsiders. So the English jokes now changed to focus on the Welsh as hypocrites. Thus it was said of a Welshman who was seeking a political appointment, "he'll pray on his knees all Sunday and then prey on his neighbours the other six days of the week."

Because of their sheer diversity, there is no simple way to sum up the various perspectives on humor discussed in this chapter. If nothing else, however, their diversity should be enough to show that efforts to come up with explanations that would apply to all people everywhere are quite hopeless. Humor is just such a deeply rooted, pervasive human quality and takes on so many different forms in different situations that it refuses to be bound by any single set of rational principles or formulas. This does not mean that we cannot understand at least some of it some of the time, though, and the following chapter examines how modern social scientists and philosophers have tried to accomplish this.

2

What Makes Us Laugh: Humor Theory and Research from Plato and Aristotle to Sigmund Freud

Everything is funny as long as it is happening to somebody else.

—*Will Rogers*

Whenever the topic of racial or ethnic humor comes up, it is usually the stereotyping that drives discussion, even though the humor is what makes the whole affair interesting. But most people react to theoretical analyses of any type of humor with either boredom or fascination. Boredom is by far the most frequent response, because the concepts involved are often seen as so far removed from everyday life as to appear useless, or the opposite: the concepts seem to be so much a matter of common sense that anybody with half a brain already understands them. Yet some of us become fascinated with the puzzle-solving nature of theory, the idea that it can help us understand why some jokes work and others fail, or why we laugh when we do not think we should, and other things that may at first seem inexplicable. In all fairness, however, it should also be acknowledged that scholars themselves react to theory with boredom or fascination. B. F. Skinner, the famous psychologist of learning, claimed that most theories were not only boring but also a diversion from mapping the concrete determinants of human behavior. The pioneering social psychologist Kurt Lewin, on the other hand, famously suggested that when studying social behavior—and what is more social than humor?— "There is nothing so practical as a good theory." I am with Lewin on this point, even if the theorizing discussed in the following text turns out to hang too heavily over the spontaneous joys of comedy. This problem also comes up when discussing research designed to test theories of humor, but it is relieved by the sheer ingenuity of many studies.

One thing that should be made clear immediately, however, is that the theories and research examined in this chapter primarily concern the *mechanics* of humor—what makes it work—rather than its larger social meaning. That will be taken up in later chapters, once we have discussed the nitty-gritty mechanisms proposed by philosophers and social scientists. By way of introduction, some attention to the remarkably simplistic early efforts to research and theorize about humor during the late nineteenth and early twentieth century can help explain why it became an intriguing topic for psychology in particular.

Toward the end of the nineteenth century, philosopher-psychologists such as William James, whose experiences with depression may have stimulated his interest, clearly saw humor as a significant challenge to the budding science of human behavior. In fact, at one point in his career James spent considerable time searching for the physiological origins of laughter by experimenting with nitrous oxide, the then-newly discovered laughing gas. But he did not get very far with this, and eventually was satisfied to merely describe laughter as an emotional expression of pleasure that has a number of physiological health benefits. The chapter on emotions in his 1890 *Principles of Psychology* text let it go at that, focusing instead on feelings of sadness and depression. At about the same time that James was trying laughing gas, other investigators attempted to study humor by doing systematic experiments on tickling. (One gets a sense here of the charming innocence that characterized the early psychology researchers.) The only substantial finding to emerge from the tickling work was that people only laugh when tickled by others; they are unable to tickle themselves into laughter. We still do not have a good explanation for this, or for the fact that some people are more ticklish than others, but the findings speak to the social nature of laughter.

There were also a handful of studies done on the ability of individuals to remember jokes, and some Darwinian writers speculated that since laughter and smiling require the baring of teeth, these facial expressions may have evolved from a primitive snarling response to aggression. Since so much humor has an aggressive quality, this idea seemed quite plausible. People do, in fact, sometimes mistake an angry grimace for a smile. Later in the 1920s and 1930s, when psychologists were increasingly concerned to establish themselves as respectable scientists, humor studies languished. There were few sources of funding for research on the topic, and it appeared frivolous compared with more significant problems such as learning and motivation.

But psychologists never entirely gave up on humor as a topic for research. Interest in the topic was stimulated in the early 1970s when a comprehensive review of humor research published by Patricia Keith-Spiegel identified several different approaches to the topic. Each approach is distinguished by a particular theme, but all have in common the underlying idea

that our humor is an instinct that must have evolved to serve some important purpose for adaptation or survival. The most persuasive evidence for this
comes from studies showing that babies generally begin smiling and laughing at about the age of four months. These early infant smiles first occur as
a spontaneous response to tickling, and soon become directly linked to pleasurable contact with the mother or primary care giver. Infants also smile spontaneously a little later on when they begin to master any significant new
activity, such as crawling or standing up. By the time they are a year old, babies will laugh when adults make funny faces for them. As might be expected,
by age two or sooner, they already seem to know that smiling calls up positive responses from adults.

But if laughter is instinctive, how did it evolve, and why do we value it?
Among the many quaint ideas that have been suggested, one that holds up
pretty well is that it began as a spontaneous expression of triumph after de-
feating an enemy or killing an animal. According to this view, laughter evolved
from hunter-warrior victory cries that were imitated by tribal or family members, perhaps something like the cheering of fans at sporting events, and eventually came to serve as an "all clear, no danger" signal for the whole group.
Laughing together then became the basis for sharing a collective sense of well
being. It has been noted that we can see the remains of such behavior today
when the leader of a group begins to laugh at something and all the others
present take this as a cue to join in, even if they do not know what the laughter is about. Research has also demonstrated that if an individual is placed in
a group where everyone else is laughing, he or she will usually join in without knowing why. Once we get past these ingenious speculations about the
origins of laughter and humor, however, several more specific explanations
for why we laugh come into play.

The earliest and most fundamental of these explanations centers on the
time-honored notion of *superiority*. This includes all of the many variations
on the theme of laughter as an expression of pleasure at feeling superior to
those who appear uglier, stupider, or more unfortunate than ourselves. The
superiority theme was already present in the writings of Plato and Aristotle,
the work of Hobbes (seventeenth century), Bergson (early twentieth century),
and many others. At the most basic level, an immediate sense of superiority
is presumably what triggers our laughter when we see someone slip on a banana peel or clowns tripping over their feet and other kinds of slapstick
humor. Their mastery of such physical humor is what made silent film comedians like Charlie Chaplin and Buster Keaton popular all over the world.
Pleasurable feelings of superiority are also why we laugh at the victims of
practical jokes. Those who sit on a tack or panic when finding a snake in their
bed are immediately rendered inferior to ourselves.

Hobbes described this pleasurable sense of superiority as a feeling of "sudden glory." This is why practical jokes seem especially enjoyable to observers if the victim has a high social status. The higher the status of the victim, the greater is the tendency to glory over making fools of them. Jokes at the expense of people who are clearly of lower status than the observers may also be enjoyed, but in this instance there is usually some need on the part of observers to reinforce their feeling of superiority. People who are uncertain about their superior position or feel a bit guilty about it are the ones most likely to enjoy witnessing the embarrassment or humiliation of others who are supposed to be inferior to them. Carried to its extreme, such humor becomes sadistic, as noted earlier when prisoners are abused by their guards. Finally, superiority theory can also be applied to account for the more subtle form of pleasure the Germans call *schadenfreud,* that is, the quietly amused feeling of gratification one may experience at witnessing a disliked colleague or supervisor being "taken down a peg" because of a poor performance or embarrassing error.

If there is any single triggering mechanism that most modern scholars and comedians agree offers the most important explanation of humor, it is encounters with *incongruity.* Even those who acknowledge superiority as a fundamental principle argue in favor of incongruity as the basis for feelings of superiority. The reasoning here is that the sense of superiority gained from observing the victim of a practical joke, for example, ultimately follows from the incongruity of the victim's situation. A tack on the chair or snake in the bed is essentially a contradiction to the normal function of chairs and beds, and suddenly plunges the victim into a humiliating experience of incongruity. Another way to distinguish between the superiority and incongruity interpretations of humor is by noting that the former is an ego-enhancing emotion within the individual, whereas incongruity refers to something outside the individual, a quality of the situation "out there," in the environment. Philosophers such as Kant, Hegel, Schopenhauer, and Bergson all discussed incongruities as a source of humor. Kierkegaard suggested that if a dramatic incongruity is seriously threatening, it becomes the basis for sadness rather than laughter. It is funny to see someone get a pie in the face, but not if there is a brick in the pie. One of the hallmarks of a brilliant clown is the way he or she can quickly cycle an audience through moments of humor and sadness.

Examples of nonthreatening incongruities that stimulate humor are commonplace. Young children laugh when they see a parent make funny faces, whereas adults enjoy the absurd routines that were a staple of the Marx Brothers comedies. Groucho could amuse an audience simply by twitching his eyebrows while making nonsensical conversation with matronly ladies. He was also celebrated for the wonderfully incongruous remark, "I would never join a club that would have me as a member." Incongruity has been a perennial source of humor in plays and films where adults act like children, animals speak good English, or males masquerade as females and vice versa. Henri Bergson's discussion of incongruity also emphasized that contradictions between physical appearances and the social character of situations were a prime condition for laughter. In some obvious cases, these involve self-contradictions, as when a high and mighty professor comes to class with his fly open or lets go a loud fart in the midst of a lecture. What the incongruity theory of humor boils down to is our apparently innate tendency to be amused by scenes that are clearly absurd or contradictory. Many cartoonists specialize in sketching such scenes. One of the most famous examples was a cartoon drawn by Bill Mauldin during World War II. Appealing to the cavalry tradition of shooting a horse with a broken leg, the cartoon showed a tearful soldier pointing his forty-five automatic at the hood of a jeep with a broken wheel. The absurdity of the scene was enhanced by the military practice of referring to its mechanized units as "armored cavalry."

The *surprise* theory of humor overlaps with incongruity, but simply focuses on sudden, unexpected positive events (finding money in the street, getting an A when you expected a C) that are experienced as a happy shock. The seventeenth-century French philosopher René Descartes noted that it was the mixture of joy and shock at the occurrence of a happy surprise that provoked laughter, and both Hobbes and Darwin also mentioned surprise as an important basis for humor. More specifically in *The Philosophy of Rhetoric* published in 1776, George Campbell discussed surprise as a function of incongruity, saying it was the essence of wit to "excite in the mind an agreeable surprise," and this could be accomplished by "debasing things pompous," "aggrandizing things little and frivolous," or arranging ordinary things in unusual ways. Comedians, of course, know very well that a good punch line to a joke should not only resolve an incongruity but also come as a surprising shock to the audience. As will be discussed in more detail later on, many stand-up comedians make strategic use of obscenities and ethnic slurs in order to produce a surprising shock effect. A relevant example was the advice old vaudeville comedians would give to beginners, to the effect that if your act is not working, you can always drop your pants to get a laugh. But perhaps the purest case of surprise humor can be seen in the delight of children when a Jack-in-the-Box pops up.

Ambivalence theory suggests that laughter occurs when we experience conflicting feelings or emotions. Such ambivalence can follow from an incongruity between emotional states. In one of Plato's dialogues, for example, he notes that laughter may result from the simultaneous experience of incompatible emotions. Specific examples suggested by modern theorists emphasize incongruities between joy and sorrow, love and hate, superiority and inferiority, and so on. A familiar common illustration of ambivalence occurs, for example, when people attending a funeral or memorial service find themselves having to stifle laughter when speakers express pious sentiments about the deceased even though many mourners in attendance remember the individual as a hell-raising atheist. Jewish Mother jokes can often generate ambivalent feelings because they call up a mixture of affection for the mother and resentment or anger at some of her domineering behavior. Another variation is the mix of emotions that attracts people to roller coasters: on the one hand fear, and at the same time excitement and mastery of the fear, resulting in uncontrollable laughter.

Cognitive theory, rather than focusing on the emotions, emphasizes the intellectual aspects of humor. In this perspective, laughter is viewed as the outcome of creative problem solving, an activity that requires some degree of information processing or the mental manipulation of symbolically represented persons or concepts. A simple example is the joke about Moses coming down from Mount Sinai and announcing to the waiting crowd, "I have good news and bad news. The good news is that I got Him down to ten. The bad news is adultery is still in." In order to get the point, you would have to know who Moses was, what the Ten Commandments were about, the meaning of adultery, and the fact that one of the Commandments forbids it. Even after processing these concepts, if you did not think people enjoyed adultery, the joke would make no sense. In his 1999 book about jokes, the philosopher Ted Cohen sums up this point by emphasizing that many jokes are "conditional"; they will only work on condition that the audience has both the knowledge and information processing ability required to understand them. Another good example of the necessity for information processing goes something like this: A fellow meets an acquaintance and announces that he is going to tell him a great new stupid joke. Knowing the usual stereotype involved in such jokes, the other guy stops him, saying, "I better warn you I'm Polish," at which the fellow replies, "That's OK, I'll tell it to you slowly." This joke may not register immediately because it takes a moment or two to process the concepts involved. Cartoons also frequently require some level of cognitive processing whereby visual and verbal information are linked together in a way that yields an amusing conclusion. A cartoon in my files by Callahan shows a priest with his arms raised toward heaven standing over a man in a wheelchair, and crying out, "Heal!" In the next box the man who was in the wheelchair is shown crouched on all fours, panting like a dog at the feet of the priest. The humor here requires a stereotyped knowledge of faith healing and recognition of the dog training command "Heel!"

In general, cognitive theory emphasizes a critically important aspect of humor that we often ignore because the mental activity necessary to get a joke happens so quickly. An interesting ramification of cognitive theory has been the effort by a few humor scholars to develop a computer program that can generate jokes. They more or less have the computer randomly matching standard straight lines with a variety of punch lines. But the results so far have not been very funny.

Release and relief theory focuses on the tension arousal and release that must accompany virtually all humor. The general principle here is that there can be no laughter without some prior arousal of tension. This is why so many jokes and comedy routines center on emotionally loaded topics such as sex, toilet behaviors, and politically incorrect ridicule of ethnic groups. ("How do you break a Pole's finger? Punch him in the nose." "What do you get when you cross a French whore with a Jewish American Princess? A girl who sucks credit cards.") Apart from jokes and pie-in-the-face slapstick routines, the tension built up in many stressful real-life situations can also be released in what we call nervous laughter. In the film and TV series *M*A*S*H*, for example, surgeons operating under difficult conditions were shown making wisecracks in order to cope. This frequently occurs in real life among soldiers, police, and others who are in stressful situations. A classic example was in the film *Butch Cassidy and the Sundance Kid*. When the two outlaws can only escape from a posse by jumping from a high cliff into a river, one of them hesitates, saying, "I can't swim," and the other replies, "Don't worry, the fall will probably kill you." Sigmund Freud's psychoanalytic theory provides the most elaborate tension release explanation for humor.

This theory first appeared in a 1905 monograph titled *Jokes and Their Relation to the Unconscious*. Major elements of Freud's humor theory are still widely accepted because of their close fit with common experience. Almost everyone is familiar with the concept of the "Freudian slip," whereby we mistakenly say something embarrassing by mixing up similar words. Typically, the mix-up yields some inadvertent expression of aggression or sexuality. I still recall an incident in junior high school, when a very attractive social studies teacher asked our class if anyone knew why the United States led the world in wheat production, and one of my friends raised his hand, shouting, "The invention of the McCormick raper" instead of reaper. Of course, according to Freud the mixing up of similar words is no accident; it represents the expression of a socially unacceptable motive or wish that has slipped past our internal censor.

Briefly, Freud's approach to humor was based on his three-dimensional view of personality in which primitive, socially unacceptable *id* impulses are inhibited or censored by the moralistic *superego*, while the *ego* or conscious self mediates between them. Accordingly, immoral or other unacceptable material that would ordinarily be inhibited can be released when the superego is evaded, or tricked by the ego's ability to package the forbidden impulse merely as humor. The laughter that follows is understood as catharsis: the sudden release of tension. In terms of everyday life, one of the implications of the theory is that we can get away with making all sorts of insulting, aggressive, or sexual remarks so long as they are delivered in a humorous fashion.

Freud's theory, therefore, has it that all jokes and witty remarks, with the possible exception of childish nonsense, like making funny faces, relates directly or indirectly to some sort of forbidden, socially unacceptable behavior. Even funny faces, such as when children thumb their noses or stick out their tongues, can often be expressions of anger or rejection. In fact, research studies have shown that the most frequent themes of jokes center on sex and/or aggression. This is obviously true of all racial, ethnic, and gender jokes, but practical jokes, like putting a tack on the teacher's chair or a bucket of water over the schoolroom doorway, are also clear examples, along with all forms of slapstick comedy. Aggression carried out in the name of fun is easy to see in various initiation rituals, when people are forced to wear buckets over their heads or recite humiliating lines ("I am a plebe; a plebe is lower than whale shit at the bottom of the ocean on a cloudy day"). Any such situation that creates enough tension to stimulate laughter by onlookers can be taken as evidence of how Freud's ideas relate to the Hobbesian theory of superiority. If the implicit presence of aggression in humor sometimes may seem obscure or debatable, no such problem exists when it comes to sexuality. We have an apparently inexhaustible supply of sexual jokes and comedy routines, where males target females, females target males, and both will often ridicule their own gender group.

In addition to jokes based on aggression and sex, there is the wide range of body processes that are considered unmentionable. Freud himself never discussed bathroom behaviors, farts, belches, and nose picking as topics for humor, but insofar as public discussion of such things can arouse tension or anxiety, they provide further evidence for his theory. A striking "pure case" demonstrating this point was comedian George Carlin's seven dirty words routine on a successful comedy record produced about thirty years ago. Carlin simply recorded seven of the obscene words that were at that time not allowed to be used on radio or TV, even though, as he pointed out, everyone had heard them. And if anyone had not heard them, or did not know what they meant, then it could do them no harm. This sort of thing would not have interested Freud, who was contemptuous of what he considered to be vulgar attempts to get laughs. In some of his later writings compiled in 1959, Freud was at pains to distinguish between higher level, healthy forms of humor, and low comedy or wisecracks. He called the former a "rare and precious gift," because it helped people to not take themselves too seriously, and could serve as a valuable defense against anger and guilt feelings. Low comedy he just called "trash."

Another aspect of Freud's theory that deserves emphasis is that our laughter at the punch line of a joke is an unconscious reflex. For the most part, we seem to either understand or not understand a joke immediately, and laughter is a reflexive, spontaneous response. Cognitive theorists would object that this appearance of things may be deceptive, but if we have to spend much time thinking about a joke in order to decide whether or not is it funny, then it usually is not.

A potent example of how unconscious processes can become a collective group experience occurs when a comedian occasionally "gets on a roll" or begins to "riff" (rapidly free associate) on a topic that resonates with the audience. Psychologically, what happens here is that the comedian's spontaneous stream of thought on a topic somehow harmonizes with that of the audience, and it is as if the performer and people in the audience become intimately linked together. The audience can be seen hanging on the words of the comedian, chuckling or giggling in anticipation of the next punch line, for as long as this sense of harmony lasts. Freud's theory receives yet another boost from stand-up comedians who say that when they are on a roll with an audience, it feels as if they are sharing a sexual orgasm with them. Comedians push the analogy even further by suggesting that the buildup to a punch line is like sexual foreplay that culminates in a rush of orgiastic laughter. When they can bring this off they experience it as a fantastic "high," superior to anything that can be obtained from drugs. Ironically, it is often because they get so high during their performances that comedians have difficulty "getting down" afterward, and they might begin to use drugs just to cool out.

The idea of a shared group unconscious relevant to humor can be further supported by observations of children (every kindergarten teacher knows this) who may begin to giggle together for no apparent reason except that one of them has started giggling. This is fairly common among teenagers as well, who may occasionally look at each other across a room and begin giggling spontaneously, even while trying not to. We have no simple explanations for such behavior. Followers of Carl Jung's analytical theory would likely appeal to his concept of collective or shared unconscious processes: something in the situation triggers off a funny thought or reaction in the collective unconscious of the people involved. More traditional Freudian theorists, however, might describe it as a form of emotional empathy, whereby people may unconsciously sense the feelings of others. For their part, behaviorist learning psychologists would attribute the phenomenon to some sort of simultaneous conditioned response to a stimulus in the situation. All of these explanations still remain as little more than theoretical speculations.

Parenthetically, it may be worth noting that while Freud's ideas about jokes have had a broad impact on the popular culture, that culture has occasionally struck back. A remarkable example of this appeared in a scholarly article by Sachi Sri Kantha published in 1999 under the title *Sexual Humor on Freud as Expressed in Limericks.* From a list of six thousand limericks available in collections such as Bennet Cerf's *Out on a Limerick,* the author identified twenty-one that specifically targeted Freud. Here are two of them.

> An early psychologist, Freud
> had the blue noses very anneud,
> saying, you cannot be rid
> of the troublesome Id,
> So it might just as well be enjoyed.

> Withdrawal, according to Freud,
> is a very good thing to avoid
> If practiced each day
> your balls will decay
> to the size of a small adenoid.

The author went on to offer a sober discussion of the possible reasons why limerick writers, many of them anonymous, might have chosen to create sexual rhymes about Freud, none of which need concern us here. But his suggestion that Freud himself would have been pleased by the attention seems appropriate.

Freud's ideas have never lacked critics, however, and in his 1983 book *Taking Laughter Seriously,* the philosopher John Morreal argues for a less complex theory of humor. In his view, our laughter depends on only three conditions. First, we must experience a shift in our thoughts or feelings, which is usually stimulated by encountering an incongruity. Second, this change must be sudden or unexpected, and third, it must be pleasurable, something that strikes us as amusing. These conditions can be seen in the following joke circulated prior to the Iraq War. A reporter spots George Bush and Colin Powell in a bar having an argument. He immediately approaches and asks what they are arguing about. Bush exclaims, "He doesn't agree with my plan to kill a million Iraqis and a blond with big tits!" "Oh," says the reporter, "why would you want to kill a blond with big tits?" Bush laughs and turns to Powell: "See, I told you nobody would care about a million Iraqis." Of course, this may be amusing only to critics of President Bush, but given the shift imposed by the incongruity between the Iraqis and the blond, and the sudden change triggered by the punch line, this joke and countless others fit the commonsense model proposed by Morreal. Yet there is still something here in line with Freud, because the tension aroused by this joke is based on aggression and sex.

Brief as it is, the foregoing review should also make it obvious that if anything, we have an overabundance of general humor theories. Each of them emphasizes one or more answers to the question of what makes people laugh, but none of them, not even Freud's theory, really covers all of the possibilities. Morreal, for example, deserves praise for offering a broadly inclusive commonsense analysis, but he has little to say about the deeper cognitive or emotional processes involved. In sum, therefore, when it comes to humor theory at large, you pay your money and take your choice, because one size does not fit all. It is partly for this reason that psychologists have tried to sort out the various theories by conducting systematic research on the question of how people typically experience humor.

Experiments, surveys, and other varieties of psychological research on humor have increased a great deal over the past thirty-odd years because the so-called armchair theories like those described up to now have been disappointing. For one thing, there are too many exceptions to the explanations they offer. For another, we now have a more effective set of research tools allowing us to come to grips with problems that could not be directly investigated in the past. Thus, as in other areas of psychology, empirical research on humor and laughter has begun to take precedence over speculative theorizing. Such theorizing served well enough to outline the general range of subject matter and mental processes related to humor, but the research findings in the following summary provide a more concrete understanding of the social and emotional conditions governing the ways humor is experienced.

This research has not grown up by accident. An excellent review by the psychologist Peter Derks has traced much of the work accomplished over the past quarter century back to an international conference on the topic organized in 1976. The conference brought together a broad range of scholars, mainly from the social sciences, literature, and philosophy, and although much of the conference was devoted to sorting out ideas from the past, its central aim was to develop a firm foundation for work in the future. This work, which was then in the future and has now been accomplished, generally fits three categories. These include personality or differences between the ways individuals respond to humor, the thematic content and structure of most humor, and the various applications of humor in daily life. These categories are not airtight, however. Some of the research findings mentioned in the following text fall in the cracks between them. Gender and age differences, for example, are usually considered relevant but not central to personality, and this is also true of our emotional states and abilities to tolerate stress. Yet all of these have been found to influence humor behavior.

Studies of how personality relates to humor often involve samples of people (usually college students) who complete one or more personality trait assessment questionnaires and are asked to rate the funniness of various jokes or cartoons. Their ratings are then analyzed according to their scores on the personality traits measured, such as aggressive versus passive, radical versus conservative, extrovert versus introvert, and so forth. The procedure is based on the idea that we tend to find material more or less funny depending on the extent to which it reflects one or more of our outstanding personality traits. The basic question, then, is, what types of people like what types of humor? and the answers are typically in line with common sense.

People who score highly on aggressiveness are more likely than others to like harsh or aggressive jokes. ("Why is the new Polish parachute unique? Because it only inflates on impact.") Those who get high scores on extro-version are more likely to enjoy sexual humor, and the same thing is true of people who claim to have an active sex life. When it comes to incongruity jokes, such as, "Why do they call camels ships of the desert? Because they are full of Arab seamen," responses to this incongruous play on words (seamen = semen) are more complex. People who score highly on conservatism do not find them very funny, whereas those who score highly on "sensation seek-ing" do. Another personality trait relevant to conservatism is "authoritari-anism," a pattern of beliefs emphasizing obedience to authority figures and strict adherence to conventional moral values. According to a 1996 study by psychologist Herbert Lefcourt, college students who had high scores on au-thoritarianism had relatively low scores on a general sense of humor ques-tionnaire. There has also been research showing that people who have an internal or external "locus of control" trait respond differently to certain types of humor. Those with an internal locus tend to believe that they can exert control over most areas of their lives, and they enjoy ambiguous or ab-surd forms of humor, such as the classic *New Yorker* cartoon showing a set of ski tracks that separate in front of a tree and come together again on the other side. People with an external locus, who believe they have little or no control over events in their lives, are usually puzzled by such absurd humor and find it meaningless.

Other studies have focused on the ecology of humor: when, where, and how frequently it occurs among different types of people. Some representa-tive results include the finding that men who fit the Type A personality pat-tern, characterized by generally hostile, competitive attitudes, laugh more often than women, presumably because they frequently enjoy disparaging jokes about others. On the other hand, among women, it is those who are low on the Type A characteristics who laugh the most. This study also found that people reported an average of eighteen laughter incidents per day, with most of them occurring in the evening, and that their laughter was mainly due to common social incidents rather than formal jokes.

Along with gender, recent research has also been concerned with how aging might affect responses to humor. In one instance, people ranging from age fifty to seventy-nine were asked to rate the funniness of a series of jokes and, contrary to what might be expected, the older individuals indicated the greatest enjoyment. A related investigation among sixty-nine- to ninety-six-year-old retired people in an assisted living facility found that those who exhibited more frequent laughter and humor had more positive, optimistic attitudes about their situation. A likely explanation suggested for these findings relates to other studies of longevity showing that people with a strong sense of humor tend to live longer into old age. Still other work, however, has yielded evidence that among socially assertive people, humor appreciation remains consistent across the life span, so it seems that both age and personality help determine reactions to humor.

Studies of how gender alone may influence humor behaviors have been somewhat ambiguous. Most research shows that men initiate humor more frequently than women, but women enjoy it more. Yet at least one study found no important differences between the levels of humor appreciation reported by men and women. The picture is further confused by other findings that although women are less likely to initiate humor, they use humor as a way of coping with stress or depression more often than men. One conclusion that all researchers agree on is that regardless of gender, a strong positive attitude toward humor is closely associated with mental health and feelings of well-being across the life span. There is also a growing consensus that personality and age are better predictors of humor appreciation than gender. The confusing results about gender differences are most likely because of changing social norms and expectations about male and female behavior. While they still differ in some respects, the gap between them has steadily narrowed. Where humor is concerned, the growing number of successful women comedians probably has helped to reduce traditional gender differences.

Further signs of this can be seen in a series of unusual investigations carried out in the early 1990s showing that both males and females who received high scores on measures of "intimacy"—willingness to reveal their thoughts and feelings to others—received high scores on measures of humor. These findings led to further work where it was found that persons rating themselves as high on the general trait of "trust," which is typically associated with high self-esteem, were also rated particularly high on humor. The important implication here is that in order to enjoy a wide range of humor, it is apparently necessary to trust or feel confident that one is not at risk of being insulted or made to look like a fool. This is an issue that can easily be observed in the tension aroused among audiences listening to stand-up comedians who use ethnic material or insult humor. As long as the comedy routine is presented as a playful manipulation of stereotypes, it remains acceptable. George Carlin is very good at this; he rarely violates the implicit trust established with his audience. Lenny Bruce, on the other hand, would begin his performances this way, but was notorious for pushing beyond the limits of what some in his audiences could accept, and suffered accordingly. By contrast, Don Rickles, who has made a long, successful career out of insult humor, manages to get away with it because he seems to have an intuitive sense of just how far he can go before audience laughter turns into anger.

Finally, although they are not closely tied to personality traits, emotional states have also been examined in relation to humor. In one experiment, for example, college students who were waiting to be tested for their ability to tolerate what they thought would be a painful electrical shock were allowed to listen to a humorous audiotape. Those who heard the funny tape showed less anxiety about the forthcoming shock than those who simply waited without hearing it. In another experiment, when individuals were subjected to increasing levels of physical pain from a pressure cuff (similar to what is used to measure blood pressure), those who were at the same time listening to a funny audiotape showed a greater degree of pain tolerance than those who did not hear the tape.

Most of the foregoing research results can be summed up as supporting three conclusions. First, a number of individual personality characteristics are clearly related to measures of humor behavior, even though such measures may not be perfect. Second, humor appreciation does not decline with aging and may even become stronger, whereas gender differences vary in ways that seem ambiguous and related to changing social norms. Third, humor appears to reduce sensitivity to pain. The practical implications of the pain research are obvious, but knowledge about how individual personality traits can influence the ways people react to various types of humor can also have quite practical implications. One of the most interesting comes from the psychotherapist Shirley Feldman Summers, who suggested that humor was an important predictor of relationships between men and women. If they do not enjoy the same kinds of jokes and comedy, they are not likely to have a happy, long-term relationship. Caution is required, however, since we are still a long way from making perfect predictions. One thing we can predict accurately is that people who are described as having an "above average" sense of humor are likely to be seen as more agreeable than others. According to the authors of a recent study demonstrating this point, a good sense of humor can therefore be an important social asset.

A second category of humor research described by Derks concerns the subject matter of most jokes and their typical structure or format. As noted earlier, the most frequent themes are sex, aggression, and relationships, between either individuals or groups. Studies confirm the commonsense view that people tend to enjoy aggressive, sexual jokes ridiculing persons or groups they dislike. This finding is in line with the superiority theory noted earlier and clearly applies to traditional racial, ethnic, and gender humor. During Bill Clinton's presidency, Republicans particularly enjoyed the many sex jokes about him, such as:

> "What do Monica Lewinsky and Bob Dole have in common? They were both upset when Bill finished first."

> "What's the difference between Clinton and the Titanic? Only 200 women went down on the Titanic."

Unfortunately for the Democrats, there are no readily available sex jokes to tell about George W. Bush, but they relish jokes about the ways he occasionally mangles the English language:

> "I am mindful not only of preserving executive powers for myself, but for my predecessors as well."

And there are also many jokes about his lack of cultural knowledge:

> "Einstein, Picasso and Bush meet St. Peter at the Pearly Gates, who asks each of them to prove their identity. Einstein explains a mathematical equation; Picasso draws a picture. St. Peter turns to Bush, 'Einstein and Picasso have proven themselves and may enter, now it's your turn.' Bush replies: 'Who are Einstein and Picasso?' 'Enter, my boy!' says St. Peter."

All presidents have been ridiculed in jokes and cartoons. Even George Washington was not immune and was frequently disparaged for what critics claimed were his high and mighty aristocratic manners.

Incongruity has been documented as the most frequently occurring structural component of most humor. It can take a number of different forms, as in jokes based on word play: "What do we call a murderer who eats a lot of fiber? A cereal killer." It is also the basis for an ethnic joke that can be applied to any identifiable group: An African American (or Korean, Israeli, Hispanic, etc.) walks into a bar with a beautiful parrot on his shoulder. The bartender sees the parrot and says, "Gee, he really looks beautiful, where did you get him?" And the parrot exclaims, "Where else but in Africa (or Korea, Israel, Mexico) you dummy!" Another variation on this joke is the blond who walks into a bar with a pig. The bartender says, "Where did you get that dumb animal?" The pig says, "I won her in a raffle." The riddle format of light bulb jokes and many of the common Polish and Jewish Mother jokes are also based on incongruities.

The third general category of humor research relates to its applications in everyday life. Most current studies are about the health benefits of laughter. Physicians as far back as Hippocrates have noted that patients with a good humored, optimistic attitude tend to recover more quickly from illnesses or injuries. But it has only been over the past twenty years or so that the idea of facilitating medical treatments and health maintenance through the deliberate use of humor has received serious attention. Interest in this idea was inspired by Norman Cousins, a well-known writer and magazine editor. When he was hospitalized for a persistent rheumatic disease but got no relief after weeks of treatment, he moved to a hotel and passed the time listening to comedy tapes. After the disease went into remission, he believed that it was because of the steady diet of laughter and wrote a popular book about his experience. The now well-accepted explanation for his recovery was that the humor had somehow strengthened his immune system, which then became better able to counteract the disease.

The work of physician Patch Adams has been another source of popular interest in the humor-health connection. Dramatized in a recent film starring Robin Williams as Adams and described in his 1998 book, *Gesundheit!: Bringing Good Health to You, the Medical System and Society through Physician Service, Complementary Therapies, Humor and Joy*, Adams has become a tireless advocate for the therapeutic value of laughter and humor. He makes personal appearances all over the country to speak about the topic and has established a foundation called The Gesundheit! Institute, "dedicated to bringing joy and friendship into health care." Adams' lighthearted enthusiasm for the benefits of humor is supported by an increasing number of research findings.

In the field known as psychoneuroimmunology, for example, substantial evidence indicates that people who frequently use humor to cope with stress tend to be more self-confident and optimistic and claim to have more enjoyable social lives, and laboratory tests indicate they have more efficient immune systems. Studies have also shown that measures of the immune system are significantly higher after people have been watching a comedy video, whereas these measures drop off after people see a video about auto accidents. Other findings show that laughter has the same general effects on the body as aerobic exercise because it gets more oxygen into the bloodstream. Moreover, although there is a rise in blood pressure during laughter, it drops below baseline afterward. Some research is beginning to demonstrate that humor can influence brain functions. A neuroscience report in *Brain Briefings* (12/01) noted that brain scans recorded while people are reading jokes or looking at cartoons reveal increased levels of activity in the frontal lobes, in the motor area related to smiling and laughter, and in the nucleous accumbens, an area associated with pleasure. The report also mentioned that frontal lobe activity only increased when people thought the jokes or cartoons were funny. A comprehensive research review lists more than a dozen studies showing that exposure to humor reduces anxiety, depression, and aggression.

Humor is also starting to be taken seriously in education, where a handful of studies confirm what many teachers have believed for a long time, namely, that a few jokes or witty remarks will always help liven up a classroom. These studies show that classroom humor improves the attention level of students, encourages flexible thinking, and improves students' ability to remember verbal and graphic material. There is no evidence, however, about whether too much comedy in the classroom might impair learning.

Like teachers, professionals in marketing and public relations have known for a long time that humor is an almost infallible attention getter, and market research studies confirm this. The only problem is that such studies also show that attention, even when accompanied by the pleasures of humor, does not necessarily translate into persuasion. Although people enjoy the humor used in advertising and political speeches, it does not consistently sell more products or influence the opinions of voters. According to Lynette Unger, who studied this issue several years ago, funny ads or commercials do not guarantee increased sales because audiences pay more attention to the humor than the commercial message. The same point relates to advertising slogans and jingles: people may remember them for years even though they never used the product. Another problem is that because tastes in humor vary, some people may not be amused by a funny commercial, and even those who are will tune it out if it is repeated more than a few times. Nevertheless, such commercials are widely used. A 1990 study reported that humor appeared in approximately 30 percent of American radio and TV messages. The percentage today is probably higher.

Politicians often try to use humor in their campaign appearances, and their speech writers usually provide them with a few funny lines designed to make them seem more likeable to the public. Some politicians do not need any help in employing humor. When he was governor of New York, for example, Mario Cuomo was well known for making spontaneous jokes and witty remarks about his Italian heritage. On one occasion, in order to emphasize his humble origins as the son of a hardworking immigrant, Cuomo told how his father had been ruined on Wall Street by the 1929 stock market crash, and then went on to explain that his father was not an investor; his pushcart was destroyed by the body of a broker who jumped out his office window. Few elections have ever depended on whether one candidate was more amusing than another, however. Noteworthy too is that in some instances, politicians may become unintentional figures of fun. After tripping in public a few times, Gerald Ford was ridiculed for his apparent clumsiness. When Dan Quayle was vice president, he attained inadvertent celebrity because of his frequent malapropisms. There are still Web sites listing some of his choice remarks:

> "It is time for the human race to enter the solar system."

> "Republicans understand the importance of bondage between a mother and child."

> "I was recently on a tour of Latin America and the only regret I have was that I didn't study Latin harder in school."

Among the three general topics discussed in this chapter—the general theories about mechanisms of humor including explanations suggested by Sigmund Freud's work, the research studies focused on situations and personality factors influencing how people react, and the practical uses of humor in relation to stress, health, and marketing—it is clearly the health benefits that have energized the growing volume of research. And if there is not much public concern with the mechanics of humor, there is still a good deal of interest in how it relates to personality and life adjustment. Consequently, work in this field is now well on its way to becoming a significant part of the behavioral sciences, even though racial, ethnic, and gender humor receives little attention because of its controversial status. Yet the research findings reviewed here clearly suggest that because humor stands as a major defense against the effects of stress, it would be particularly important for minorities who have traditionally suffered from prejudice and discrimination. The more we learn about the practical benefits of humor, the more obvious it becomes why so many of our major comedians have emerged from minority groups. Some of the implications of this view are worked out in the following chapter concerning theories and research specifically focused on racial and ethnic humor.

3

Prejudice, Pride, and Play in Ethnic Comedy

Humor is an affirmation of dignity, a declaration of man's superiority to all that befalls him.

—*Romaine Gary*

Humor is just another defense against the universe.

—*Mel Brooks*

Most discussions of stereotype humor and comedy routines fall far short of the existential insights expressed by Romaine Gary and Mel Brooks. Conventional analyses often just brush over the subject by referring to the humor theories summarized earlier and emphasizing the superiority theme—that by ridiculing others, people enhance themselves. Freud's psychoanalytic concepts are also frequently cited, since so much of racial, ethnic, and gender humor involves sex and aggression. This is not wrong, and much of it is useful, but the aim of this chapter is to show there is a great deal more to be said about humor based on stereotypes. Scholars who have studied stereotype humor in depth suggest that, rather than being primarily associated with prejudice, such humor is more frequently a matter of pride and play with important social functions in minority groups. The arguments to be made in support of this claim owe a great deal to the pioneering research of Christie Davies.

As the author of many articles and books, including the most authoritative collection of ethnic jokes available in print, *Ethnic Humor Around the World* published in 1990, Davies has probably done more to clarify popular misconceptions about such humor than anyone else. One of his major insights is that ethnic jokes in all societies have traditionally been aimed at peripheral groups, those who live at the margins of the mainstream society. This may seem like obvious common sense, but it has only been established as a general principle through painstaking, worldwide research. Furthermore, based on his examination of thousands of ethnic jokes, Davies found that their basic structure depended on the use of polar opposite adjectives. In connection with his first principle, it is pointed out that most if not all societies contain two types of peripheral groups. On the one hand, they can be either immigrants or older inhabitants who, as a matter of pride more than necessity, refuse to fully accept the values and attitudes prevailing in mainstream society. Conspicuous examples of such groups in the United States who have more or less chosen to maintain their identity as members of a distinctive minority would include some, but certainly not all, of our so-called hillbillies, as well as Native Americans, Cajuns, Hispanics, and Asians. In Canada, prominent examples are French Canadians ("canucks") and Newfoundlanders ("newfies"). One characteristic common to all such groups is that they typically have a language or dialect of their own, as well as a lifestyle marking them as different from the mainstream majority. Then, too, as outsiders they are likely to be suspicious of strangers and poor, have an unusual cuisine, and have limited access to good schools. So these and other associated characteristics are frequently the basis for stupid jokes (How did the newfie freeze to death? Because he went to the drive-in movie to see "Closed for the Winter") and cleanliness jokes (How do you hide money from a newfie? Put it under a soapdish).

On the other hand, traditional forms of discrimination have imposed a peripheral status on minorities like Jews and African Americans despite their efforts to enter mainstream society. This is not to say that they do not take pride in their ethnic identity, or that some do not choose to deliberately maintain a distinctive lifestyle, but the great majority actively seek assimilation to the mainstream. Moreover, for Jews and blacks, ethnic slurs such as kike and nigger carry much stronger negative implications than hillbilly, redskin, or newfie. Although to my knowledge there is no such thing as a measure of the relative degree of insult experienced by people subjected to various ethnic slurs, the long histories of violence and persecution suffered by Jews and blacks are easily evoked by terms like kike and nigger, and these are especially potent forms of insult.

Such slurs are often thought to be a typical component of ethnic humor, but for the most part they are little more than window dressing. Davies and other humor scholars have not found them to be central or essential features of the jokes. Like the obscene language many comedians sprinkle through their routines, ethnic slurs are employed for their shock value, and do not in themselves generate laughs. But this is a topic that will be examined more fully in a later chapter. In the present context, it is enough to note that peripheral groups and minorities also create their own slurs and stereotype humor aimed at ridiculing mainstream values and lifestyles. Much of the humor in TV sitcoms such as *The Beverly Hillbillies* and *Green Acres*, for example, involved country bumpkins—another type of ethnic slur—who made fools of urban sophisticates. Davies does not give this issue much attention, however, and his second general principle is focused instead on the pejorative language of traditional ethnic humor.

The important insight here is that most disparaging jokes involve polar opposite adjectives such as "stupid versus canny" (or shrewd), "dirty versus clean," "miserly versus generous," and "cowardly versus brave." But as can be seen in the following illustrative jokes, only the negative end of the pair is emphasized; the positive end always remains implicitly understood as characteristic of the "superior" joke teller. For example, Davies has shown that almost every society on earth targets at least one peripheral group with stupid jokes. In England, it is the Irish: "Why was the wheelbarrow invented? To teach the Irish how to walk on their hind legs." In Sweden, it is the Finns and Norwegians; in Russia, the Ukrainians; in Canada, Newfoundlanders. In the United States, the targets of stupid jokes are often Poles, blonds, African Americans, and others in different regions of the country. So in Minnesota there are many dumb Norwegian jokes: "A Norwegian driver entered the Indianapolis 500 but had to make fifty pit stops; three for gas and oil and forty-seven to ask directions." But of course in Texas, the racing car driver would be Mexican. The most widely distributed stupid jokes throughout the United States concern Poles. We seem to have an infinite supply of Polish jokes.

"What is the thinnest book ever written? The history of Polack culture."

"How many Poles does it take to change a light bulb? Five. One to hold the bulb and four to turn the ladder."

"Why does the Pope not allow dogs into the Vatican? Because they like to pee on Poles."

There is no generally accepted, clear-cut explanation for the prevalence of stupid Polish jokes in our society, although one writer has suggested that it is because Americans of Polish descent were so eager to assimilate to American society that other ethnics began to single them out for ridicule. The folklore authority Alan Dundes, however, points out that a traditional stereotype of Poles in Germany portrayed them as stupid and dirty, et cetera, and that German immigrants probably brought this stereotype with them to the American Midwest. The Nazis encouraged this, and one elderly German immigrant recalled a typical joke from her childhood during the Nazi period: "How do you catch a Pole? By slamming the toilet lid on his head while he's taking a drink of water."

Another, seemingly plausible explanation is that the word "Polack" simply sounds funny and works well in jokes, while at the same time it is not burdened with particularly vicious implications that might upset mixed audiences. Research studies have shown that people who laugh at Polish jokes have no particular dislike of Poles. This idea gains some further credibility from Dundes, who suggests that as white racism became less acceptable to many Americans, Polack jokes may have become a popular substitute for Sambo and Coon jokes. Yet another view mentioned in Davies' book *The Mirth of Nations* is that these jokes originated as insult humor exchanged between rival groups of Polish immigrants living in different areas of Milwaukee.

Davies also makes the point that many stupid jokes, Polish or otherwise, involve a play on language. The targeted group has either a comical accent that shows up in dialect jokes or just a poor knowledge of the dominant language leading them to make "stupid" mistakes. Thus, a Pole explains to a judge that he wants a divorce because his wife is planning to murder him.

> Judge: "How do you know?"
> Pole: "Because I find bottle in bathroom says Polish Remover."

In England, the Irish are typically ridiculed in language jokes, as in the one about the Irishman who buys a bar of soap, and when the salesperson asks, "Do you want it scented?" the Irishman replies, "No, I'll take it with me." A little collection of Norwegian jokes published in South Dakota contains the following example:

> Lena got a phone call from her husband Lars announcing he had purchased a condominium. "Good," she replied, "Now I can throw away my diagram."

The rural versus urban polarity shows up in jokes about the supposed backwardness of students attending state agriculture universities:

> "Why did they drop driver education at State Tech? Because the mule died."

> "What is the difference between culture and agriculture? About eighty miles" (the distance between the University of Kansas and Kansas State University).

Another frequent polarity is miserliness versus generosity. In this category we find all the traditional jokes based on stereotypes about cheap or miserly Jews, Scots, and in many Asian and African countries, the ethnic Chinese. What these groups have in common is that they are often traders, peddlers, or shopkeepers who must pay close attention to nickels and dimes in order to survive and thus end up stereotyped as miserly. These groups are also often ridiculed for being rich and flaunting it. The comedian Jack Benny—born Jewish as Benny Kubelsky—joked about both stereotypes. On a visit to Israel, when his tour guide said it would cost ten dollars to sail across the Red Sea, he supposedly replied: "Ten dollars! Now I know why Jesus walked on water!" On another occasion, when General Motors issued a recall notice for Cadillacs on the eve of a Jewish holiday, he remarked, "I've never seen so many Jews walking to synagogue."

Throughout his writings on the subject, Davies consistently argues against the idea that derogatory ethnic jokes always indicate hostility or hatred of the targeted group. When criticized for ignoring the anti-Semitic implications of jokes ridiculing Jews, for example, Davies replied that he could find no evidence showing that most of those who made up or told such jokes hated Jews, and that he found many of the jokes originated among Jews themselves. He maintains that ethnic jokes are usually told and enjoyed for their own sake because they are clever and entertaining and can provide a momentary sense of amusing superiority even among those who may belong to the group being ridiculed. The point of such jokes, he claims, is not aggression, but a way of "playing with aggression." This is a remarkably important observation because it helps explain why Jews enjoy telling jokes about Jews, Catholics about Catholics, blacks about blacks, and so on. Many stand-up comedians begin their routines by joking about their own ethnic origins. Parenthetically, it is a truism in psychology that to laugh at some aspect of your own behavior or that of your family or ethnic group can be an essentially healthy way of releasing conflicted, negative emotions. It allows us, at least momentarily, to rise above them. But the reasons why minorities may enjoy jokes applied to their own group have not received detailed attention from Davies. His master work is primarily concerned with the underlying principles of pejorative ethnic humor, and it in no way detracts from his achievement to point out that he does not emphasize the ethnic humor enjoyed within ethnic groups. Useful perspectives on this issue, however, appear in the work of Arthur Asa Berger.

In his 1993 book *An Anatomy of Humor*, Berger discusses ethnic jokes and comedy routines in a way that generally resonates with Davies' views. For example, Berger suggests that much of ethnic humor does not necessarily imply disdain for a particular group, but might be aimed more narrowly at ridiculing certain elements of their lifestyle. So Irish men might be ridiculed in jokes based on their tradition of heavy drinking, rather than simply because they are Irish. Jews might be ridiculed because of their traditional concern with money, not their religion. Berger's general view is that at least one function of ethnic humor is to criticize unacceptable lifestyles or habits, that is, to disparage the sin, not the sinner. This idea carries over to the issue of why minorities frequently tell jokes that ridicule members of their own group: it can serve an implicit educational or corrective purpose and relate to a number of other issues.

Self-critical humor thus can serve a defensive purpose by helping to prepare group members to cope with the prejudices they are likely to encounter in the larger society. The idea is that if you become familiar with this kind of thing in advance, you can develop some protective defense mechanisms—emotional insulation—against its effects on your self-esteem. Then again, since most ethnic groups are quite diverse, often divided by social class, religious, and cultural differences, the jokes they tell among themselves and about themselves will often reflect their own prejudices. For example, during the first half of the twentieth century, German Jews told jokes about Polish and Russian Jews who, in keeping with Davies' theory of polar opposites, they considered to be stupid, dirty, and greedy. Similar attitudes were prevalent in the jokes that northern blacks told about southern blacks, as well as in the jokes assimilated immigrants would tell about newly arrived "greenhorns" from their own ethnic group. In short, even though a group as a whole may be the target of prejudices, this does not mean that they are free of prejudices themselves or will not amuse themselves by disparaging members of their own group, or even their own family.

A more serious dark side of self-critical humor can be seen occasionally when it crosses the border into self-hatred. Psychiatric case histories show that there are always a few minority individuals who work out their neurotic problems by developing vicious attitudes toward their own group. A conspicuous example is the chess champion Bobby Fisher, whose mother was Jewish. While still a young man he won the world grand master title, and then became a recluse, emerging only occasionally to publicly express rabid anti-Semitism. William P. Gale, whose father was a converted Jew, preached violent anti-Semitism throughout the Midwest in the 1970s and early 1980s. The same sort of thing occurs in other groups. Prior to the Civil War, there were a few blacks who became well known as runaway slave catchers. More recently, Leo Felton, an "Aryan" activist convicted of trying to blow up African American memorials, was revealed as the son of a black father. But it would be wrong to associate these rare cases of self-hatred with self-critical ethnic humor, because such humor almost always stands as a defiant gesture *against* prejudice.

Many accounts show that by sharing jokes that repeat or exaggerate the stereotypes used to insult them, members of ethnic groups are in effect pro-claiming a form of ethnic pride: "Sticks and stones may break my bones but stereotypes can never hurt me." The laughter that oppressed individuals enjoy by making ironic jokes about their situation can provide an outlet for feel-ings of anger and frustration. During the 1930s, for example, when Jews were being forced to leave Germany and found it difficult to enter other countries, the Zionist leader Chaim Weizmann remarked: "There are two sorts of coun-tries in the world—those that want to expel the Jews and those that don't want to admit them." More extreme examples of such ironic, in-group humor have been reported by survivors of the Holocaust. One such joke involved leaders of the Jewish community in the Netherlands named Asscher and Cohen, who claimed that by cooperating with the Nazis, some of their brethren might be saved. As more and more Jews were deported to death camps, the joke has it that eventually, Asscher and Cohen are the only ones left. When the Nazis still demanded that another fifty percent of the Jews be handed over, Cohen says to Asscher: "It had better be you, Abraham, lest worse befall the rest of us." (An eclectic collection of Holocaust humor can be found in Steve Lipman's 1991 book, *Laughter in Hell: The Use of Humor during the Holocaust*.)

Berger's view of ethnic humor includes the fact that minority groups typically have their own characteristic forms of in-group humor. American Jews provide a noteworthy example. In no other ethnic group is there such a clear pattern of jokes based on contrasting stereotypes about mothers and their daughters. The Jewish Mother cooks, sacrifices for her family, and saves money, whereas the Jewish American Princess orders out, is self-centered, and is a spendthrift. Traditional Jewish fool or stupid jokes provide another ex-ample. They focus on the so-called schlemiel, who is a clumsy loser and al-ways dropping things, and the schlemazl, who is always in the wrong place at the wrong time and gets things dropped on him. These examples offer fur-ther evidence for Davies' idea about the importance of polar opposites in eth-nic humor.

Finally, in one of his more original theoretical suggestions, Berger of-fers a four-point outline that can be applied to analyze the structures of all ethnic jokes. It requires a breakdown allowing the identification of (1) the *subject* of the joke, usually a specific group; (2) the *form*, which is typically a story or a riddle, as in the case of light bulb jokes; (3) the *technique*: does the joke involve an appeal to incongruity, use of a comical dialect, or a play on similar sounding words; and (4) the *theme*, which is usually a stereotype about the subject, such as stupid Poles, miserly Jews, and so forth. Among these four components Berger singles out technique as being the most important. Con-sider the following ethnic joke from the 1950s (in Berger, p. 71):

"A Southerner walks into a bar in New York with an alligator on a leash. 'You serve niggers here?' he asks. 'We serve Negroes, yes,' answers the bartender testily.

'Fine,' says the Southerner. 'I'll have a bourbon. Give my alligator a Negro.'"

The subject of the joke is racist southerners and the form is a story. The technique, however, involves use of the ethnic slur N-word, the incongruity of an alligator on a leash, and a play on the word "serve." Finally, the theme is a stereotype about the brutality and prejudice of southern racists. Note in addition that this joke is clearly obsolete, because the 1950s stereotype of southerners as prejudiced racists is no longer current. But a strikingly similar technique involving a play on the word "serve" occurs in a joke that emerged during the civil rights movement in the 1960s:

"A black student sitting in at a lunch counter in the South is told by the waitress, 'We don't serve Negroes here,' and he replies, 'That's good, because I don't eat them.'"

In general, Berger agrees with other scholars of ethnic humor who feel that it is particularly prevalent in the United States and Canada because these societies are made up of so many diverse ethnic groups. As previously mentioned, he suggests that such humor can have beneficial effects for both minorities and mainstream society. In particular, such humor allows for the relatively harmless release of social-emotional tensions within and between groups, although he acknowledges that it may occasionally contribute to prejudice.

Berger and Davies both approach ethnic humor in a more or less global, commonsense fashion, drawing on a mixed bag of established social science concepts as well as their own original analyses of stereotype jokes. By contrast, sociologists such as Gary Alan Fine, Marvin Koller, and Michael Mulkay discuss humor in general, including ethnic humor, as a more or less formal social process serving specific social functions. Thus, unlike Berger and Davies, who do not examine the meaning of ethnicity as such and simply accept popular views, Koller and other sociologists point out that ethnicity is a complex issue. Ethnicity can mean different things to different people, even to those who readily identify with one or another ethnic group. But many do not. Surveys conducted with hundreds of students have consistently shown that many are not quite sure what to say when asked about their ethnic identity. Their initial response is simply "American." When prompted, quite a few say they are not sure, but they think one or another grandparent or great-grandparent may have been from Italy, Ireland or Eastern Europe, and so on.

A majority of students, however, report mixed ethnic backgrounds. One parent may be of German descent and another Irish, one Jewish and another Italian. There are many such combinations of Mexican, African American, Native American, Swedish, Polish, and so forth. Moreover, there are others who report three or four lines of descent from grandparents as well as parents. One student described herself as a "Heinz 57," because she had one grandparent who was an orphan raised in a German family, another who was a Louisiana Cajun, and a mother who was Japanese.

Students with mixed backgrounds also have interesting ways of deciding how to select an ethnic identity. Often it is based on family dynamics, so that one of them, whose father came from a Polish family and whose mother was descended from Scots, said that she identifies with the Polish side because her father enjoys telling Polish jokes. Those with African American and Mexican or Native American parents say they identify as African Americans if they are relatively dark skinned, or Mexican or Native American if they are lighter skinned. In this case, they tend to choose the group that fits the way they are generally perceived. It follows that the humor within their family and ethnic group of choice, as well as the humor that may be directed against it, can have a number of significant implications that are not always obvious to casual observers. Some of these have already been touched upon by Berger and Davies, but the perspectives to be discussed in the following paragraphs bring a distinctive sociological focus to the study of humor.

Primary to this focus is the assertion that it is essentially a social activity. Individual personality qualities are also considered important, but sociologists have a powerful argument in the fact that people who are alone do not tell themselves jokes or create witty remarks in order to make themselves laugh. At a very basic level, this assertion is borne out by the research mentioned earlier showing that people cannot tickle themselves in order to bring on laughter. More to the point is research showing that people find it hard not to laugh when they are with others who are laughing, or when they are exposed to an audiotape of others laughing. (This is why some TV sitcoms come with canned laughter.) Of course, we may laugh aloud when we are alone reading something funny or watching it on TV, but then we are in the symbolic presence of others. On those occasions when we are alone and might laugh at ourselves because we have done something particularly silly, sociologists would say that we are simply taking the role of the other, acting as an observer of ourselves. Another curious outcome of such situations is that we often cannot wait to tell someone else about our foolish behavior. How many times have you heard someone start a conversation with something like, "Wow! Did I do something dumb today!"

The reason why many of us will go out of our way to ridicule ourselves in this fashion is because it can provide obvious social benefits. That is, people will typically exploit self-disparaging humor because it is a way of gaining attention, acceptance, or improved social status with someone else or within a group. To tell jokes on yourself, or by extension, your own ethnic group, is to show you are a regular guy who can enjoy a little self-ridicule. President George W. Bush is quite good at this, and easily jokes about his occasionally mispronounced words or confused grammar. This is also one of the sometimes "innocent" reasons why some people will tell jokes disparaging another individual or group; they claim it is to see whether or not "they" are regular guys. The interesting psychological principle here is that in both cases the humor can serve the same general purpose, as a type of social testing (can "they" take a joke without getting upset?) or self-enhancement (I can tell a joke on myself without getting upset). Sociologists also point out that those who habitually tend to use humor as a way of relating with others or gaining acceptance in a group are likely to adopt one or another of the following social roles: the *clown*, the *fool*, the *wit*, or the *joker*. Each of these roles implies a different behavior pattern. The clown does silly things to provoke laughter (recall the class clowns in every grade school). The fool will often adopt a deliberately exaggerated stupid attitude. The wit comes up with sarcastic, usually cruel but amusing remarks, and the joker is one who is always telling jokes or planning practical jokes. A single individual may act out more than one such role. The class clown and fool I recall from grade school would fart, belch, and offer deliberately silly answers to our teacher's questions.

Sociologists further emphasize that shared jokes, whether self-critical or critical of others, can provide an important means of establishing group cohesion. This occurs among children and adolescents in sports teams, clubs, and gangs, as well as among adults in ethnic groups and various occupations: police, firefighters, doctors, paratroopers, et cetera. The more distinctive the ethnic group or hazardous and stressful the occupation, the more likely it is to have distinctive forms of insider jokes and humor. Studies have shown that a high level of group cohesion, pride, and morale usually goes with a feeling of superiority to other groups, or, in the extreme, with disparagement of anyone who is not a member of one's own group. Thus, newcomers to any cohesive group frequently have to show that they can tolerate a certain degree of ridicule without getting upset, in order to prove themselves worthy of acceptance.

The social context of humor can be a critical determinant of whether or not people will accept or laugh at any joke, including ethnic jokes. Professional comedians, for example, can get away with all sorts of racial or ethnic slurs and insults when in front of an audience that has come primed to laugh and where there is an implicit, shared understanding that the material is all in fun. A good example is how a minority audience will enjoy comic routines containing insulting stereotypes about their own group. As long as the insults are not pushed too far, they can be enjoyed as an expression of pride or group solidarity. So a successful Mexican American comedian always gets applause from Mexican American audiences when he proclaims that Anglos are wrong about Chicano teenagers always stealing hubcaps, because "We don't take hubcaps, we take the whole car." Jews enjoy the joke about the Jewish man returning from being turned down for a job as a radio announcer. When asked why he did not get the job, he replies: "S-s-same old th-thing, p-p-prejudice."

In general, sociology studies show that humor is usually initiated and directed downward from those with higher to those with lower social status. The higher status individual (supervisor, boss, military officer, etc.) will typically make a humorous remark or tell a joke, to which the lower status person may then respond, but it is rarely the other way around. As will be noted later in connection with gender humor, in the past, it was usually males who initiated humor with females. Any female who took the initiative to joke with men was at risk of being labeled a "loose woman." The same principle applies to higher versus lower status ethnic or racial groups. In the Old South, whites might initiate humor with blacks, but blacks who "knew their place" would hardly ever do this with whites.

A related sociological finding is that people generally laugh more and rate jokes as funnier when they ridicule members of an out-group rather than members of their own in-group. But as noted earlier, there are many exceptions, such as when a Jewish comedian tells Jewish Mother jokes in front of a Jewish audience. There are some jokes with an ethnic flavor that seem to play well with everyone because of their universal appeal. The following is a good example.

> "A traveling salesman comes to a small town in the Midwest and notices a sign 'Don't miss the Amazing Goldstein performing tonight at the Fairground.' With nothing to do that evening he wanders over to the Fairground where he sees the stage lit up, and on it a table with three walnuts. Soon, an announcer introduces the Amazing Goldstein. Onto the stage comes a little middle-aged man who goes up to the table, opens his fly, and proceeds to crack open the walnuts with his penis. The audience bursts into astonished applause, and the salesman is amazed. Fifteen years later the salesman is at another little town and again sees a sign advertising the Amazing Goldstein. He goes to the show, where the same little man comes on stage only this time he cracks three large coconuts with his penis. The salesman can't believe it. He goes backstage

where he finds Goldstein and asks, 'The walnut act was incredible, so how come you are now doing coconuts?' to which Goldstein replies: 'Vell, I tell you, mine eyesight ain't so good anymore.' "

The noteworthy thing about this joke is how it combines the elements of incongruity, surprise, and ethnicity. It works particularly well because Goldstein is obviously Jewish, and the surprising punch line is innocently amusing rather than disparaging.

Taken together, the theories of ethnic humor and the related sociological perspectives reviewed both emphasize the instrumental importance of ethnic humor within ethnic groups. Despite the politically correct view that such humor may contribute to prejudice against minorities, Davies and others argue there is little or no concrete evidence for this, and a good deal that indicates the contrary. Yet research on ethnic jokes and comedy routines has largely been relegated to the back of the general humor bus because of its apparent connection with prejudice. The majority of scholars are not eager to publicly challenge this view even though it is contradicted by substantial research findings. When the contents of a large sample of ethnic jokes were scrutinized in a 1979 study, for example, it became clear that they were mainly about the behaviors of ethnic groups that deviated from commonly accepted social norms or values. It was the deviations that provoked the laughter, rather than any strong dislike or prejudice concerning the ethnic groups. The conclusion was that most ethnic jokes and comedy routines amuse large audiences because they emphasize common human foibles appreciated by everyone. A similar general conclusion was reached by J. M. Olson and two associates in 1999. They carried out an experiment to see if disparaging humor about men would influence the attitudes of college women toward men, and found no effects. In further research they found that when college men and women were exposed to disparaging jokes about lawyers, their view of lawyers did not change.

Another study carried out a few years ago in Hawaii is particularly striking because in this multiethnic society, humor based on ethnic stereotypes was reported to be not only acceptable but also desirable by a large sample of the population. That is, people in Hawaii apparently have an implicit understanding of how such humor helps to defuse potential conflicts between various groups, and have developed a form of social etiquette involving self-ridicule as well as jokes about others. The relatively benign quality of most ethnic humor was also discussed in a 2001 report by the scholar Harvey Mindess. He studied the jokes and funny stories popular among various ethnic groups in America and found little evidence for the idea that such material contributes to prejudice. Instead, his general conclusion was that it had beneficial effects, such as bolstering the morale of ethnic minorities and fostering mutual understanding between them. An excellent example confirming this point appeared several years ago in an Israeli survey of immigrants from the Soviet Union. They shared jokes and anecdotes about the prejudices and other difficulties they experienced while adjusting to their new environment, and most of them said this helped them deal with their anxieties.

As is clear from the foregoing, some social scientists are beginning to reluctantly give up on the commonsense idea that disparaging jokes promote prejudice. For example, in their 2004 review of current experimental research, Thomas Ford and Mark Ferguson concluded, "It does not appear that exposure to disparagement humor reinforces negative images of the targeted group." But they did not say anything about the potential benefits of ethnic humor, a point I will emphasize later on. For the moment, it seems clear enough that the work reviewed in this chapter can be summarized in two general statements: first, there is no significant malice associated with laughter at jokes based on stereotypes, and second, such material is generally popular within minority groups. This does not mean that minorities never wince or feel insulted when their group is singled out for ridicule. Considerable social research done in the 1930s, 1940s, and 1950s demonstrates that painful reactions were common in the past, when prejudice and discrimination against minorities and women were widely accepted. Some of that persists in the present. But the climate in our increasingly multiethnic society is very different today, so much so that it is not unusual to hear of white males complaining about discrimination. In the following chapter, however, we take a step backward to examine the less attractive elements of racial and ethnic humor.

4

The Origins and Psychology of Stereotypes and Slurs

> Good taste and humor are a contradiction in terms, like a chaste whore.
> —*Malcolm Muggeridge*

There is no denying that stereotypes and ugly slurs are the mother's milk of racial, ethnic, and gender humor. Although most of us are quite familiar with them, taking them for granted like air pollution as one of the less attractive elements of our environment, some consideration of their origins and uses can provide important perspectives on their significance. Yet just because slurs like kike, spic, nigger, and gook are so familiar, it is fair to ask, why should we bother with them? The obvious "intellectual" argument would have it that since vulgar slurs and stereotypes are not only part of our own culture but are also found all over the world, we ought to know something about them. Where did they come from, why can we not get rid of them, and why are they so much a part of popular humor? While this rationale is good enough for openers, there is something much more concrete to be gained. By confronting slurs and stereotypes head on through social and historical discussion, we strip away most of their harmful emotional power. This power to manipulate the feelings of others explains why, throughout human history, competing groups have been using insult and ridicule against one another, and also among themselves.

It is within groups, however, that we can frequently see the most vicious use of slurs and stereotypes. If any member of a group fails to show proper enthusiasm for whatever struggle or rivalry happens to be going on—anything from a football game to a major war—the others will usually turn on that person with insults comparable to those directed against "the enemy." In this case, however, it is the enemy within, the indifferent slackers who will not pull their weight toward the group's goal, or the awkward, ineffectual individual whose behavior is an embarrassment to the group, that becomes the target of slurs and ridicule. On a broader scale, within every dominant majority group there are slurs and stereotypes applied to its own members who do not live up to its standards. "White trash" and "trailer trash" are two examples of slurs that have been used against people seen as inferior by the dominant members in society. While it is usually true that the ultimate aim of stereotypes and slurs is disparagement, in many situations such disparagement serves a variety of functions. Certainly in the extreme cases of war and national rivalries, slurs and stereotypes are employed to dehumanize one's opponents, or at least reduce them to a laughably inferior status. Within nations and groups, disparagement may also be used to enforce conformity to dominant standards of behavior. There are also occasions when positive and negative stereotypes can be pitted against each other simply in order to generate a humorous incongruity. So in general, slurs and stereotypes can be more complex than we usually think, and this comes up immediately when considering the difference between them.

Ethnic slurs are defined as "insulting or disparaging remarks" that serve as a kind of shorthand way of referring to the negative qualities associated with any particular group. They are quite specific. Hispanics might be called "spics" and Jews "kikes"; each term would stand for a specific cluster of traits assumed to be typical of Hispanics and Jews. This of course raises the question of how to quickly insult Hispanic Jews—would they be "spic kikes" or "kike spics"? We can let that go, although there is a relevant cross-over joke: "What do you get when you cross a kike with a spic? A medical student who steals hubcaps." This example shows how shorthand group insults or slurs can evoke contrasting stereotypes that make for a surprising incongruity. We also have a broad range of group insults to choose from. The first formal dictionary devoted to slurs referring to nationality was published in England in 1785. It contained approximately fifty derogatory terms, mostly referring to the Scotch, Irish, and Dutch. By 1944, when the Harvard psychology professor A. A. Roback published his *Dictionary of International Slurs*, he included nearly three thousand disparaging references to various national and ethnic groups. In 1983, the sociologist Irving Lewis Allen found that more than a thousand different slurs, which he called nicknames, had been applied to ethnic groups living in North America. The sheer volume of this special vocabulary is enough to make one pause to wonder at the dark ingenuity of our species. When it comes to the uses of slurs in humor, however, quality rather than quantity is what counts. Some ethnic slurs are apparently more insulting than others, and many of them have had such limited historical or regional currency as to be unrecognizable today.

For example, Irving Lewis Allen's "lexicon of ethnic epithets" includes a long list of insulting references to African Americans that would be meaningless to most, if not all, blacks and whites today. Who would know that a "jaybee" is someone who looks jet black? Or that an African American might be called a "moke"? This term goes back to the 1850s when freed black slaves were called "smoked Yankees"; it was later reduced to "smokes" or "smokeys," and finally abbreviated to "mokes." The physical features shared by many members of an ethnic group are the most easily identifiable basis for slurs. Native Americans were "redskins" (even though their skins were not red). Jews were thought to have long noses and accordingly called "eaglebeak" or "schnozzola," whereas the hair texture of African Americans lent itself to "burr-head" and "wooly-head." Asians were called "slant-eyes" or "slants," although during the Korean War American soldiers came up with the generic term "gook" for Koreans, and this was later applied to all Asians. The curious thing about this term is that it originated with Koreans and referred to Americans. According to one of my students who was raised in Korea, the Korean word for Americans is "mi-gook-in." So it seems that when GI's heard this, they took it as "me gook" and generalized "gook" to all Koreans.

Another, rather uglier slur passed on to me by a former law enforcement officer from the Southwest is the term "tonk," applied to illegal border crossers from Mexico. He explained this was based on the sound made by a three-cell flashlight when it strikes the head of a tonk! Those protecting the southern U.S. border also sometimes refer to illegals as being "wet," or "wets," presumably from wading across the Rio Grande, and this term figures in at least one violent joke that can be heard along the border: "How is a 'wet' like a cue ball? The harder you hit him, the more English you get."

When distinguishing appearances are not available, slurs often focus on food habits: "limeys" for the English because their sailors were traditionally fed limes to prevent scurvy, "krauts" for Germans who ate sauerkraut, "frogs" for the French who ate frogs' legs, "mackerel snappers" for Catholics who were supposed to eat fish on Fridays, and "spaghetti benders" for Italians. In the American military, members of elite special operations units trained to live off the land have been called "snake eaters." Some slurs have less apparent origins and are applied to more than one group. Any Mexican, Italian, or Filipino could be called a "spic." One theory is that the term evolved from the phrase "no speak (spic) English." A more impressively esoteric slur is the word "pickaninny," referring to small African American children. It is said to have originated from mispronunciation of the Portuguese "pequenino," meaning little one.

The best known, most insulting ethnic slurs in contemporary society are those reserved for the groups with the longest histories of oppression, blacks and Jews. In his admirably detailed 2002 book titled *Nigger: The Strange Career of a Troublesome Word,* the African American Harvard professor Randall Kennedy notes that the N-word is derived from the Latin "niger," meaning black. After discussing the various meanings that have become attached to the word, some of which can be affectionate as well as insulting, Kennedy also explains that some black entertainers, athletes, and writers are trying to detoxify the N-word and claim it as a token of pride. The psychology of this process is considered later in this chapter, but disparaging use of the N-word has been traced back to the seventeenth century. This is when the early Spanish and Portuguese explorers who reached black Africa referred to the people they encountered as Negroes. Mispronunciations by the slave-trading whites who soon followed yielded "nigra" and "nigger." There is no clear explanation of just why this corruption of the Portuguese and Spanish word for black should have become the most insulting of ethnic slurs. Nor is it clear why the N-word should have been used in the past to create odd, pejorative metaphors that most of us would not recognize today. Until informed by a knowledgeable African American colleague, for example, I never knew that based on former segregation practices in public places, the upper balcony of a theater was called "nigger heaven," or that a "nigger toe" was slang for a brazil nut, and someone receiving a financial windfall was said to be "nigger rich." Some authorities suggest that the N-word has been such a powerful, all-purpose term of insult and abuse because it lends itself to a particularly contemptuous tone of voice; it simply sounds especially ugly. Others think that it may have taken on an extreme insulting quality because it became widely used by blacks themselves to disparage other blacks. Randall Kennedy's personal reflections on the word include his grandmother's habit of referring to disreputable Negroes in this fashion.

There is something of a parallel here to the way "kike" has evolved as the most frequently used insulting slur for Jews. Scholars agree that it is a Yiddish term first used in America during the 1880s by Jewish immigrants from Germany as a way of expressing their contempt for East European Jewish immigrants who were often illiterate. There are several different theories about its origin, but the one most widely accepted is based on the fact that the Yiddish word for circle is "kikel." The story goes that when asked to sign documents, illiterate immigrant Jews who had been persecuted by Christians were reluctant to make their mark with the usual "X" because they saw it as representing a crucifix. Instead, they would sign with a circle, and soon became known as "kikels" or "kikeleh," which after a time was abbreviated to kikes, and was applied to all Jews. It is also said that as government inspectors on Ellis Island noticed how immigrant Jews frequently signed papers with a circle, they would remark, "Here comes another kike." An interesting alternative

explanation suggests that it was based on the word "keek," a Yiddish term referring to individuals who were hired by tailors and clothing manufacturers
to spy on the new designs in production by their competitors. I can add a
parallel to Randall Kennedy's observation about his grandmother: my own
Jewish mother often referred to ill-mannered Jews as kikes.

Another ethnic slur that may have originated within the group it refers
to is "wop." Italian Americans and many others believe that it came into use
in the 1890s when some Italian immigrants could not legally document their
status and were accordingly designated with the acronym WOP, meaning
"without papers." However, scholars maintain that it was more likely derived
from the Southern Italian word "guappo," for a show-off or bully, and then
pronounced in America simply as wop. Here too, other derivations have been
suggested, such as "working on pavement," because many Italian immigrants
worked on road construction crews, as well as the fanciful idea—undoubtedly based on some comedian's routine—that wop is the sound made when
a pizza is thrown against a wall.

If immigrants and minorities were often the source of ethnic slurs that
were used to demean them, they were also not entirely passive victims and
were well able to respond in kind. In Mexico and other Latin American countries, North American whites are called "gringos." Jews have the Yiddish slur
"goy" for gentiles. African Americans and other minorities of color refer to
Anglo and other European whites as "honkys," a term first applied to Hun-
garian immigrants with the abbreviation "hunky" and later generalized to all
whites in African American slang as honky. Blacks also appropriated southern white slang expressions to refer to whites. The term "peckerwood" was
originally used by upper-class whites to disparage poor whites in the 1930s,
and blacks began using it in the same way. "Redneck" is similarly derivative:
woodpeckers have a red mark on their necks, and poor whites who worked
outdoors were likely to be sunburned on the back of their necks.

Slurs and the obscenities often used to enhance their insulting impact
both seem to be universal. There is hardly any national, racial, or religious
group that does not have some sort of insulting name attached to it, just as
there is hardly any language in the world that does not have its own vocabulary of obscenities. Scholars of obscene language—yes, there are language ex-
perts who specialize in the origins and uses of dirty words—have identified
approximately 1,200 words referring to sexual intercourse, and the American
motion picture industry has a list of seventeen words that automatically trigger an R rating for a film. The word "fuck" is apparently the most popular
and has the widest range of uses. It is believed to have originated in Latin as
futuo and then in French as *foutre,* and was first used in English in 1503 by a
Scottish poet. It can be used to designate disgust (fuck this), indifference (fuck

it), frustration (fuck me), abuse (fuck over), playfulness (fuck around), as well as in acronyms, such as FUBAR (fucked up beyond all recognition) and SNAFU (situation normal, all fucked up). Its use by stand-up comedians has become almost mandatory in relation to all varieties of ethnicity, including white Anglo-Saxon Protestants ("fucking WASPS"), as well as men and women. (Gender humor is considered in detail in a later chapter.)

Given these facts of life, there is good reason to believe that human beings everywhere have a deep-seated need to demean others with slurs and obscenities; why else do we all have these linguistic tools so readily available? Yet why is it that most of us try not to use them, or feel more or less guilty when we do? There are superficial answers to these questions that relate to conventional social norms and campaigns for political correctness, but psychoanalytic theory would maintain that our conflicted feelings about using or even listening to obscenities and ethnic slurs run much deeper and reflect a persistent conflict between the components of our personality. The instinct-driven, impulsive id is attracted to the primitive pleasures associated with obscene slurs, whereas the moralistic superego prohibits them. So Freud's theory would argue that our laughter at much of racial and ethnic humor is a release of the tension between our id and superego. But there is usually some tension left over in the form of guilt feelings. We know it is wrong, yet it is our awareness of this that makes the insulting language attractive as a primitive form of self-assertion. Merely by hearing or saying "fucking kike, nigger, honky, spic," or some other ethnic slur, many of us can experience a momentary sense of power or satisfying feeling of superiority. It follows that such phrases will be most appealing to people at the low end of society frustrated by their lack of power or to others who feel abused in situations where they cannot assert themselves. So if you get a traffic ticket from a black or white policeman or a bad grade from a Jewish teacher, you can at least take a momentary symbolic revenge by muttering some obscene slurs under your breath. Some people exhibit this vengeful type of behavior when they see someone they dislike on TV and make nasty remarks to the screen.

Humor provides one of the only acceptable ways for us to freely indulge in the guilty pleasures associated with morally unacceptable topics and language. More important, it is comedians who pave the way for us to dip into this domain of negative emotions and anxieties. They take it upon themselves to bring up sexual, racial, and other forbidden topics, and by situating them in the context of humor, the tensions that are aroused can be released as laughter. Thus, with a few exceptions such as Bill Cosby, who has vowed to never use ethnic slurs or obscenities, most comedians exploit such material because they know it stimulates the tensions that are necessary to generate laughter. This can be a risky game, because having once taken the responsibility to push their audience toward a direct confrontation with forbidden material, if comedians fail to convert the tension they have created into humor with a clever punch line, the disappointed audience is likely to become angry and release its tension upon the comedians themselves. The rise and fall of the stand-up comedian Andrew Dice Clay is a noteworthy example. He achieved some initial success doing raunchy sexual and gender routines targeting women. But as time went on, his act seemed to consist mainly of obscene slurs about women that were not very funny. The result was that women, and many men too, began to boycott his shows; influential women performers refused to appear on the same venue with him, and his comedy career ended. On the other hand, no matter how raunchy their material may be, if comedians can wrap it in humor, audiences will accept and applaud them, even if the audience itself is being ridiculed. Richard Pryor, for example, could emphatically ridicule the social and sexual behaviors of white middle-class men and yet have these same men rolling in the aisles. Part of his success may have been due to his apparent impartiality, because he often would ridicule the behaviors of black men as well. Eddie Murphy and Chris Rock can also do this successfully, whereas George Carlin has successfully ridiculed almost every aspect of mainstream American culture, as well as making many Catholics laugh at his routines about attending a Catholic grade school.

Carlin is one of the few comedians today who has tried to seriously defend the uses of slurs and obscene language in humor. His arguments boil down to the claim that words, unlike sticks and stones, are essentially harmless. They only have meaning insofar as we choose or have been conditioned to endow them with meaning. Carlin is not the first comedian to make this argument, however, and he would probably not hesitate to nominate Lenny Bruce for this dubious honor. During a relatively short career that ended with his death in 1966, Bruce was arrested at venues in Hollywood, Chicago, New York, and San Francisco because he violated local obscenity and so-called public decency laws by uttering words like "fuck" and "cocksucker" while performing in nightclubs. To make matters worse, instead of just paying fines imposed by the courts, he would demand a trial, claiming that obscenity laws were fundamentally unconstitutional. One the more notorious ways that Bruce defended himself in court was by claiming that since God had endowed all of us with sex organs and desires, anyone who found mention of these things objectionable should really take it up with Him. Bruce also argued that the definition of obscenities or filth lay in the eye of the beholder. Years later, Bruce's position was vindicated by Supreme Court decisions leading to the abandonment of most obscenity laws.

Carlin simply claims that he uses obscenities such as "motherfucker" as little more than a form of punctuation in his routines. Carlin also argues that as such words are frequently repeated they begin to lose their shock value. Like Lenny Bruce, in 1972 Carlin was arrested for violating public obscenity laws. During his act at an open air concert in Milwaukee, he used the words "fuck," "fucker," and "motherfucker," and since the police claimed that children might have been in the crowd, he was charged with corrupting the morals of minors. Carlin went on, however, to make the comedy record mentioned in a prior chapter, containing a routine famously titled "The Seven Words You Can't Use on Television." (They were "shit," "piss," "fuck," "cunt," "cocksucker," "motherfucker," and "tits.") The record became a milestone in the culture war over obscenity, and when a radio station played it on the air the FCC threatened to withdraw its broadcasting license. This led to a series of lawsuits ending up in the Supreme Court, which ruled in 1978 that although the words were "indecent," they were in fact "speech" within the meaning of the First Amendment, and the FCC could only ban them from radio during hours when children were likely to be listening. Carlin became a hero to his fans over this issue. He once tried to sum up his position on the multiple meanings of indecent language with a line proclaiming: "I don't take no shit 'cause I don't give a shit."

Carlin's general "sticks and stones" argument can also be applied to the uses of racial and ethnic slurs. In this view, depending on the circumstances when they come up, words like "wop," "kike," "nigger," and "honky" may lose their culturally conditioned insult value. Some humor scholars such as Alan Dundes tend to agree, and suggest that in certain instances, ethnic groups have converted slurs into positive statements. The best example of this occurred during the civil rights movement of the 1960s when African American activists coined the phrase "black is beautiful." Until that time, the term "black" was taken as a slur when applied to Negroes. And of course, most African Americans are not literally black. Yet by defiantly throwing the term "black" into the teeth of white society, the civil rights fighters were able to put such an effective positive spin on this formerly insulting slur that today it is widely accepted, whereas the once-acceptable "Negro" now seems a bit like a throwback to the days of slavery. Another case in point occurred some time ago at the inspiration of a young Jewish musician in Texas named Kinky Friedman. Having grown up in an area where there was a good deal of popular anti-Semitism, he was able to gain publicity for his band by calling it *Kinky Friedman and the Texas Jewboys*. Used in this fashion, the ethnic slur became an attention grabber and a defiant gesture of pride in the face of prejudice. The same technique has been employed by the rap music group called NWA, which stands for "Niggas With Attitude." As this manuscript is being written, two additional examples have been mentioned in the news. A Jewish motorcycle club in New York has deliberately asserted their identity with the name "kikes on bikes," and at a recent gay pride rally in San Francisco a lesbian motorcycle group paraded under the name "dykes on bikes."

Within many ethnic groups, slurs can sometimes be used as a sign of affection or comradeship. Among blacks, the phrase "say what, nigger" can be a token of intimacy or comradeship. The black comedian Dave Chappelle has been criticized for his frequent use of the N-word in his performances but claims that he uses it as a gesture of solidarity with other blacks. Randall Kennedy mentions that the soul singer James Brown is sometimes praised by blacks for being "a straight-up nigger." Among Italians, Jews, and Irish, terms like "wop," "kike," and "mick" can also be either insulting or affectionate depending on the context. One of my Italian American colleagues who grew up in Cleveland in the 1950s tells me that he and his friends did not mind being called "dagos" and would use that term among themselves, but they would fight if called "wop." This distinction may have originated from the fact that "dago" is thought to have been derived from "Diego," a popular first name among Spaniards that was mistakenly applied to Italians, as in, "he's another Diego," and was not seen as particularly insulting.

In sum, one of the more interesting psychological aspects of ethnic slurs and insults is their ambiguity. The old cowboy movie cliche, "Smile when you say that, pardner," captures this phenomenon very nicely. It is no mere accident that when some old friends or relatives meet they are likely to exchange insulting or obscene remarks by way of greetings. This sort of thing clearly stands as testimony to bonds of affection so strong as to allow people freedom to violate conventional behavior norms. The violation itself (e.g., "how are you, you old wop/kike/black/sonuvabitch, etc.") becomes a literal token of intimacy. Of course, common experience indicates this does not occur very often except among fairly young men, who—if they are seriously macho— are also likely to show their feelings by laughingly greeting each other with a punch in the arm or stomach. It is interesting, however, because there is no established psychological explanation for this contrarian behavior. Psychoanalytic theory would suggest that it is a defense mechanism protecting the ego against strong emotions, and sociologists might suggest it is a way for close friends to show their contempt for middle-class values, a gesture of superiority over conventional sentimentality. The humor scholar Elliot Oring touches on this issue in a recent essay where he argues persuasively that one of the features of modern life has been the "suppression of sentiment." As an example, Oring points to the way greeting cards have changed over the past fifty years. Instead of expressing sentimental feelings on the occasion of a birthday or anniversary, greeting cards are now more likely to contain funny cartoons and ironic remarks. Oring believes that in other contexts as well humor has come to serve as a substitute for sentiment.

In any case, it should be clear that slurs and obscenities can be used in a variety of contradictory ways to express feelings that are not always negative. It would be absurd, however, to argue that disparaging slurs have no shocking or significant emotional impact; if they did not, comedians would not use them, and they would not show up in conversations between intimate friends. But as suggested by the work of Christie Davies, the use of such slurs can be understood as one of the ways in which people play with aggression. It is also arguable that slurs and stereotypes can be ridiculed when they are pitted against each other in ethnic jokes:

> "How can you tell if an Irishman is queer? If he prefers women to drinking."

> "What's the difference between a Jewish American Princess and a Puerto Rican woman? The Puerto Rican woman has real orgasms and fake jewelry."

Walter Lippman first introduced the term "stereotype" in a book about public opinion published in 1922. It is now formally defined as "A standardized mental picture held in common by members of a group and representing an oversimplified opinion, affective attitude, or uncritical judgement (as of a person, a race, an issue, or an event)." Lippman appropriated the term from printers who used a metal casting called a stereotype in order to produce exact copies of texts. In some respects, slurs and stereotypes are similar to each other because they are based on what appear to be the typical characteristics of specific groups. They differ, however, because slurs are usually based on particular physical or behavioral qualities and aimed at insult, whereas stereotypes can involve more complex values, attitudes, or personality traits and are not necessarily negative. Thus a common North American stereotype is that Asian students are inherently very good at math, and there are ethnic jokes to the effect that when an Asian student enters a math class, the grading curve will immediately go up. This essentially positive stereotype might be upsetting to some Asian students, but it is difficult to construe as insulting.

Another relatively benign stereotype widely accepted during the 1970s and 1980s, when Japan was considered to be an economic powerhouse, portrayed the Japanese as extraordinarily successful at business, particularly in the auto industry. Although there was substantial resentment at the time—unemployed American auto workers would occasionally bash Hondas and Toyotas—there was also a good deal of envy. In a cartoon of the period, a woman was shown gazing at her toddler playing on the floor and saying to her husband, "I do hope Junior grows up to be someone successful, like a doctor, lawyer or a Japanese." There was also a light bulb joke: "How many Japanese does it take to change a bulb? One, but first he buys the building." My personal favorite from this period was a cartoon sketch of a typical Western saloon. A Japanese man in a business suit carrying a briefcase is shown entering through the swinging doors, and the grizzled bartender looks up saying, "Howdy stranger . . . or should I say pardner?" (This cartoon appeared when Japanese corporations were in fact buying up a good deal of ranch land throughout the western United States and Canada.) In all of these cases the stereotype is obvious but not clearly insulting. Finally, the strongest evidence I know of for the fact that ethnic stereotype humor can be benign or even affectionate is the success of Garrison Keillor's Lake Wobegon monologues that often emphasize stereotypes about Norwegian bachelor farmers, Lutherans, Catholics, and Unitarians living in Minnesota. A typical Keillor joke is one he told about why, as compared with Catholic and Lutheran funerals, Unitarian funerals are particularly sad: "Because the deceased is all dressed up with nowhere to go." Most Minnesotans, including Unitarians who reject notions of heaven and hell, apparently enjoy such humor and are not offended.

Then again, it is clearly true that at the international level, stereotypes about national character are the basis for an endless variety of disparaging jokes. Such jokes have been studied by the folklore scholar Alan Dundes, and the following examples are from his 1987 book *Cracking Jokes: Studies of Sick Humor Cycles and Stereotypes*:

> "An Englishman an Irishman and a Scotsman each finds a fly in their cup of tea. The Englishman gets a spoon and scoops it out before drinking. The Irishman takes the fly out with his fingers before drinking, and the Scotsman carefully picks up the fly and wrings it out before drinking."

> "An Englishman, a Frenchman, a Texan, and a Mexican are in an overloaded plane that can only carry one passenger safely. The Englishman cries 'God Save the Queen' and jumps out. The Frenchman cries 'Vive La France' and jumps out. The Texan cries 'Remember the Alamo' and pushes out the Mexican."

> "Two men and a woman are shipwrecked on a desert island. If they are Spanish, the men will fight a duel and the survivor gets the girl. If they are French, one man becomes the husband and the other the lover. If they are English, nothing will happen because no one is there to introduce them so they won't speak."

Note how the stereotypes of miserly Scots, violent, prejudiced Texans, and overly formal Englishmen all refer to assumed traits or behavioral tendencies.

Dundes adds that the structure of such jokes is always the same. A case in point is the following joke I heard when living in Norway for a year. It is based on Scandinavian stereotypes about Norwegians as roughnecks, Danes as comfort-loving, and Swedes, like the English, as concerned with good manners.

> "Following a shipwreck, there are two Norwegians, two Danes, and two Swedes stranded on an island. When the Norwegians encounter each other, they get into a fist fight; when the Danes meet, they start planning to open a restaurant, and when the Swedes meet, they ignore each other because they haven't been properly introduced."

Dundes claims that in order to dramatize the relevant stereotypes, people representing them—usually just three or four because more than that might be asking too much of the audience—are placed in a standard situation allowing their different reactions to be contrasted. He also emphasizes that within many nations, regional stereotypes are the basis for disparaging jokes. In the United States, Germany, and Italy, for example, such jokes involve contrasts between hardworking northerners and lazy southerners, presumably because the north is more heavily industrialized than the south. But it is the opposite in Brazil, where industry is concentrated in the south and it is the northerners who are stereotyped as lazy.

Another type of national stereotype joke identified by Dundes is called the "crossbreed riddle" that targets two or more nationalities:

> "What do you get when you cross an Italian with a Mexican? A gangster on welfare."

> "What would the son of a Jewish mother and a Polish father be? A janitor in a medical school."

> "What are the three shortest books in the world? Italian War Heroes, Jewish Business Ethics, and Who's Who in Puerto Rico."

Finally, some forms of disparaging national stereotypes take the form of epigrams:

> "One German is a philosopher, two Germans is an organization, three Germans is war."

> "A Hungarian and a Rumanian will both sell you their grandmother, but only a Rumanian will deliver her."

In addition to the types of ethnic jokes based on national and regional stereotypes, Dundes suggests that there are stereotypes about stereotypes. This can take the form of generalizations about the patterns or styles of stereotype humor that appear to be typical of different nations. Such national styles have been studied by the Israeli scholar Avner Ziv. In the collection of essays on this topic he edited in 1988, Ziv mentions research showing that American students enjoy hostile jokes more than Japanese students, sexual humor is more prevalent among the French than the Belgians, and there are many Irish jokes about drinking and fist fighting but practically none concerning these themes in Israel. Ziv further observed that the value associated with humor is different in various countries. Business and government leaders in the United States use humor more often than leaders in France and Italy, and TV humor programs are more common in the United States and Britain than elsewhere. Ziv's anthology includes a number of articles by humor scholars on the types of ethnic jokes popular in different countries, some of which are briefly summarized in the following paragraphs.

Australia: According to the article by Davis and Crofts, the main targets of traditional Australian humor were middle- and upper-class Englishmen, commonly called "pommy bastards." The basic stereotype, going back to the time when the British used Australia as a penal colony, has been of Englishmen as arrogant stuffed shirts who look down on Australians as inferior provincials. Thus, "A pompous pommy is trying to find the subway in Sydney and asks an Aussie for directions, saying 'Excuse me old fellow, could you tell me how to get underground?' to which the Aussie replies, 'Sure thing, drop dead you pommy bastard.'" Other groups disparaged in Australian humor include the indigenous people called "Abos" (from aborigines) and recent immigrants from Asia. Because most of the original European population of Australia was made up of rough-and-ready males, women also became a traditional target of jokes:

> "An Aussie approaches a young lady and says, 'What about sex?'
> 'No,' she answers.
> 'Well then, would you mind lying down while I have some?'"

France: The essay by Baudin et al. points out that the traditional victims of ridicule in French humor were women, the Catholic clergy, government officials, provincials, and immigrants. Women were often disparaged for deceiving their husbands, although a husband who is deceived by his wife was also a stereotyped figure ("cuckold") to be laughed at. During much of French history, the Catholic clergy was a dominant force in society, and contradictions between their secular and religious activities became the basis for disparaging humor. During the Napoleonic era and afterward, the French government became very centralized, attempting to impose uniform standards throughout the country, and this made government bureaucrats the object of ridicule. Finally, immigrants and people from the various French provinces are often ridiculed for their regional or foreign accents.

Italy: In his contribution to Ziv's anthology, Paolo Consigli describes the stereotypes that are the basis for much Italian ethnic humor. Sicilians are the butt of jokes about their family honor and the Mafia; Genoese are ridiculed for stinginess, Romans about their love of feasts, and the women of Bologna about their "special sex services." Disparaging stereotypes are also the basis for humor about misbehaving Catholic priests, fanatical Communists, corrupt politicians, and the police (Carabinieri), who are singled out for stupid jokes.

Israel: Ziv's own work on Israeli humor emphasizes historical changes in the ethnic groups targeted. Early on, there were many jokes about the British, who governed over what was then called Palestine. Later, when Israel became a separate state and many Jewish immigrants arrived, the Rumanians were stereotyped as thieves, Moroccans as knife fighters, and Germans as overly formal snobs. Surviving Holocaust victims were sometimes called "soap," because body fat from Jews slaughtered by the Nazis was supposedly used to make soap. As the new state matured, disparaging humor focused on politicians and the many different religious and secular groups competing for power. Oddly, despite their history of conflict with Palestinians, Israelis have not generated much in the way of popular jokes aimed at ridiculing Palestinians or other Arabs.

America: In many respects, American ethnic humor follows the same general pattern found in other countries, insofar as minorities, immigrants, politicians, and often women have traditionally been the butt of jokes. As Davies concluded in his studies of ethnic humor around the world, the underlying patterns seem to be virtually universal, but the ways in which they are played out in different societies vary depending on specific historical and cultural factors. An example of this can be seen in how American stereotype jokes emphasize "dirty." This disparaging term does not appear in most other societies because they are less concerned with cleanliness as a moral value. On the other hand, as Ziv has suggested, historical factors probably account for general similarities between humor in Australia and America. Both countries were once part of the British empire and were populated by immigrants, and they share similar frontier values emphasizing self-reliance, individualism, dislike of rules and regulations, and skeptical views about authority figures.

According to Don and Aleen Nilsen's contribution to the Ziv anthology, three major, traditional types of prejudice have been responsible for most stereotype humor in the United States: prejudice against people of color, prejudice against newly arrived immigrants, and prejudice against regional, peripheral groups. During the nineteenth and the first half of the twentieth century, jokes and theatrical performances disparaging people of color, including slaves from Africa, Native Americans, Mexicans, and the Chinese re-cruited to build railroads, clearly served as a popular way of justifying their exploitation. By making these people the butt of jokes showing them to be stupid or lazy, dirty, dishonest, or sexually promiscuous, it became easier to view them as inferior beings only fit for manual labor. In other words, such humor contributed to the acceptance of prejudiced attitudes and helped to soothe the moral conscience of white Christian Americans who profited from racism.

There were certainly other whites, most notably Mark Twain, who used ironic humor and satire in attempts to subvert this trend. Prevalent public opinion, however, was very similar to that of the Europeans who colonized Africa. They viewed the natives of color as childlike barbarians and them-selves as benefactors bringing the natives Christian civilization as part of "the white man's burden." This was clearly the attitude of most whites in America, including those who, even while they opposed slavery and were sympathetic to blacks, nevertheless freely joked about their behavior. Abraham Lincoln himself was a celebrated storyteller who was not above using jokes at least mildly disparaging of blacks. As reported in an 1888 memoir by William D. Kelley, at a meeting during the Civil War some of Lincoln's visitors com-plained about the excessive number of casualties suffered by the Union army in recent battles. Lincoln responded that they needed to reconsider the num-bers according to "darky" arithmetic. Puzzled, they awaited Lincoln's expla-nation, which consisted of the following story:

> "Two young contrabands, as we have learned to call them, were seated together when one said, 'Jim do you know 'rithmetic?' Jim answered 'No what is 'rithmetic?' 'Well,' said the other, 'it's when you add up things. When you have one and one, and you put them together, they makes two. And when you subtracts things, if you have two things, and you takes one away, only one remains.' 'Is dat 'rithmetic?' 'Yes.' 'Well 'taint true den; it's no good.' Here a dispute arose, when Jim said: 'Now, you s'pose three pigeons sit on that fence, and somebody shoot one of dem, do t'other two stay dar? I guess not, dey flies away quicker'n odder feller falls.'"

Lincoln then went on to explain to his still puzzled listeners that darky arith-metic applied to the figures reported after every major battle. Any men not responding to roll calls following the action were listed as casualties, but in fact, these figures were always wrong because many of the men had just be-come separated from their units and would soon find their way back.

Another example of Lincoln's ethnic humor was recorded in the diary of his Navy Secretary, Gideon Welles. Published in 1911, the diary includes an entry for February 2, 1864, recounting that when Welles approached Lincoln about a potential problem concerning the Spanish oppression of Dominican Negroes, the President said it was a dilemma: he could not afford to antagonize Spain, but neither could he afford to lose credibility with those supporting the Negro cause. He continued on, remarking that the problem reminded him of the story about a Negro preacher who tried to warn one of his flock named Joe to mend his wild ways, by telling him that he was on two roads, one leading straight to hell, and the other to damnation. Joe replied that he would not take either road, but go through the woods. Lincoln concluded the story by saying that he would go neither for Spain nor the Negro, "but shall take to the woods."

The second major dimension of ethnic humor in America was focused on immigrants. No other country in the world has been populated by such huge waves of immigrants with different cultural values and languages. Consequently, much ethnic humor in the United States came to be based on jokes about the dialects and linguistic errors of successive waves of newcomers. Such jokes have been interpreted as both a way to allow those who got here earlier to feel superior and a way to encourage the so-called greenhorns to hurry up and learn proper English. Other immigrant behaviors and values related to food preferences, table manners, and personal cleanliness (many of the nineteenth- and early twentieth-century immigrants had never seen indoor plumbing and only took a bath on special occasions) were also ridiculed. Noteworthy too is that there was no love lost between various immigrant groups. Finding themselves immersed in the rough-and-tumble, free-wheeling American society where the operative rule, especially in the nineteenth century, was something like "Anything goes as long as you don't get caught," different groups had no choice but to compete for jobs and housing. Young male immigrants in the urban ghettos banded together in gangs that later became the basis for Irish, Italian, Jewish, and other crime "families," and mutually derogatory humor employing ethnic slurs and stereotypes was common. The Italian American situation has been portrayed so often in popular films emphasizing organized crime that the Mafia stereotype still remains current and is routinely exploited by stand-up comedians. One of Jackie Mason's jokes along this line is about his half-Jewish and half-Italian friend: whatever he cannot buy wholesale, he steals.

The third leg of the traditional American ethnic humor triangle extended beyond people of color and immigrants to regional or peripheral groups such as New England Yankees, Appalachian hill dwellers, Swedes and Norwegians in Minnesota, Texans, southerners in general, and in the past, Mormons in Utah. Such groups typically had, or still have, one or more distinguishing characteristics that are easily translated into disparaging stereotype humor. Unlike most immigrants who usually try to fit into mainstream society, many of these groups maintain a sense of pride in their distinctiveness. As a result, they can take on the status of permanent aliens who become stock characters in all varieties of comedy. Thus, New England Yankees are portrayed as shrewd, tight lipped, suspicious of strangers, and set in their ways. Al Capp's long-running comic strip *Li'l Abner* was based on stereotypes about hillbillies who are supposed to be ignorant, superstitious, violent, gullible, and partial to eating possums and squirrels. The characters he developed for his comic strip—Abner was strong and simple minded, Mammy Yocum was the tough old grandmother who smoked a pipe, and Sadie Hawkins was the sexy young woman out to entrap Abner—were later more or less reproduced in the *Beverly Hillbillies* TV series.

The writer and comedian Jeff Foxworthy has made a career out of redneck jokes ridiculing the southern white males he grew up with. One of his best-known routines specifies that "You might be a redneck if:

You thought the unabomber was a wrestler.

The biggest city you've ever been to is Wal-Mart.

You remarry three times and still have the same in-laws.

You mow the lawn and find a car.

You missed graduation from sixth grade because you had jury duty.

One of my students from the South who is a Foxworthy fan remarked in class that his northern friends seem to think that as soon as a guy moves to the South he goes to live in a trailer and tries to marry his sister.

In the nineteenth century Mormons were ridiculed for their practice of polygamy. The humorist Artemus Ward said of their leader, Brigham Young, that he "loved not wisely, but two-hundred well" and "Pretty girls in Utah mostly marry Young." Swedes and Norwegians who settled in Minnesota have been ridiculed for their accents, stolid temperaments, love of ice fishing, and ability to eat ludefisk (overly ripened codfish). Among the many jokes about the latter told in Minnesota is one about the Norwegian who asks a Dane if he has ever eaten ludefisk. "No," replies the Dane, "but I think I stepped in some once."

The major social factors responsible for the development of traditional American ethnic humor have been covered in the foregoing discussion. Deliberately omitted are critically important contributions to contemporary American humor that are almost entirely due to the reactions of groups that were ridiculed: immigrants, people of color, Native Americans, and others considered marginal to mainstream society. All of these groups created their own stocks of slurs and stereotypes aimed at the white gentile majority. This will be taken up in later chapters emphasizing the central role of Jews and African Americans.

Before we leave the present chapter, however, a relatively unique national style of ethnic comedy—calypso—deserves attention because it apparently violates some of the generalizations described up to this point. Rather than having emerged from a context of prejudice against minorities or conflicts between them, calypso seems to have developed in Trinidad as a rhyming musical style of ridicule humor that could be directed against anyone. According to a detailed study carried out in the 1970s by James Jones and Hollis Liverpool, a remarkable blend of cultural, historical, and ethnic traditions has made calypso an important way of life in Trinidad. Briefly, folklore has it that calypso began in the late eighteenth century among African slaves who worked on a plantation owned by Pierre Begorrat. At some point, probably in order to help celebrate a special occasion, Begorrat's slaves were encouraged to create and perform rhyming songs emphasizing his virtues as well as joking comments about other plantation owners. A few particularly talented slave performers were so good at this that they were given special privileges by Begorrat. As their reputations spread, slaves at neighboring plantations began to emulate them. In some instances, these performers were emboldened to make up humorous rhymes with double meanings that were actually critical of their owners. They could often get away with this because their rhymes were mainly done in a mix of French slang and slave vernacular and were highly entertaining. But this was risky behavior; some of the slave masters caught on to the ridicule and meted out severe punishments to performers who went too far. Instead of discouraging the calypso singers, however, the risk of punishment only seemed to make them try harder. As time went on, many of the plantation owners came to enjoy the creative routines invented by their slaves and would reward singers who could make up rhyming songs that ridiculed rival plantation owners. The practice spread, and it became a major form of entertainment throughout the island.

When slavery ended in 1834, the more outstanding liberated performers took it upon themselves to continue creating musical commentaries on current events. Known as "Calypsonians," they expanded their material to include satirical rhymes about sexual behaviors, politics, and race relations. Their performances also became a major feature of the annual Mardi Gras carnival parades. With the rise of tourism in the twentieth century, visiting vacationers were treated to amusing parodies of themselves. The Calypsonians achieved a special status in Trinidad, becoming known as verbal warriors who used humor to criticize government officials and voice the needs of the poor. Noteworthy too is that while calypso remains a unique ethnic synthesis between humor, poetry, and music, a clear parallel can be seen in the growth of rap music in the United States. Both were developed by people of color at the low end of society (rapping began in prisons and urban ghettos). Both emphasize clever rhymes about sexual, social, and political issues, use double meanings, and typically criticize prominent institutions such as the government or police. A final striking parallel between calypso and rap is that despite their focus on criticism and ridicule of established institutions, both successfully entered mainstream white society. The same thing is true of the Jewish and African American traditions of humor examined in the following chapters.

In sum, while many people will undoubtedly continue to be offended by the slurs, obscenities, and stereotypes inhabiting all humor traditions, I would hope that after having some of their surprising origins and sundry uses held up to the light, their power to insult and intimidate has been reduced. This is what I have observed among many students when they began to appreciate that language itself is a somewhat messy human invention that has never been static or antiseptic. It is rather more like a smelly compost pile that slowly cooks to generate much of the linguistic fertilizer that writers, musicians, and comedians rely upon in creating the works that shape and feed our culture.

5

The Dominant Role of Jews and African Americans: Lenny Bruce, Richard Pryor, and the Culture of Irony

All my humor is based on destruction and despair. If the whole world were tranquil, I'd be standing on the breadline right in back of J. Edgar Hoover.

—*Lenny Bruce*

The title of the piece was "The Yiddishization of American Humor." Was this yet another variation on *The Protocols of the Elders of Zion* claiming that Jews were out to take over the world? Or at least elements of American culture? No, it was the title of a 1965 article in *Esquire* magazine pointing out, quite correctly, that nearly all popular comedy in our society was now either being created by Jewish writers, comedians, and producers or being heavily influenced by them. This was at a time when it was estimated that Jews amounted to only 3 percent of our population but were responsible for 80 percent of our humor. If the article had been written a dozen years later, it could have proclaimed with equal justice: "The African Americanization of American Humor," because by the late 1970s the generation of black writers and performers who would further revolutionize comedy were making their mark. Thus, in addition to the slurs and stereotypes discussed in the prior chapter as the raw material of racial and ethnic humor, most culture commentators today agree that over the past half century, American humor has largely been the creation of Jews and African Americans.

When you think of it for a moment, the astonishing fact is that in hardly more than the lifetime of many senior citizens today, Jews and blacks have gone from being the most prominent targets of ethnic jokes and prejudice in general to become the most successful, widely imitated humorists—stand-up comedians, writers, TV personalities, and Hollywood stars—in our society, and much of the Western world as well. This remarkable transformation should be obvious to anyone familiar with our popular culture, which now includes as near standard English some of the language disseminated through Jewish and African American humor. Most of us know, for example, what is meant by phrases like "Jewish Mother" or "Jewish American Princess" and Yiddish-isms like "shmuck," "schlemiel," or "shiksa." So too are we familiar with black slang like "gimme five," "uncle Tom," "say what," or "shuckin and jivin." We even have widely accepted and imitated models or prototypes of contemporary Jewish and black comedians in the images projected by Woody Allen and Seinfeld, on the one hand, and Bill Cosby and Eddie Murphy, on the other. In this context, the stage name Whoopi Goldberg can be seen as a stroke of genius.

How did this happen? How did the humor associated with Jews and blacks change from focusing on them as objects of ridicule and prejudice to being created by them and focused on the ridicule of not only white gentiles but everyone—including themselves? To answer this question in depth would take another book, but to entirely ignore it would be to miss some of the ways in which humor is profoundly linked with the dynamics of social change. It should come as no surprise, therefore, that humor scholars have devoted a great deal of attention to the study of Jewish and African American humor and to the implicit question of how their ethnic styles and perspectives have become virtually synonymous with present-day American humor. The literary scholar John Lowe had already anticipated this question in a comprehensive discussion of ethnic humor published in 1986, where he suggested that Jewish and black comedians were responsible for the general sense of humor that currently prevails in America. So how did they do it?

When faced with such questions, historians and others who study social change invariably emphasize explanations appealing either to cultural processes and events that alter "the climate of the times"—the so-called Zeitgeist theory—or to the impact of outstanding individuals—the "great man" theory. It will be argued here that both of these theories clearly apply to the transformation of ethnic humor, although scholars may disagree about which one has been more important. There is little disagreement, however, about why Jews and blacks have become the dominant sources of contemporary humor. They, more than any of the other groups in our society, have suffered from the most intense forms of prejudice. Unlike prejudice against the Irish, Hispanics, Italians, Asians, and other ethnic groups, prejudice against Jews and blacks has been far more severe because it was, and in some ways still is, based on both religious and pseudoscientific grounds.

Where Jews are concerned, their persecution throughout most of the history of Christianity centered on their presumed responsibility for killing Christ. As if that were not enough, with the rise of science in the nineteenth century, racist biology contributed the idea that Jews were genetically inferior to white gentiles. The same combination of factors has been responsible for the persecution of blacks. On the authority of certain passages in the Bible, blacks have been labeled as "the children of Ham," inferior beings fit only for manual labor. This was thought to be confirmed by racist scientific findings purporting to show that blacks were mentally and emotionally inferior to whites. As a result, and because historically both minorities were too weak to resist by taking direct action, Jews and blacks have had the greatest need to develop traditions of humor as a means of coping with their situations. Today it is well understood that humor tends to be most appreciated and valued when people find themselves in stressful, precarious circumstances. So the long history of persecution experienced by Jews and centuries of slavery endured by blacks helps explain why humor has been such an important feature of their cultures. But it does not mean that as some sort of "compensation" for their oppression every persecuted group will inevitably develop a strong tradition of humor. There are all too many such groups around the world that demonstrate the contrary. What has been relatively unique about Jews and African Americans is that their suffering was never so extreme as to prevent them from holding on to meaningful values, traditions, and a vernacular language of their own.

But if their respective histories can account for the high value Jews and blacks have placed on humor, this does not yet explain why or how their traditional styles of humor have become characteristic of mainstream American society. The Zeitgeist theory suggests two plausible reasons. First is the obvious fact that the "climate of the times" has profoundly changed over the past half century. Following World War II, which revealed the horrors associated with Nazi racism, previously common practices of prejudice and discrimination were increasingly seen as irrational and unfair and thus a contradiction of basic American values. It also became particularly important to uphold American values of justice and equality in the context of the cold war in order to show our superiority to the Soviet Union. In short, it became unacceptable to maintain a racially segregated military and to post signs or run ads saying "whites and gentiles only" or "no Jews or Negroes need apply." During the 1960s, the civil rights movement led by Martin Luther King Jr. succeeded in dramatizing the oppressive effects of white racism as well as finally undermining the legal mechanisms that had supported discrimination. By the end of the 1970s, if most forms of discrimination based on race, religion, or gender had not entirely disappeared, they had at least become illegal.

In addition to these profound social changes, a more subtle culture trend emphasizing the use of irony began to emerge in our culture during the 1970s. Irony is easier to describe with examples than it is to define, because it can take many different forms. One of the most common is when someone says the opposite of what they really mean, such as when hearing bad news, we may respond "Swell!" in a flat tone of voice. A more clear-cut illustration of irony was the phrase "Kill for peace" that some American soldiers in Vietnam stenciled on their helmets. These examples fit the dictionary definition of irony as "a mode of speech, the intended implication of which is the opposite of the literal sense of the words." But there are many other forms of irony. A recent *New Yorker* cartoon, for example, shows two studious-looking young women sitting at a restaurant table where one is saying to the other, "I first became a vegetarian for health reasons, then it became a moral choice, and now I do it just to annoy people." On some occasions, too, serious public statements attain the status of ironic punch lines if they seem obviously questionable. When Bill Clinton first ran for president he acknowledged that he had once smoked marijuana and then added, "but I didn't inhale." This phrase was quickly seized upon by comedians who used it as an ironic punch line in various routines "I beat up my wife but I didn't inhale," etc.). The same sort of thing has overtaken the military phrase "collateral damage." Certain lines from classic films—"We don't need no stinking badges" (from *The Treasure of the Sierra Madre*) and "I was misinformed" (from *Casablanca*)—have also become standard items in the vocabulary of irony. Nor is irony limited to verbal remarks. Andy Warhol's famous painting of a Campbell's soup can was considered to be a breakthrough ironic statement about the meaning of art. The famous novel and film *Catch-22* provides an elaborate illustration of irony in the scene where Yossarian, the antihero airman, complains to his squadron physician that flying combat missions is making him crazy, and the physician replies by saying that this proves he is sane and therefore must go on flying.

Another approach to the appreciation of irony can be found in its derivation from the Greek word *eironeia* meaning to dissemble or speak falsely. In the ancient Greek plays there was often an actor performing the role of an eiron, someone who pretended to be weak or foolish in order to trick his or her adversary into making a fool of himself. This is a time-honored tactic of many women who have learned to play the dumb blond role when relating to powerful males. Judy Holiday and Marilyn Monroe both did this very effectively in some of their films, and Goldie Hawn first gained celebrity by acting the dumb blond on Rowan and Martin's TV show *Laugh-In*. Irony is also frequently presented as an attractive feature of powerful male movie heroes such as James Bond, who always has ironic remarks available for every occasion of sex or violence. In fact, popular films and movie stars provide a clear demonstration of the increasing presence of irony in contemporary society. One need only compare such he-man stars of the past like John Wayne and Gary Cooper, who were rarely given ironic lines in their films, with those today like Sean Connery, Arnold Schwarzenegger, and George Clooney, who invariably salt their films with ironic comments and asides. Indeed, irony has now become a virtual necessity for the portrayal of any attractive film character, and it is no wonder that bright teenagers today try to emulate this behavior when talking back to their parents.

The ultimate expression of the current prevalence of irony appeared in a 2002 *New York Times Magazine* article by Laura Miller describing the rise of a form of irony called "meta." This term has come into use to describe witty critical comments about any ongoing action or performance, such as when an actor may step out of character and offer an ironic remark about the role he or she is playing. Another example offered by Miller would be a TV sitcom about the making of a TV sitcom. Meta humor would also be illustrated by a stand-up comedian making jokes about being a stand-up comedian. In effect, irony reaches the ultimate level of meta when it can be turned against itself and ironic remarks are made about . . . ironic remarks.

The point of this discussion about irony is that it marks a cultural change that has occurred over the same period that saw the decline of prejudice and discrimination against Jews, African Americans, and other minorities. The striking thing about these two trends is that they have occurred within the same time frame and appear directly related to one another. A good case can be made for the idea that as Jews and blacks have gained increasing prominence in society, and particularly the mass media, their traditions of ironic humor have gradually trickled down throughout society.

Also relevant is that society was clearly becoming more receptive to ironic humor as events over the past fifty years were making people increasingly skeptical about the official pronouncements of government, industry, and science. That is, government assured us that the Vietnam war was necessary until it became clear that it really was not; President Nixon assured us that he was not a crook until the Watergate scandal indicated that he was; science assured us that nuclear power plants were safe until the Three Mile Island accident showed that they were not; President Clinton claimed that he did not have an affair with a White House intern until he admitted that he did; and more recently, we have had the spectacle of major corporate financial scandals and sexual abuses by a number of Catholic priests. These events, and many others as well, have eroded the credibility of traditional institutional authorities. The result is a widespread public attitude of distrust that easily lends itself to ironic and sometimes cynical humor. But while it can be difficult to tell them apart, there is a useful formal distinction that should be made between irony and cynicism.

Cynicism has been described as the attitude of one who typically expects only the worst of human behavior. It takes the form of bitter jokes or remarks about the human condition, such as: "A man on trial is in the hands of twelve people who were not smart enough to get out of jury duty," or "The rule of life is, eat the dinner or be the dinner." Irony is a near relative to cynicism, but usually goes beyond bitterness to express a value or redemptive truth about the human condition, as in Voltaire's famous remark, "If God did not exist it would be necessary to invent Him," or this Hanukkah joke circulated among assimilated American Jews: "Hanukkah is like most of the other Jewish holidays: they tried to kill us, we survived, let's eat."

The Jewish and African American humor traditions are predominantly ironic because they developed in historical contexts that were never completely hopeless, and rather than only expressing cynical feelings of bitterness or despair, their humor served as a defense against them. This is why it is arguable that in our present climate of social distrust, the type of protective, ironic humor traditionally associated with Jews and blacks has become appealing to almost everyone, although it is still most significant for those who feel abused. Contemporary Native Americans, for example, have moved beyond their traditional animistic humor and coyote trickster stories to ironic jokes about their condition. According to Kenneth Lincoln's 1993 review of Indian humor, this occurred as part of the Native American "renaissance" in the 1960s and may be seen in the works of Vine DeLoria and N. Scott Momaday. A discussion by DeLoria included the following one-liners:

> When asked how come the Indians were the first ones on this continent, an Indian replied:
> "We had reservations."

> What did the Indians call America before the white man came?
> "Ours."

> A missionary in New Mexico was explaining the concept of hell to an Indian. "It is a place for the wicked where all sinners end up. Do you understand?" "Yes," replied the Indian.
> "And what do we call that place?"
> "Albuquerque."

There is no way of knowing for sure if Native Americans began using ironic humor because of their exposure to the ethnic routines of Jewish and African American comedians that circulated widely in the 1960s, but it seems like a good bet.

In general, when fleshed out with the historical events and examples of culture trends outlined in the previous paragraphs, the Zeitgeist explanation for Jewish and African American domination over contemporary humor is quite persuasive, because their styles of ironic humor have a close fit to the climate of our time. But there is also a strong case to be made for the "great man" theory of social change (great women in humor are covered in a later chapter). While most historians tend to downplay the idea that any one individual, male or female, can singlehandedly change the course of history or alter the values and attitudes of a society, they will usually acknowledge that at least some important changes could not have occurred without the presence of a single, apparently indispensable individual. A few classic examples would include George Washington during and after the American Revolution, Winston Churchill in the early days of World War II, and Abraham Lincoln during the American Civil War. In physics we have the example of Albert Einstein, and within psychology, Sigmund Freud and B. F. Skinner. All of these figures stand out as great because they broke new ground, opened up new pathways of thought or action or both. While it clearly requires a long leap down the scale of major human events to go from wars and science to comedy, there is no doubt that the great man principle can be applied here as well.

When considering the remarkable influence of Jews and blacks on American humor, many scholars and critics agree that the outstanding figures during the early 1960s and 1970s, respectively, were Lenny Bruce and Richard Pryor. Their status as the metaphorical fathers of current American humor is not only based on the opinions of culture commentators and humor scholars; no less an authority than comedian Jerry Seinfeld has a similar opinion. He was quoted in *Time* magazine (11/4/02) as flatly declaring, "Today's style [of comedy] started with Lenny Bruce," and he referred to Richard Pryor as "perhaps the greatest artist of all standups." But there are some dissenters. In a recent popular study of innovative comedians, *Seriously Funny: The Rebel Comedians of the 1950s and 1960s,* Gerald Nachman suggests that Mort Sahl was a more significant pioneer of the free-wheeling, spontaneous style of stand-up comedy than Lenny Bruce. Nachman also gives priority to Stan Freberg, Tom Lehrer, and a few others for pushing the boundaries of humor well beyond the carefully scripted performances of the earlier headliners like Bob Hope and Jack Benny. Nachman more or less dismisses Richard Pryor as a latecomer who only arrived in the 1970s after the new styles of comedy had already been established. This may well be correct so far as the general development of stand-up comedy is concerned, but when it comes to racial and ethnic humor, I would still argue for the overriding importance of Bruce and Pryor. Mort Sahl was certainly a brilliant innovator, but he was never primarily known for head-on engagement with racial and ethnic material. In any case, if it is granted that this view, along with Seinfeld's, is at least approximately correct and that the obscure Jewish guy from Long Island, New York, and the poor black guy from Peoria, Illinois, were somehow able to catch the wave of social change and use it to create new paths for American humor, the question becomes, what did they do and how were they able to do it?

There are a few quick and easy answers. What Bruce and Pryor did was bring the essence of Jewish American and African American ironic humor out of the ethnic/racial closet, and they were able, each in his own way, to do it by turning loose their deep consciousness of ethnic minority experience. This means that in the context of humor, they found ways to speak to their audiences about issues that had previously been publicly unspeakable, namely, the contradictions, hypocrisies, and absurdities of prejudice and sexuality, not only among white gentiles, but also and most uniquely within their own minority groups. Mort Sahl was very good at some of this too, but he generally stayed with intellectual and political humor. By contrast, Bruce and Pryor had an electrifying effect on audiences as they delivered what was thought to be outrageously obscene, controversial material in a conversational, stream of consciousness style—as if they were simply thinking out loud to a group of friends. Both of them, for example, defied the prevailing standards of decency, let alone good taste, by doing routines about interracial sex, homosexuality, and cunnilingus; they ridiculed patriotism, racism, and organized religions that catered to the middle and upper classes while ignoring or exploiting the poor. Lenny Bruce even had a routine about Jesus returning to earth and being shocked to discover the grandeur of St. Patrick's cathedral while people nearby were living in poverty and another bit ridiculing the hypocrisy of a prominent Jewish rabbi. Richard Pryor was famous for his parodies of fundamentalist black preachers, southern redneck sheriffs, and urban ghetto winos, thugs, and other persons of low social status. Furthermore, because they were both talented actors, they could literally embody the characters they would create on stage, sometimes acting out the voices and body language of two or three characters in a single routine.

Most of this, of course, is no longer considered startling or innovative, because so many comedians have followed in the pathways that Bruce and Pryor opened up. But when their style of comedy first gained attention, it was seen as both shocking and entirely new, light years removed from the traditional humor provided by established, mainstream comedians, as well as many of the "rebels" cited by Nachman, few of whom would ever get down and dirty about sex, ethnicity, religion, or patriotism. Bruce and Pryor, therefore, stand out because of both the substance and the style of their work. But a more complex question still remains: how did they get to the point of challenging the familiar patterns of mainstream American humor? What drove them to run the risks of rejection and condemnation? The only answers seem to lie in their strangely parallel life histories.

   Despite having been born into different generations (Lenny in 1925 and
Richard in 1940), raised in different regions of the country (New York and
Illinois), and exposed to very different ethnic cultures, their childhood and
adolescent experiences followed similar patterns. Lenny Schneider—Bruce
was his stage name—and Richard both had difficult childhoods. According to
Albert Goldman's account of Lenny's life and career, his mother was a
stagestruck young woman who neglected him, divorced his father when he
was about eight years old, and only saw him sporadically after that. He was
farmed out to relatives, and a few years later he was brought back to live with
his father and stepmother, a woman he never got along with. His schooling
was fragmented because of frequent moves. He was a bright child but a poor
student with few friends and often the target of anti-Semitic taunts by his
mainly gentile schoolmates. When he dropped out of high school to join the
Navy at age seventeen, he had only made it through tenth grade. Up to that
point, the brightest spots in his life consisted of either his fantasies, stimulated by movies and radio programs, or the occasions when his mother would
turn up and take him to see shows in the city.
   Richard Pryor's mother was a prostitute. She left most of his upbring-
ing to his paternal grandmother who ran a whorehouse in Peoria and raised
him with strict discipline involving a good deal of physical punishment. Being
from the wrong side of town and attending school with mostly white children, he experienced the usual racial taunts and became something of a little
wisecracking troublemaker. Recognizing his ability to get laughs, his sixth
grade teacher allowed him to do a ten-minute comedy routine at the end of
each school day if he would behave in class. When he was thirteen, he attracted the attention of Julia Whittaker, the director of a local community
center. She arranged to have him perform in a show put on at the center, and
this experience apparently stimulated his lifelong interest in acting. The
source of his flair for comedy is said to have been the hours he spent hanging around his grandmother's house where he enjoyed listening to the stories
told by customers, many of whom were musicians and comedians passing
through town. Neither Richard nor Lenny ever completed high school. As a
teenager, Richard already had a reputation with the local police for minor of-
fenses. After being expelled from high school for hitting a teacher, at age eighteen he joined the Army.
   On the face of it, given their different ethnic roots and childhood environments, there appear to be few similarities between Lenny and Richard's
early life experiences, but the social and emotional parallels are unmistakable.
Both emerged as alienated young adults attracted to the idea of finding a career in show business because this had been their primary source of pleasure
while growing up. And the parallel between them continued. Lenny spent

three hard years in the Navy during World War II, part of the time on a cruiser that saw heavy action in Europe. In 1945, when his ship was being refitted in Brooklyn, he was desperate to get out and was given a dishonorable discharge after successfully pretending to be homosexual. During Richard's two years in the Army he became a chronic discipline problem while stationed in Germany and was discharged in 1960. Following their experiences in the military, both of them began to build their careers, but at this point the parallel between them breaks down somewhat because Lenny had a more difficult time of it. He spent a few months in California attending an acting school and then returned to New York where his mother helped him get started as a comedian.

Working under the name Sally Marr, she had progressed from being a barmaid to doing jokes and introducing acts at small New York nightclubs. She introduced him to agents, gave him some of her comedy bits, and encouraged him to perform in amateur shows where he occasionally won prize money. This went on for a few years while Lenny took odd jobs and spent much of his time hanging out in a luncheonette where he traded jokes and gossip with other aspiring comedians. His first big break came in 1948 when his mother arranged a spot for him on the Arthur Godfrey talent show, where he won first prize doing impressions of famous actors using a comic German accent. For the next several years Lenny slowly worked his way up the comedy ladder playing nightclubs and summer resorts. He gained recognition doing dialect humor, impressions, and parodies of movies imitating various actors, a routine he essentially copied from Sid Caesar. It was all more or less mainstream, journeyman work, however. His major, innovative breakthrough to a new style of radically obscene racial and ethnic humor did not occur until 1958.

Richard Pryor's career accelerated much more quickly. After discharge from the Army he returned to Peoria, and with encouragement and help from his former mentor Julia Whittaker, he began performing in local nightclubs. (He never forgot her; when he received an Emmy award for TV work in 1973, he gave her the statuette.) By 1962 he was playing in clubs throughout the Midwest, and then moved on to New York clubs doing an act that was modeled on that of Bill Cosby, who was already a major star. Like Cosby, he steered clear of the obscene language and ethnic parodies that characterized his later work. Appearances followed on TV talk shows and Ed Sullivan's variety show. This exposure got him small parts in Hollywood films as well as bookings in Las Vegas during the next few years. But along with quick success came personal problems. During the late 1960s and early 1970s he developed a serious cocaine habit, was sued by the IRS for nonpayment of taxes, was accused of assault by his wife, and gave up performing to immerse himself in the Berkeley, California, counterculture movement. Yet by the end of 1972 Richard made a comeback. He developed a sensational new racial/ethnic nightclub act and for the next several years progressed through one important success after another, writing comedy pieces for films and TV shows and taking major roles in a number of hit movies.

One of the most impressive parallels between the careers of Lenny Bruce and Richard Pryor is the "creative moment" they both experienced about midway through their careers. This apparently occurred when, in the late 1950s and early 1970s, respectively, both of them were in or near San Francisco involved with drugs and radical, avant garde musicians, artists, and writers who were rebelling against mainstream American society. For Lenny in the late 1950s it was the so-called beat generation or "beatniks"; for Richard about fifteen years later it was the hippie movement that had morphed out of the beatniks. Both Lenny and Richard were deeply into these movements. Although the beatniks and hippies had different styles, fundamentally they shared the same antiestablishment values calling for sexual liberation, racial equality, and, for want of a better term, social justice for everyone including legal access to any drugs of one's choice. (All that remains of these heady ideas today is a bit of nostalgia carried by the cliche "sex, drugs and rock and roll.")

At the time, however, Lenny, and later Richard, absorbed these ideas and used them as the basis for unprecedented comedy routines. In Lenny's case, the professional breakthrough came at a San Francisco nightclub in 1958 with his performance of a satiric act called "Religions, Inc." It was an extended play on his whimsical notion of what it would be like if all the major religious, political, and media leaders were really just cynical Broadway hustlers and were having a sales meeting to figure out new ways to fleece the public. He mimicked the stereotyped voices of all the participants, such as the southern evangelist who wanted to promote new products: a "genyewine Jewish-star-lucky-cross" cigarette lighter, and cocktail napkins printed with the saying, "Anothuh mahtini for Mothuh Cabrini." He parodied Pope John talking on the phone to Oral Roberts, who spoke like a typical New York show business agent ("Hey Johnny, what's shakin, baby!") and was arranging a series of lucrative public appearances for the Pope while assuring him that nobody would know he was really Jewish. The routine went on with parodies of other revered celebrities in outrageous ways that had never been done before on stage, and it became an immediate smash hit among leading figures in the San Francisco counterculture and show business community. As reported by Albert Goldman, everyone who was anyone in the city, including college students, professors, and priests and ministers, flocked to catch the act and loved it. Executives from the Fantasy Record company saw Lenny perform and signed him for a comedy album.

Over the next few years he became immensely successful. By 1960 he had sold almost two hundred thousand records and was earning three thousand dollars a week in nightclubs, and the name Lenny Bruce had become a virtual household word among culture critics, intellectuals, and everyone who considered themselves to be "progressives." His act was meanwhile expanding as he improvised monologues on themes seemingly aimed at ridiculing and offending almost every group in society. Jews were among his most frequent targets. Thus, he would elaborate on the theme that Hitler might have been successful in show business if he only had been discovered and managed by a Jewish booking agent. Or that the secret ambition of most prominent Jews was to be mistaken for gentiles, or that Jews turned against Christ because he refused to become a doctor or lawyer, and that Jews were rarely shown as bad guys in the movies because the studio heads were Jewish. He also created whimsical dialect routines, such as the one about the genie in the neighborhood candy store:

> When a Jewish candy store owner opens an old bottle a Genie pops out and offers to grant him a wish. The storekeeper says he would like to take the day off if the Genie would mind the store, and the Genie agrees. Soon after a regular customer enters and asks the Genie what he is doing behind the counter. The Genie explains that has taken over the store for a day and he can do anything. "Is dat so," says the skeptical customer, "so let's see you make me a malted," whereupon the Genie goes "Va Voom! You're a malted!"

In much of his humor, Lenny was breaking new ground for comedians by not only acknowledging his own ethnic identity in a way that comedians in the past had never done (most Americans at the time did not know that Jack Benny, Milton Berle, George Burns, and the Marx Brothers were all Jewish), but also, and most remarkably, using his ethnic identity as one of the foundations for his act. Being Jewish, in effect, gave him license to ridicule the Jews, just as their ethnic identity now allows contemporary Asian American, African American, and other comedians to do routines about their own groups. But of course, many assimilated middle- and upper-class Jews were offended by Lenny's in-group humor. They saw his use of obscene expressions and Yiddish-isms not as a defiance of anti-Semitism, but an encouragement of it. Richard Pryor was later criticized in the same general way for embarrassing African Americans with some of his routines, and this pattern still continues. Some Korean Americans, for example, criticize Margaret Cho's routines about growing up in a Korean American family.

Lenny would also dominate audiences by delivering his monologues in a rapid-fire style that became known as "shpritzing," a Yiddish term for a sudden outburst, as when a bottle of soda is shaken up and allowed to spray outward. A 1987 article by Sanford Pinsker explains that Lenny learned the shpritzing style from one of the neighborhood characters he had known in New York, and with his increasing success he began using this technique to improvise on a given theme in the same way jazz musicians would improvise on a given melody. Pinsker's article (pp. 97–98) provides the following examples of Bruce shpritzing about sex:

> "Now, lemme hip you to something. Lemme tell you something. If you believe that there is a god, a god that made your body, and yet you think you can do anything with that body that's dirty, then the fault lies with the manufacturer."

> "To a lady [cheating] means kissing hugging and liking somebody. You have to at least LIKE somebody. With guys, that doesn't enter into it . . . like, a lady can't go through a plate glass window and go to bed with you five seconds later. But every guy in this audience is the same—you can IDOLIZE your wife, just be so crazy about her, be on the way home from work, have a head-on collision with a Greyhound bus, in a DISASTER area. Forty people laying dead on the highway—not even in the hospital, in the AMBULANCE—the guy makes a play for the nurse."

One important effect of this technique was that it kept audiences on edge because they never knew what might be coming next. For Lenny Bruce, however, after a few brief years at the pinnacle of his career, what would come next was a crash dive into self-destruction. In this respect there is yet another, uncanny parallel to the career of Richard Pryor.

Richard reached the pinnacle of his success as a stand-up comedian and film star during the mid-1970s. Although there were similarities between his work and Bruce's—both took on the same sacred cows in society, and both excelled at dialect humor directed toward their own ethnic groups—Richard's major comedic breakthrough was based on his acting talent. On a bare nightclub or theater stage, he was able to create fully believable characters representative of the black underclass: elderly winos, hustling preachers, drug addicts, hoods, and everything in between. His genius was in capturing the voices, street vocabulary, and even the body language and gestures of these characters, and placing them in common situations allowing their natural, spontaneous humor to emerge. As one respected commentator noted in a *New York Times* article, through his "speech and movements, he can create a scene that is comic and at the same time recognizable as profoundly human." But like most new art forms, his was controversial, especially among middle-class blacks, including Bill Cosby, who found his frequent use of obscenities and the N-word worse than

embarrassing. They viewed his act as encouraging white prejudices and stereotypes. This is quite understandable, given some of his famous routines about
how ghetto black movie audiences watching horror films would shout warn-
ings and obscenities to characters on the screen, or how black teenagers would
respond with farfetched excuses when arrested and brought into court. It made
matters worse that he freely used the N-word on his five award-winning comedy records. In 1974 the Grammy Award record was titled *That Nigger's Crazy*,
and in 1976 the award was for *Bicentennial Nigger.*

So it is not surprising that many blacks, and some whites as well,
thought he was exploiting prejudice to advance his career and sell millions of
comedy albums. But his routines also included brilliant parodies of rednecks,
tough cops, and white liberal social workers talking down to blacks. In one of
his most successful one-man performances, the 1979 film *Richard Pryor in
Concert*, he mimicked a wide range of middle-class white speech patterns and
contrasted their body movements with that of streetwise blacks. Another
noteworthy feature of this film was the extraordinary humor he created by
acting out the heart attack he had suffered the previous year. During these
high-intensity years, however, Richard was on and off into hard drugs. His
major self-destructive crash occurred in 1980, when he was on a cocaine jag
and claims in his autobiography that for reasons he still cannot explain he deliberately set himself on fire after pouring a bottle of brandy over his head.
Following a long, painful recovery from severe burns, he performed in a few
undistinguished films, but later required heart surgery, was diagnosed with
multiple sclerosis, and lives today as an invalid, by all accounts a mere shadow
of the remarkably creative artist he once was.

For Lenny Bruce, self-destruction came much more quickly and
abruptly. He was using a wide range of hard drugs during his success in the
early 1960s, while at the same time being sued by the government for back
taxes and fighting various indictments for public obscenity associated with
his performances in New York, Chicago, and other cities. By the time of his
death he had been arrested more than a dozen times on obscenity charges. In
1964, he was convicted and sentenced to four months in a New York City jail.
At the time this chapter was written, it was announced that the governor of
New York has granted Lenny a posthumous, retroactive pardon for his 1964
misdemeanor conviction.

Frank Kofsky, a historian whose book about Bruce's humor described
him as an important "social critic and secular moralist," claimed he was
hounded to death by the authorities because of his extreme ridicule of conventional values. During his final years, he did in fact complain to friends that
FBI and CIA agents were following him and tapping his telephone. No proof
of this has ever been discovered, but Lenny certainly added to his troubles by

defiantly adhering to a semi-outlaw lifestyle. His behavior, already erratic because of heavy drug use, increasingly fit the pattern of paranoia. By 1965 he was broke and in debt to lawyers and drug dealers. His nightclub act began to fail as he spent time on stage reviewing his legal problems with little or no humor, and he died of a drug overdose in 1966 at the age of forty-one. Richard Pryor was forty at the time he set himself on fire and began his subsequent decline. The final question, then, is how can the eerie parallel between their careers be understood?

The sociologist Georg Simmel would have found Lenny and Richard to perfectly fit his theory of "the outsider," the individual who seems destined from childhood to never quite fit in and always remain a stranger to his own society, even to his own family. According to Simmel's analysis it is the outsider—individuals like Franz Kafka, Vincent Van Gogh, and Friedrich Nietzsche—who is best able to see the problems in society that pass unnoticed by most people. But as the fate of such creative outsiders demonstrates, while they may eventually be recognized as culture heroes, this creativity comes with a heavy price tag. Growing up poor and Jewish and poor and black, Bruce and Pryor were outsiders right from the start. Their alienation was reinforced by their inability or unwillingness to conform as schoolboys or when serving in the military and later on as performers. So although their breakthroughs to a new style of unabashed, critically ironic and confrontational humor may not rank with the achievements of Kafka or Nietzsche, they clearly fit Simmel's outsider concept.

The outsider theme also relates to the ancient Greek concept of hubris, and quite directly to Joseph Campbell's work on the myth of the hero. Anyone familiar with Campbell's analysis can hardly fail to see how closely the careers of Lenny and Richard match the pattern he described. The analogy may be a bit strained, yet like the mythic heroes, both of them emerged from obscurity in their youth, experienced years of hardship and "testing" in raunchy clubs, and eventually attained important public success (the ancient Greek metaphor was "stealing fire from the gods"). Hubris comes into play because those jealous gods would punish human heroes who pushed their luck too far and began acting like gods themselves, by imposing self-destructive penalties upon them. Like the heroes of mythology, however, Lenny and Richard left behind them a precious gift. In this case, their precious gift was not fire or treasure but a powerful new form of humor allowing those who came after them to transform race and ethnicity from an issue laden with prejudice—something most Jews and blacks had previously repressed or tried to resist with rational arguments—to an occasion for ironic laughter and assertion of pride. The black author Langston Hughes must have had this in mind in 1957 when writing about racists in our society: "Since we have not been able to moralize them out of existence with indignant editorials, maybe we could laugh them to death with well aimed ridicule."

What their critics did not realize was that by openly confronting and ridiculing stereotypes and slurs rather than denying them, Lenny and Richard were deflating them, draining the emotional poison out of them, and allowing laughter to enter where before there had only been aggression or anger. This is not to say that there were no other minority performers contributing to the transformation of ethnic comedy. Dick Gregory, Shelley Berman, Joan Rivers, and Godfrey Cambridge were also pushing the conventional boundaries at about the same time. But none of them had anything like the dramatic impact of Lenny and Richard, who are seen by comedians today as the patron saints of contemporary American humor. Neither of them was purely self-invented, however, because both were able to draw upon background traditions to be considered next as the "roots humor" of Jews and African Americans.

6

Jewish and African American Roots Humor: Saving Grace in the Face of Oppression

> Humor is laughing at what you haven't got when you ought to have it.
> —*Langston Hughes*

> If I had no sense of humor, I would long ago have committed suicide.
> —*Mahatma Gandhi*

To speak of the "roots humor" of any group is to speak of the language and thought patterns that have evolved in that group and given birth to its characteristic humor. Or, to put it more directly, roots humor refers to the type of humor that grows out of the historical and cultural experiences of a particular group and becomes typical of that group. For a simple example, consider the military. The military is not an ethnic group, to be sure, but certainly is a group that has a distinctive culture of its own, particularly in combat units, where the characteristic humor is usually obscene and sometimes violent. In my own unit many years ago, it was considered perfectly hilarious when someone got on the battalion radio net for an unauthorized minute and did an obscene parody of our commanding officer. Practical jokes causing embarrassment or minor injuries were also popular. One of the high moments in my squad occurred when we knew an emergency alert was due early in the morning and we nailed our sergeant's boots to the barrack floor while he was asleep. It was also thought to be quite funny that during a training exercise one of our tanks ran over a German civilian's Volkswagen when he ignored our road guards. If all this seems rather ugly and nasty, that is the point about the roots humor of soldiers. Jewish and African American roots humor is far more complex, but the underlying principle is the same, insofar as their cultural experiences have been the basis for their traditions of ironic humor.

Different as they are in so many other respects, the main characteristics that Jews and African Americans have in common are centuries of oppression and, at least in North America, a more or less successful struggle against prejudice. But apart from this, the historical origins of their humor have remained controversial. Seeking the ultimate source of ironic Jewish humor, for example, some writers have exhaustively studied the Old Testament looking for evidence that irony was already present in the texts of the ancient Hebrews. Most scholars reject this notion, pointing out that the few examples found are not convincing and that while the themes of Jewish humor are often ironic, they are also often self-critical, aimed at deflating pretentious behavior or focused on the fact that pain and suffering are inescapable. Irony and self-criticism are combined, for example, in the joke about three Jews who are about to be shot by a firing squad. When the officer in charge offers each of them a blindfold, the first two bow their heads and accept it, but the third defiantly says no, at which point one of the others whispers to him, "Don't be a troublemaker, take the blindfold."

Efforts to trace the sources of African American humor back to remote tribal cultures or to ancient Egypt have also been disappointing. There are, to be sure, elements of humor and laughter to be found in African folklore, but nothing that approaches the subtle uses of irony that developed as part of the slave culture in America. The reason for this failure to find clear evidence of their characteristic humor in the early histories of both Jews and blacks is very simple: they just did not need it. As a matter of common sense as well as social psychology, it should be obvious that the oppressive social and emotional pressures encouraging people to turn inward and employ subtle forms of humor as a defense mechanism or covert source of self-esteem do not accumulate within groups that are independent and capable of self-determination. Free peoples can directly assert themselves against threats of oppression, maintaining their values and beliefs by direct action. Indeed, the Jews of the Old Testament and the precolonial tribes of Africa both have impressive histories of warfare. It was only with the loss of their freedom, when Jews became the pariahs of Europe and many black Africans were forced into slavery in the New World, that their condition would gradually stimulate the development of ironic humor.

There is no definitive explanation of how this type of humor developed across many generations. We can approximate how it most likely occurred, however, by appealing to the psychological finding that when direct, reflexive reactions against abuse or oppression are blocked, they are turned inward and become a source of emotional tension. Release of such tension can take various forms—withdrawal into fantasies, self-abuse, and in extreme cases a type of indifference called learned helplessness—all of which are often associated with alcoholism and drug addiction. But the most common way we release tensions that cannot be expressed openly is through passive aggressive behaviors. We can do this directly by acting as if we are too slow or stupid to understand what is going on, or indirectly by ridiculing the oppressive situation and the oppressors themselves behind their backs. A trivial example is the way schoolchildren make faces when their teacher is not looking. It is therefore easy to understand why various passive aggressive techniques of this sort, acquired and ingeniously refined over the years, became an important feature of Jewish and African American humor. The historical knowledge available easily supports this view.

Where Jewish humor is concerned, most scholars agree that its characteristic features can be traced to nineteenth-century Yiddish speakers living in Eastern European ghettos. Briefly, this was the environment of segregation, poverty, and persecution dramatized in the show and film *Fiddler on the Roof*. Because Jews were essentially powerless under these conditions (they were allowed to live in peace most of the time so long as they did nothing to anger the authorities), they adopted a passive aggressive coping strategy. Their feelings of fear, anger, and frustration were released by ridiculing gentiles among themselves. Thus, a typical phrase used by ghetto Jews to admonish other Jews who seemed a bit dense or slow on the uptake was to accuse them of having a "goyishe kopf," literally meaning a gentile head. There was also a good deal of ironic, self-critical humor, as could be seen in *Fiddler* when Tevya sings "If I were a rich man" or expresses his frustrations by engaging in one-way conversations with God. The psychological significance of such humor is that it nurtures self-esteem. By turning inward to explore their dilemmas, ridicule their oppressors, and verbalize the ironies involved to themselves, people are able to gain a sense of detachment that makes it easier for them to cope. The commonsense logic here is that when we cannot do anything about a nasty situation we can at least assert ourselves and rise above it by laughing at it.

Another, more specific feature of Jewish folk humor that emerged in the nineteenth-century East European ghettos was focused on pain, as can be seen in the old joke line, "It only hurts when I laugh" or the Yiddish proverb, "If you want to forget your troubles just wear a pair of shoes that are too tight." The chronic anxiety associated with their precarious situation in Eastern Europe was expressed in the classic Jewish response to any important event, "Is it good for the Jews?" For example:

"Have you heard that two Americans have built a flying machine?"

"Yes, but is it good for the Jews?"

As will be discussed in the following text in connection with African American humor, Jews also developed a strain of ironic humor aimed at deceiving or making fools of those who looked down on them. A good example is this joke circulated on the Internet:

"There were two beggars sitting side by side on a street in Mexico City. One had a Christian cross in front of him, the other one the Star of David. As people passed by they only put money into the hat of the one sitting behind the cross. A priest came along and told the beggar behind the Star of David, 'Don't you understand? This is a Catholic country. People aren't going to give you money if you sit there with a Star of David in front of you, especially when you're sitting beside a beggar who has a cross.' The Star of David beggar thanked the priest and then whispered to the Christian cross beggar: 'Moishe, look who's trying to teach us marketing.'"

There are many one-liners emphasizing the same sort of deception or superiority theme, such as, "Why did God make so many Gentiles? Because somebody has to buy retail."

During the nineteenth and early twentieth century in America, however, Jews were less often the practitioners than the targets of ethnic humor. In his 1973 study of Jews in early American humor, Rudolf Glanz cited typical examples of the jokes that appeared in publications of the period. Most of them ridiculed Jews for their concern with money and attempted to parody their dialect. Thus, from the magazine *Puck* in 1898:

"Isaacs: You t'ink der Anglo Saxons vos going to rule der eart?

"Cohenstein: Vell, mey be dey mighd, but dot von't brevent der Hebrews from owning id!"

A number of the jokes focused on the idea that when their businesses were failing, Jews would set them on fire to collect insurance. Another one from *Puck* in 1895:

"Isaacstein: Vot vos der cause of der fire?

"Burnupsky: Der insurance."

The stereotyping usually included a play on Jewish-sounding names, such as Burnupsky, or writing Bernstein as Burnstein. The 1898 volume of *Puck* also had a joke in which a Jew is asked to name his favorite poet and replies with

"Burns." As can be seen from these examples, most of the jokes cited by Glanz seem quite primitive and not very funny. Slightly more sophisticated is one from 1899, where a visitor solicits Burnupsky for a contribution to the Disabled Firemen's fund, and he responds: "Mit pleasure, but how vas you going to disable dem!" Another popular vein of anti-Semitic dialect humor portrayed newly successful, pretentious Jews as looking down upon the up-and-coming Irish. Several jokes had Jews complaining about the uncouth Irish immigrants who were moving into their neighborhood or ruining the atmosphere at their favorite summer resorts. This idea, whereby the moment a group settles into what they begin to see as their own urban or rural territory, they view new arrivals from any other group as running it down, seems to be a universal phenomenon and a perennial theme for humor. (In what might be the ultimate joke along this line, the Native American author Vine Deloria tells about the two Indians who are watching Columbus coming ashore, and one finally says to the other, "There goes the neighborhood.") Glanz also identified a wide range of nineteenth-century cartoons containing the classic stereotyped image of Jews: stoop shouldered, hook nosed, and bearded, very similar to illustrations of Shakespeare's Shylock and Dickens' Fagin. In fact, one cartoon shows a Jewish Fagin teaching American boys how to become pickpockets.

This was the general type of humor that millions of East European Jews encountered when they reached North America during the late nineteenth and early twentieth century. But all the anti-Semitic stereotypes portraying them as greedy, pushy, underhanded, and so forth, were relatively easy to cope with compared to persecutions they had left behind. Once they were settled in the bustling cities of the New World, many of them were attracted to the music halls and vaudeville theaters that were the chief source of mass entertainment.

The term "vaudeville" itself has a curious immigrant history. It is defined as a "stage entertainment consisting of various unrelated acts following one after the other: singers, comedians, jugglers, magicians, etc." Some authorities claim that the term is based on the French phrase *vaux de vire*, used to describe satirical songs that were composed as early as the fifteenth century in and around the town of Vire in northern France. In any case, such songs became known as *voix de ville* (voices of the town or streets). The phrase migrated to America, and in the early 1880s, was changed to "vaudeville" by John Ransone, who used it as the title for his troupe of itinerant entertainers. Its widespread use, however, is attributed to Benjamin Keith, a Boston showman who opened a theater for family-oriented variety shows in 1883 and called it vaudeville. Later on, as he and his partner E. F. Albee opened a string of such theaters, performers who moved from town to town were said to be playing on the Keith vaudeville circuit.

Much of the entertainment presented on the Keith circuit and in other variety theaters was essentially ethnic humor based on stereotypes. According to a study by Lawrence Mintz, between 1890 and 1910, comedy routines and sketches based on ridicule of immigrant dialects, misunderstandings of English, and stereotyped behaviors were the mainstay of vaudeville theaters. Comedians presented the Irish as drunks and brawlers, the Italians as carefree, irresponsible and operatic, the Germans as rigidly conservative, blacks as lazy and dishonest, Jews as devious, cowardly swindlers, and all of these ethnic types as stupid: dumb greenhorns or cotton pickers with only a primitive grasp of English. One of the surprising things about this situation is that most working-class immigrants, especially their children, enjoyed this material because it spoke directly to their experience. They tended to accept the gross stereotyping as self-evident, amusing exaggerations of everyday realities. Some of these ethnic youngsters, particularly the Jews and Irish, soon realized that they could get paid for making people laugh by going on stage with routines ridiculing their own and other groups. (Blacks did the same thing in their minstrel shows.) They began doing dialect humor on the vaudeville circuits, usually emphasizing the stupid and amusing behavior of greenhorns. A typical example is the bacon tree and ham bush story:

> "A pioneer wagon train is lost in the old West when the leader spies an immigrant Jew sitting under a tree. He rushes up to him and asks for help because the pioneers are starving. The Jew says 'dere is a bacon tree over de next hill but I vouldnt go dere if I was you.' The leader returns to the wagons and guides them toward the hill, explaining to the others that they will find bacon but the Jew cant eat it because it isn't kosher. On the other side of the hill is a party of Indians who attack the wagons and kill everyone except the leader who escapes and makes his way back to the Jew. Fiercely indignant, he asks, 'why did you tell me there was a bacon tree down there,' to which the Jew replies, 'Oi veh! I tink I made a mistook,' and begins paging through his English dictionary. 'Here,' he finally says proudly, 'I meant to told you dere vas a hambush down dere.'"

Another example is the joke about the Jew who goes to his rabbi claiming he needs a divorce because his wife has such filthy habits. Pressed by the rabbi to explain what they are, the man finally says that every time he goes to pee in the kitchen sink he finds it full of dirty dishes. There was also an endless string of one-liners:

> "Why did Moses accept the Ten Commandments? Because they were free."

"What is the favorite Jewish football cheer? Get the quarterback!"

"What did Mr. Mink give Mrs. Mink for Christmas? A full length Jew."

At first performing in small-time vaudeville and burlesque theaters mixing Yiddish with English for comic effects and using material making fun of their own group, the more successful Jewish comedians with stage names like Weber and Fields and Smith and Dale gained national reputations, and by the 1920s were followed by Fanny Brice, Eddie Cantor, the Marx Brothers, and Jack Benny, the most successful of all. Benny's career stands as a good example of the path followed by many Jewish performers.

His father, Meyer Kubelsky, came to America from Lithuania in 1889, stayed with family friends in Chicago, learned English in night school, and then with a rented horse and wagon began peddling household goods through small towns in Wisconsin. He saved enough money to buy a combination saloon and pool parlor in Waukegan and married, and in 1894 his son Benjamin was born. Started on violin lessons at age six, by the time Benjamin was fourteen he was first violinist in the high school orchestra, playing with a local dance band, and on his way to being expelled from high school for repeatedly failing all his classes. Like many other teenagers destined to become famous comedians, Benjamin apparently could not care less about school work. His father, who had sold the saloon and bought a more respectable haberdashery store, put him to work as a clerk but soon fired him because of his indifferent attitude toward customers and then tried sending him to a local business school, where he quickly flunked out. So by the time he was sixteen, Benny was considered to be a failure everywhere except at a Waukegan theater where he was admired for his virtuoso violin playing by the orchestra leader, a pianist named Cora Salisbury.

When the theater closed in 1911, Cora suggested that she and Benny could go on the vaudeville circuit with a music act. Billed as "Salisbury and Kubelsky, From Grand Opera to Ragtime," the act worked well. They toured throughout the Midwest, but after Jan Kubelik, a better-known professional violinist, accused Benny of trading on the reputation of his similar-sounding name, Benny took the stage name of Ben K. Benny, later changing Ben K. to Jack. The act broke up after Cora's mother needed her at home. Benny found another pianist, Lyman Woods, to take her place, and as "Bennie and Woods," they performed all over the country for the next five years. They finally broke up in 1917, when Benny's mother became ill and he returned home. After America entered World War I, he joined the Navy, where his first accidental experience doing comedy occurred in the context of a sailor's amateur show at the Great Lakes Naval Training Base. As he played a serious violin piece, the sailors started booing. From backstage, one of his buddies told him to drop the violin and say something. Acting on impulse, Benny said that some people thought that the Swiss Navy was bigger than the Irish Navy, but so far as he was concerned, the Jewish Navy was bigger than both of them put together. The sailors erupted in laughter, presumably because of the absurd incongruity, and Benny was thrilled. He went on to do comedy turns performing in *The Great Lakes Revue*, a traveling Navy benefit show.

Following his discharge in 1919, Benny developed a one-man vaudeville act mixing jokes with his violin playing, but when it became clear that the humor was going over better than the music, he focused entirely on comic monologues. Over the next few years he became one of the top acts in vaudeville, and by 1926 he was performing in a Broadway show. This was followed by small parts in Hollywood films, more work on Broadway, and in 1928 his first appearance on a radio program sponsored by Canada Dry, where he was introduced as the "Canada Dry Humorist." By 1934 a newspaper poll listed Jack Benny as the most popular comedian in America, and as his humor became definitively "mainstream," so did he. That is, neither he nor his wife, the former Sadie Marks who performed on radio with him as Mary Livingstone, was widely known to be Jewish. The same was true of other major Jewish comedians, like George Burns, born Nathan Birnbaum. Benny's career on radio and later on TV continued through the 1960s, and he was still doing "specials" almost until he died in 1974.

In sum, from the 1920s onward, the type of humor prevailing during the beginning of the twentieth century with its heavy-handed appeal to Jewish, Irish, Italian, German, and other stereotypes and ridicule of immigrants in general gradually lost its central place in mainstream entertainment. Restrictive immigration laws passed in the 1920s dramatically reduced the flow of newcomers, and for the next thirty or more years, the popular melting pot ideology emphasized by politicians and schoolteachers discouraged gross ridicule of ethnic groups. Prejudice and slurs still remained, particularly with respect to blacks (as will be noted later), but once movies and radio began to replace vaudeville and burlesque, ugly slurs and ridicule became too risky. The sponsors of radio shows and producers of films had too much invested to risk offending any substantial number of their customers. Even the popular *Amos 'n' Andy* radio program of the 1930s and 1940s targeting African Americans with trivial dialect and "stupid" routines avoided the more extreme forms of hostile humor.

By the 1940s and 1950s, what remained of ethnic humor in the mass media was becoming benevolent, or at least not clearly insulting. A good example of this could be seen in the popular radio shows of Fred Allen during the 1940s. Allen had a standard routine in which he would walk down "Allen's

Alley," knocking on doors and asking the stereotyped characters who answered for their opinions about some contemporary issue. The characters included a southern windbag politician named Senator Claghorn; Mrs. Nussbaum, a Jewish housewife; a conservative New England Yankee called Titus Moody; the combative Irishman Ajax Cassidy; Falstaff Openshaw, a poet who spoke in rhymes; and finally John Doe, the typical middle-class American. All of them would respond to Allen with amusing opinions delivered in accents appropriate to their one-dimensional stereotypes. Their silly humor went over well with the mass radio audience, and no one was offended. Allen himself was Irish. His real name was John Florence Sullivan and he got started in vaudeville as a teenager doing a comedy juggling act.

In the early 1950s, a new generation of Jewish comedians and comedy writers (Milton Berle, Sid Caesar, Buddy Hackett, Mel Brooks, and many others) had become so "American" that, like Jack Benny, they were no longer widely identified as Jews. Their style of humor was still fundamentally Jewish, but it was presented in a form that masked its traditional origins. Jack Benny's style provides a good illustration. Much of his humor was based on the radio and TV persona he created. It combined, in an American context, the comic characteristics of the traditional East European Jewish "schnorrer"—the greedy, miserly type always seeking some financial advantage—and "schlemiel"—the socially and physically awkward type always getting into embarrassing situations. Benny was also widely acknowledged by other comedians as the grand master of timing, his ability to draw out or "time" a routine until exactly the right moment to deliver a punch line. This ability, still rare among many comedians although conspicuous in the work of Bill Cosby, was apparently based on Benny's experience as a musician.

The general point about the "Americanization" of Jewish humor is directly in line with views expressed by the humor scholar Elliot Oring. Oring argues that apart from its content, traditional Jewish humor has three different levels of meaning. As mentioned earlier, these include "transcendence," which allowed Jews to rise above the effects of persecution, and "defense," whereby they could ridicule or disparage their persecutors. Oring also discusses a third level of meaning, sometimes viewed as a neurotic symptom, whereby feelings of anger and aggression can be turned inward and result in a more or less obsessive preoccupation with telling self-critical jokes and stories. This interpretation is based on Freud's influential analysis suggesting that such behavior can be a symptom of self-hatred, a problem that he could see among some assimilated Jews in turn-of-the-century Vienna. On the other hand, Oring notes that Freud also believed that self-critical jokes can have a liberating effect, allowing people to transcend criticism. This is accomplished through the use of irony, whereby criticism is converted to humor. The following example is from a text by Nathan Ausabel:

> Anti-Semite to Jew: "All our troubles come from the Jews!"
> And the Jew responds: "Absolutely! From the Jews—and the bicycle riders."
> "Bicycle riders! Why the bicycle riders?"
> "Why the Jews?"

The philosopher Ted Cohen provides another illustration of defensive irony in the joke about how Abe and Sol one day pass by a church with a sign saying, "$1000 to anyone who will convert." Abe wonders what it is about, so he asks Sol to wait while he goes in to inquire. He returns after an hour and Sol asks, "What happened? Who are they trying to convert? Did you get the $1000?" Abe replies indignantly, "Money! That's all you Jews think about."

Oring's analysis does not culminate in any grand conclusions, only that we may best understand Jewish humor as an intertwined product of its transcendent, defensive, and neurotic qualities. Ironic takes on neurotic anxiety can be seen in the following "principles of Jewish Zen."

> "Wherever you go, there you are. Your luggage is another story."

> "Be aware of your body. Be aware that not every physical sensation is a symptom of a terminal illness."

> "Be patient and achieve all things. Be impatient and achieve all things faster."

Ted Cohen suggests that Jewish jokes are often characterized by the ways they seem to focus on the absurdities of life, although he adds that it seems impossible to pin down exactly what defines the essence of Jewish humor. Other writers on Jewish humor tend to agree, but most also emphasize the wide range of ironic Jewish takes on suffering, guilt, and pride. Some good examples appeared in a recent collection of Jewish Haikus:

> Suffering: "Her lips next to my ear, Aunt Sadie whispers the name, of her friend's disease."

> Guilt: "Yom Kippur—Forgive me Lord, for the Mercedes, and all that lobster."

> Pride: "Beyond Valium, the peace of knowing one's child, is an internist."

When we turn to the origins and development of African American roots humor, parallels to the Jewish experience are immediately evident. Both emerged from a context of oppression and were initially expressed covertly, in languages that were not understood by their oppressors: Yiddish on the one hand, and slave vernacular on the other. Jews referred to gentiles with the Yiddish word "goyim"; blacks referred to whites as "Mr. Charley," "the man," and "ofays" or "fays." But there is clearly no comparison between the prejudices facing immigrant Jews and the much more severe conditions of chattel slavery endured by African blacks. The stereotypes leveled against the two groups were also very different. Gentiles typically drew on the figure of Shylock to stereotype Jews as greedy, sly, clannish, and untrustworthy, while southern whites created the image of Sambo to stereotype blacks as lazy, childish, dumb, and irresponsible. Prior to the Civil War, the Sambo stereotype of black males was popularized in minstrel shows that toured the country. These shows featured white performers wearing exaggerated blackface makeup while doing comic songs and dances ridiculing the supposedly primitive speech patterns and shuffling body language of black males. Black women were stereotyped either as silly incompetent servants, as can be seen in the role played by Butterfly McQueen in *Gone with the Wind*, or as obedient, stout "Mammys" who lavished affection on the families of their white masters.

These stereotypes served as justifications for slavery by portraying blacks as inferior but happy, amusing creatures who were fortunate to be cared for by their benevolent white masters. Elements of such stereotypes persisted into the twentieth century, most conspicuously in the *Amos 'n' Andy* radio and TV shows, the shuffling routines of the black actor known as Step'n fetchit, and the advertising creation Aunt Jemima. While in slavery, however, blacks developed forms of humor based on exploiting these stereotypes in order to deceive their owners or gain some advantage. Some types of hardships could be avoided or reduced by acting like an ignorant Sambo who could not understand directions, which exemplifies the passive aggressive technique. In other instances, slaves could share jokes using their private language or ridicule a master by using an exaggerated Sambo dialect or body language. A variation on this theme was illustrated by the black comedian Redd Foxx in a nightclub routine where he described how slaves learned English. The white boss might say, "Hey boy, bring dat dere here, chunk it nigger," and the slave responds, "Ooba gooba," which Foxx then translated as "Chunk that shit yo'self!" Along the same line was his remark, "Negroes have fooled whites for years with that 'Yassuh Boss' stuff, but boss spelled backwards is double SOB." Deception and humor also had survival value for slaves. Folklore has it that slaves would sometimes improve their food rations by feeding chickens or other livestock harmless plants that made them appear diseased and unfit for their owner's table. The supposedly sick animals were then left to the slaves. Deception extended to the meanings that certain Christian hymns had for the slaves. When they sang "Go down Moses . . . let my people go," they were referring to their own situation, and it is thought that "Swing low sweet chariot, comin' for to carry me home" referred to the underground railroad that helped runaways escape to the North.

Slave humor was also expressed in the context of music and dance. On most plantations it was common for slaves to gather for an evening to chant, sing, and dance to the rhythm of improvised drums. The plantation owners allowed this because they thought it was a good morale builder that resulted in more effective work during the day, and many of the owners found it entertaining. Slave dancers invented a parody of their masters called the cakewalk, whereby dressed in the cast-off clothing of their white owners, they would pose and strut to the rhythm of the drums in exaggerated imitations of their self-important masters. As time went on, the plantation slave gatherings evolved into more elaborate shows that were put on for visiting dignitaries and neighbors. By the 1830s and 1840s some of the more talented performers were highly valued for their musical abilities and clever parodies of whites and other slaves.

The minstrel shows that became popular in the 1840s and anticipated the rise of vaudeville apparently grew out of the patterns established by slave entertainers. Individual white performers had earlier billed themselves as "Ethiopian Delineators," and wearing blackface makeup they performed songs, dances, and jokes based on slave behavior. The origin of minstrelsy has been traced back to Danny Rice, one of the white performers who was anxious to build up his act. The story goes that he happened to see a crippled black stable hand singing a catchy song and doing a little dance as he worked. Rice memorized the song and dance steps, bought the black man's ragged clothing, and took it all on stage, hopping and twisting to the following lyric:

> Wheel about, turn about and do jus' so,
> And every time I wheel about, I jump Jim Crow.

The act was an immediate success. People wanted to learn the dance, and Rice became known as Jim Crow Rice. (The term "Jim Crow" acquired a new meaning following the Civil War when it became associated with regulations enforcing racial segregation, known as "Jim Crow laws.") Rice added more material to his act as other blackface performers began doing similar routines. It was only in 1843, however, that four of these Ethiopian Delineators who found themselves out of work decided to pool their talents and perform together as the "Virginia Minstrels." They did cakewalks, foot stamping, knee slapping, and an intricate dance called the juba, and included jokes and

riddles in the show. A typical example of the humor was a routine in which
Mr. Bones would ask Mr. Interlocutor:

> "Does us black folks go to hebbin through dem golden gates?"
> "Mr. Bones, you know the golden gates is for white folks," and
> Bones replies:
> "Well, who's gonna be dere to open dem gates for de white
> folks?"

Minstrel shows proliferated, but all of the performers remained whites in
blackface, except for a remarkable black dancer named Juba Lane, who is considered to be the creator of tap dancing.

In general, it should be clear enough that prior to the Civil War, African
American roots humor basically developed from the struggles of slaves who
used the techniques of passive aggression, irony, and parody to cope with their
white masters. Indeed, when Gilbert Osofsky published a collection of slave
experiences in 1969, he chose to title it *Puttin' On Ole Massa: The Slave Narratives of Henry Bibb, William Wells Brown, and Solomon Northrup.* These narratives contain a treasure trove of ingenious slave lore. Northrup, for example,
was required to whip other slaves, and claimed to be so skillful that he could
make a vicious looking show of it without ever really touching his victims.
There are also many accounts of how slaves escaped all the way to Canada by
disguising themselves as women, stowing away on ships, riding the undercar-
riage of trains, and in a few instances hiding in packing crates or barrels mailed
to Canada. Having once gained their freedom, escaped slaves sometimes sent
sarcastic letters to their former owners ridiculing their ignorance and oppressive behaviors. Another aspect of slave humor showed up in songs, such as:

> I fooled old Master seven years,
> Fooled the overseer three,
> Hand me down my banjo,
> And I'll tickle your bel-lee.

William Wells Brown reported another rhyme that was popular during the
Civil War:

> If de Debble do not ketch
> Jeff. Davis, dat infernal retch,
> An roast and frigazee dat rebble,
> Wat is de use of any Debble?

Noteworthy too is that both before and after the war, the popularity of white
Ethiopian Delineators and minstrel shows had an indirect but significant effect
on African American humor. It encouraged whites throughout the country to

accept the Sambo stereotype, and at the same time influenced blacks either to act out the stereotype—better to be viewed as a lovably entertaining clown than as a mere beast of burden—or to manipulate it for whatever advantage might be gained. Henry Bibb spoke for most slaves and ex-slaves when he wrote: "The only weapon of self defense I could use successfully, was that of deception." This in effect required blacks to lead a double life, showing themselves as respectful and compliant to their white masters, while working the system for whatever advantages were possible. The humor they created helped to relieve some of the social and emotional strains of such a double life.

After the Civil War, freed slaves organized minstrel shows of their own, reproducing the same stereotypes, songs, humor, and dances that white audiences had come to expect. Billy Kersands, one of the better-known black minstrels, was famous for singing a song called "Old Aunt Jemima." Many of these black performers like Kersands, and later on the famous Bert Williams, even used blackface makeup to exaggerate their appearance. At the same time, however, newly freed slaves were perceived as a major threat to southern society, and a new, threatening stereotype emerged of the "buck niggah," labeled "Zeb Coon." The opposite of easygoing Sambo, Zeb Coon was the stereotype of a powerful brute out to rob and assault white men and rape their women. Billy Kersands apparently played up to this stereotype with a song titled "Mary's Gone with a Coon," in which a black man laments the fact that his daughter has married one. This potent stereotype became a source of the worst forms of southern racism, up to and including lynching. In more recent times, it was used to stigmatize Malcolm X and members of the Black Muslim movement, but it was also deliberately exploited by leaders of the Black Panthers in order to intimidate whites. In general, blacks who stood up for their rights or were seen as troublemakers could be disparaged as Coons, whereas those who did not could still be demeaned as Sambos. This double-bind pattern of prejudice, whereby African Americans could be stereotyped either way, is parallel to the double-bind pattern applied to Jews: those who were working-class activists were disparaged as troublemaking Communists, and those who were rich as blood-sucking capitalists.

From the late nineteenth through the first half of the twentieth century, the humor African Americans shared among themselves in segregated clubs and on the black vaudeville circuit continued to focus on "fooling Mr. Charlie" routines and parodies of the Sambo and Coon stereotypes. Blacks also followed the general American trend to ridicule immigrants, particularly the Irish and Jews. According to Lawrence Levine's 1977 book chapter "Black Laughter," the Irish were targeted with various stupid jokes and the Jews with jokes about their greediness. Levine suggests that such jokes were popular among blacks because they allowed them to freely ridicule and feel superior to at least some groups of whites without antagonizing the white majority.

A major star who emerged in black variety shows during this period was Bert Williams, best known for his songs and ironic humor such as, "It is no disgrace to be a Negro, but it is very inconvenient," and a line he attributed to white employers of black domestic workers: "Come after breakfast, bring along your lunch and leave before supper time." Williams' variety act was so successful, however, that he was the first black performer to be booked into white vaudeville theaters. In 1910, over the objections of most white theater producers, he was hired to perform comedy on Broadway in the Ziegfeld Follies, and he continued to work successfully in later Broadway shows. Another important black comedian who was getting started about this time was Moms Mabley, but she only began to appear in mainstream white venues toward the end of the 1960s.

At the beginning of the twentieth century, young African American males also developed a self-critical type of insult joking that became known as "playing the dozens." Typically acted out in small groups of teenagers, the content of such humor was usually based on an exchange of clever, insulting sexual remarks about an individual's mother, wife, or girlfriend. As described in a 1987 review by Joseph Boskin, this was usually done in rhymes like the following:

> "I saw your Momma walking down the railroad track, She had a Pullman mattress under her back."
> "Man, don't let it make you nervous, I saw your Momma yelling curb service."

If the person on the receiving end of these remarks was unable to respond in kind and lost his temper, everyone in the group would burst out laughing at him. There is no simple way to account for the development of such abusive insult humor. One explanation is that it served the purpose of training young black men to put up with the sorts of insults they would encounter from whites without losing their tempers and provoking a violent attack. Another interpretation has it that since young black men could not show open aggression against whites but had to release it somehow, they simply turned it against themselves. Yet another explanation for playing the dozens follows from its reference to the word "play." Thus, it has been seen as an instructive game in which the players could learn verbal skills while dealing with feelings of anger or anxiety. Parenthetically, it has also been suggested that the obscenity "motherfucker" was coined in such games and traces back to slavery when white owners exploited black women (often mothers) for sex. The word has outgrown its origins and is now commonly heard in many films and stand-up comedy acts.

There is no doubt that the self-critical insult humor exchanged among blacks, like the self-critical jokes told by Jews, can be interpreted in a variety of ways depending on the specific context. Clearly, such humor in any minority group can help desensitize them to prejudice. It should not be ignored, however, that in this case such humor may indicate a wish to escape being identified with a stereotyped minority. One type of evidence often cited to support this view involves the efforts of some blacks and Jews to change their appearance. Jews have occasionally had cosmetic surgery to change their long, Semitic-looking noses; blacks sometimes use products designed to straighten their hair or lighten their skin. There is even a vein of ethnic humor about this issue: jokes about Michael Jackson's complexion getting lighter and Barbra Streisand's nose getting shorter. A joke aimed at ridiculing the idea of self-hate was a perennial favorite among black comedians and was even acted out by Whoopi Goldberg in a famous HBO concert performance. It describes a little black girl who ties a white towel around her head and announces to her mother and father that she now has blond hair and is white. Outraged, her parents send her to her room as punishment. Lying on her bed, she mutters to herself: "I've only been white for five minutes and already I hate two niggers." A similar type of joke is aimed at Jews who change their names and convert to Christianity. When other Jews suggest that they still look Jewish, the punch line is, "I've only been gentile for one day and already I hate the kikes." Such jokes are popular among the groups involved because they disparage those who would deny their ethnic heritage.

Just as Jewish comedians brought a modified style of their ethnic roots humor into mainstream society in the 1930s and 1940s, African American comedians began doing this in the late 1950s and early 1960s. In the context of the growing civil rights movement, some of them, like Redd Foxx, George Kirby, Mantan Moreland, and Nipsey Russell, who had previously only worked in segregated clubs and theaters now began to appear in front of sympathetic white audiences. Younger black comedians such as Dick Gregory, Godfrey Cambridge, and Bill Cosby soon followed. Cosby steered clear of aggressive race comedy, but the others did routines based on their traditional roots humor, as well as jokes ridiculing racist stereotypes. Some examples of their ironic routines include the following cited by Joseph Boskin.

> "A white family moves into an all black neighborhood, and later that night a watermelon is burned on their front lawn."

> "A white official is visiting a black village in Africa. As the chief shows him around the official seems worried that his baggage

might be stolen. The chief reassures him, saying that there is nothing to worry about because there are no other white men anywhere in the area."

"A white politician trying to get blacks to vote for him explains at a news conference that he has so many famous black friends that he is writing a book about them. When a reporter asks for the title of the book the politician replies 'Famous Niggers I Have Known.'"

At the height of his popularity in the early 1960s, Dick Gregory had a stand-up routine in which he explained to white audiences that his daughter did not believe in Santa Claus because even at two years old she knew that no white man would come to their neighborhood at midnight. He had another line pointing out that blacks loved baseball because it was the only time a black man could shake a baseball bat at a white man without starting a race riot.

The parallels noted earlier between the origins and development of African American and Jewish roots humor were easy to see when these traditions began to converge and blend together during the late 1960s and 1970s. This became apparent as black and Jewish comedians both increasingly employed similar, ironic styles based partly on the breakthrough performances of Lenny Bruce and used material focused on similar themes. Usually presented in extended monologues, a primary theme that would also be adopted by Hispanic and Asian American performers dealt with their experiences growing up in ethnic families. Most of it centered on the behavior of long-suffering mothers, harsh or impatient fathers, rivalries with siblings, and ethnic foods. Buddy Hackett, who grew up on Jewish cuisine in Brooklyn, joked, "Until I was 21, I thought it was normal to have heartburn after every meal." Richard Pryor talked about his childhood experiences in the whorehouse run by his grandmother, Billy Crystal about his Jewish storekeeper grandfather who insulted his customers, Bill Cosby about the playmates he had growing up in the projects in Philadelphia, and so forth. Another type of ethnic family humor designed to ridicule prejudice was presented in TV sitcoms such as *All in the Family* and its black spinoff, *The Jeffersons*.

The second important theme running through ethnic humor in the 1960s and 1970s was criticism and distrust of the government and other institutions. A reflection of events in the larger society—the civil rights movement, student sit-ins at universities, and protests against the Vietnam War—these events were grist for the mill of Jewish and black comedians, who could draw on a long tradition of humor based on persecution at the hands of established authorities. In one of his films, Woody Allen's character is asked if his grandmother was a good cook or housekeeper, to which he replies, "I don't know, she was too busy being raped by Cossacks." It is easy to see how this line could be reworked to fit the black context: "She was too busy being raped by the white slave masters." Convergence between the routines performed by African American and Jewish comedians was further promoted by their similar traditions of deception, as in this fire insurance joke, where two Jews meet on the street and one says to the other, "I hear you had a fire in your store last week," and the other says, "Quiet! It's not until next week." Also noteworthy in this context is a more unique use of ethnic humor by African American civil rights activists during the 1960s. A study published in 1968 reported that they employed satiric humor to help maintain their sense of group cohesion. As might be expected, their jokes targeted racist whites but went further to disparage blacks reluctant to support the movement. In some instances, this included challenging people of color to stand up and assert themselves against the slurs used against them. Thus comedian Dick Gregory, who was an active participant in the movement, titled his 1964 autobiography *Nigger,* and dedicated it to his mother with this ironic inscription:

> "Dear Momma—Wherever you are, if ever you hear the word 'nigger' again, remember they are advertising my book."

There were other plays on the N-word. Mantan Moreland used the line, "For years I thought people mistook me for Roy Rogers' horse. I thought they were calling me 'Trigger.'"

The 1974 film *Blazing Saddles* provides the most dramatic evidence of convergence between the African American and Jewish humor traditions. In this film, written by the Jewish comedian Mel Brooks in collaboration with Richard Pryor, the hero is a black cowboy who encounters a wide range of discrimination and persecution situations but invariably triumphs by deceiving or outwitting his antagonists, who are led by a stupidly arrogant white racist gentile. The film itself is essentially a series of more or less elaborate sketches, each of which is designed as a parody ridiculing common stereotypes as well as cowboy movie cliches. In one sketch, Mel Brooks performs the role of the state governor in the style of a traditional Jewish fool. In several of the sketches the black hero wins out by adopting the exaggerated dialect and behavior of a traditional Sambo. In another instance, he and his family are saved by the intercession of a Yiddish-speaking Indian chief, also played by Mel Brooks.

Despite the general pattern of convergence between Jewish and African American humor, some of their particular ethnic qualities are still in play. Throughout the period from the late 1960s to the 1980s and on into the present, for example, most of Woody Allen's films have retained as their central figure his representation of the awkwardly insecure New York Jewish liberal.

This stock character, like Charlie Chaplin's little tramp, always finds himself caught up in frustrating situations or in conflict with more robust individuals, but whereas the tramp escapes and evades using physical slapstick tactics, Allen's character is relatively passive and copes with his problems by turning inward. His defense against adversity lies in humorous intellectual critiques, ironic comments, and self-critical remarks. In this respect, more than any other contemporary comedian, Allen puts a clever contemporary face on the type of humor associated with Jews in the nineteenth-century East European ghettos. Another Jewish comedian, Rodney Dangerfield, known for his standard line, "I don't get no respect," also made a specialty of self-critical humor, but used it in a more aggressively simplistic fashion.

Similarly, current variations of much of the traditional "puttin' on ole massa" and "foolin' Mr. Charlie" African American humor can still be seen represented in some of the films directed by Spike Lee, others starring Eddie Murphy and Chris Rock, and the comedy sketches presented by Damon Wayans on the TV show *In Living Color*. All of them in one way or another make strategic, tongue-in-cheek use of the Sambo and Zeb Coon stereotypes as well as the Step'n Fetchit dialect and shuffle. Other types of contemporary African American humor reach well beyond stereotypes to more thoughtful commentaries on the situation of blacks. Joseph Boskin illustrated this in his 1987 article by describing a dialogue-with-God joke, in which a black man asks why he has dark skin, nappy hair, and long legs. God replies that all these features were designed as an adaptation to the environment in Africa, whereupon the man says: "Then tell me, Lord, what the hell am I doing in Chicago?" Richard Pryor, moreover, drew deeply on the African American roots tradition to create the character he called "Mudbone," a wise, world-weary old black man who had survived hard times and could offer ironic philosophical comments on the human condition, black or white. In fact, Richard assumed the character of Mudbone when he wrote a revealing self-critical introduction to his autobiography.

Finally, if there is any general pattern to be seen after scanning the origins and subsequent development of Jewish and African American roots humor, it seems most clearly to be the one worked out by Lawrence Mintz. Writing about the history of Jewish humor in 1977, Mintz suggested a four-stage scheme that fits the African American experience, as well as that of other ethnic groups. In the first stage, Jews and blacks were simply the targets of heavy-handed ridicule by those in power over them. During the second stage, this ridicule was to some extent internalized, and their humor became self-critical. Mintz describes the third stage as "realism." This refers to the period when Jews and blacks used deception and covertly made fun of their oppressors among themselves. The fourth stage is more or less where we are now, when Jews, blacks, Hispanics, Asians, and others have come full circle and can use humor to directly confront and ridicule those who formerly ridiculed them.

As already noted, the turnabout here can be traced to various historical events and social conditions fostering a general culture movement toward irony. But it has not been merely a tit-for-tat reversal, such that white gentiles are now disparaged in the same ways that Jews and blacks were in the past. Instead, contemporary racial and ethnic humor is broadly inclusive. It invites whites, gentiles, and everyone else to join in ridiculing the stereotypes and slurs of the past. Once again, it deserves emphasis that much of this change is due to the ironic style of comedy popularized by Lenny Bruce, Richard Pryor, and several others. They were not alone in changing the face of humor in our society, but they had a great deal to do with the transformation of Jewish and African American roots humor into mainstream American humor. The effects of that transformation, as well as other aspects of contemporary comedy, particularly gender humor, are examined in the following chapter.

7

Males versus Females, Gays versus Straights, and the Varieties of Gender Humor

It's not the men in my life that count, it's the life in my men.

—*Mae West*

I don't know the question, but sex is definitely the answer.

—*Woody Allen*

You could easily get into an endless scholarly debate about whether jokes and comedy routines ridiculing males, females, gays, and straights belongs in a discussion of ethnic humor. Strictly speaking, of course, a person's masculine, feminine, or homosexual identity has nothing to do with their ethnic origins, although the meaning of gender and the humor associated with it can be quite different in various ethnic groups. But since all gender humor is based on slurs and stereotypes and serves the same social and emotional purposes as humor focused on racial and ethnic differences, it demands attention. It is also particularly interesting because more of it goes on within, rather than between ethnic groups.

Nevertheless, there are some exceptions, most notably the Jewish Mother and Jewish American Princess (JAP) jokes that were popular and cir-culated all across our society in the 1980s. Yet even in this case, most of these jokes originated with Jewish comedians and were aimed at Jewish audiences who readily understood the relevant stereotypes. A joke such as "The only way to be sure that a Jewish American Princess is having an orgasm is if she drops her nail file" would be meaningless to someone unaware of the idea that well-off young Jewish women are supposed to be sexually unresponsive and ego-centric. The stereotype became so well known, however, that some African

American comedians began doing variations aimed at the so-called Black American Princess or BAP. On the other hand, the vast range of jokes and comedies ridiculing males and females in ways that have nothing to do with race, religion, or national origin shows that gender itself is a sufficient basis for disparaging stereotypes. Since most if not all of the other defining qualities of stereotype humor can be seen in the jokes men and women tell about one another, the nature of gender humor seems no less worthy of discussion than African American and Jewish humor.

At least three generalizations about gender humor are usually acknowledged by all authorities on this topic. First, it is virtually universal: if there is any society in the world where men and women do not tell some sort of disparaging stereotype jokes about one another, it is a well-kept secret. Second, men typically tell jokes ridiculing women more frequently than women do about men. Third, women are more likely to laugh at jokes told by men than men are to laugh at jokes told by women. While this last point is less true today than in the past, it helps explain why women in our society have found it more difficult to become comedians and there are fewer of them. The imbalance in favor of males is much greater in societies outside of North America, however, especially in the more traditional sexist societies of Eastern Europe, Asia, and the Near East. Even in North America, though, women have not found it easy to succeed as comedians. Their struggle will presently be discussed in detail.

A more immediate question is why gender humor is apparently universal. The fundamental answer suggested by common experience as well as all authorities on the subject basically comes down to sex and power. Where sex is concerned, it is not necessary to know anything about Freudian theory (although it helps) to appreciate the fact that wherever there are men and women, there is always some degree of latent or manifest sexual tension between them. Nor do such tensions require close contact with the opposite sex; sometimes the same sex will do, as in gender-segregated situations such as prisons. So it is easy to understand why the tensions associated with sexual needs and desires lend themselves to the creation of jokes such as: "What are the first words Adam spoke to Eve? 'Stand back! I don't know how big this thing gets.' "

Yet there is much more to gender humor than gross sexual jokes and comedy routines. The universal anxieties and conflicts between men and women extend beyond sexuality to the social power differences that have traditionally separated them. Here we run into a broad range of issues including the social roles prescribed for males and females, the norms specifying acceptable masculine and feminine behaviors, and the developmental processes whereby people acquire a masculine, feminine, or homosexual sense of identity. Distinguishing between jokes that are related to sexuality and jokes that are related to gender power can be difficult because both sexuality and gender power are often involved, but as may be seen in the following one-liners, it depends upon the primary focus of the joke.

"What's the definition of a perfect woman? One that after you're done screwing, she turns into a six pack and a roast beef sandwich."

"Why did God invent women? Because sheep can't cook."

Blatantly sexist jokes like these are more concerned with gender stereotypes about power—whose going to provide the food—than about sexuality as such. This point about the traditional male focus on power is perfectly captured in the following one-liner by comedian Elayne Boosler: "When women are depressed they either eat or go shopping. Men invade another country."

The second generalization noted, that men tell more jokes deriding women than women do about men, plainly follows from the historical pattern of male domination. Although sexism has been reduced in contemporary American society to a greater extent than elsewhere, it is still a problem that generates a good deal of ironic feminist humor, as in the joke about a woman who tells her husband that she wants to take a job outside their home. He responds quite seriously and without any awareness of the contradiction: "Stick to your washing, ironing, and cooking. No wife of mine is going to work!" Such unconscious male sexism was discussed by the feminist scholar Elizabeth Janeway, who gave another example of how men often fail to realize sexist contradictions by telling the presumably true story about a woman being interviewed on a radio program. The male host says, "Good morning Mrs. Blank, tell me something about yourself. What does your husband do?"

The well-documented tendency for men to enjoy telling disparaging jokes about women apparently helped to justify their dominance. By evoking stereotypes about the inferiority of women, such jokes provided reassurances of male superiority. The familiar and sometimes overworked analogy is to the way whites employed jokes about blacks in order to justify discrimination. In both cases, of course, when people show excessive pleasure at such humor, it is understood as a way of covering up their feelings of anxiety and insecurity. Many social scientists today believe that as women have been gaining a greater degree of equality with men in our society and entering traditional male occupations, men are becoming more insecure about their status and have accordingly been behaving more aggressively toward women. Sexist humor is a perfect instrument for the symbolic expression of aggression, and as will be noted in the following text, women are aware of this and well able to respond in kind.

The question raised by the third generalization about gender humor—that women are more likely to laugh at jokes told by men than men are to laugh at jokes told by women—involves both the tradition of male domination and the ways that women have typically been socialized to deal with it. In the first instance, research studies show that regardless of gender, starting in childhood most of us learn to defer to those with greater power or higher status. Where humor is concerned, this means that we have a near automatic tendency to ingratiate ourselves with authority figures by acting as if we appreciate their jokes or humorous remarks. Other things being equal, we are likely to believe, or act as if we believe, that a joke told by a high-status individual is funnier that one told by someone of lower status. This is why common experience confirms studies showing that college students are more likely to laugh at jokes told by professors than by students, nurses are more likely to laugh at jokes told by doctors, and enlisted men are more likely to laugh at jokes told by officers rather than the reverse. Research also shows that because higher status individuals are usually in control of the situation when dealing with others, they are the ones who are more likely to initiate humor. Why? Because they can be confident that their humor will be well received, and if not, then it will do them no harm. But if lower status people initiate humor, they run the risk of drawing attention to themselves in a way that may be seen as inappropriate. Their peers may feel as if they are showing off and their superiors may view them as pushy, and if their joke or remark goes over badly, they are likely to be thought of as fools. So the conventional social science wisdom has it that in most situations, particularly those involving men, most women have been reluctant to run the risk of initiating humor and eager to ingratiate themselves by appearing to appreciate the humor of men.

Much of this reasoning clearly applies to males as well. New young faculty members, for example, are unlikely to initiate humor with older tenured professors and are more likely to laugh at their jokes. Yet as between young male and female instructors, the males are less inhibited about joking with senior colleagues. The same is apparently true about males and females in all sorts of other situations. A number of feminist writers on this topic suggest that the explanation for this "humor bias" favoring males lies in the ways young women have been taught (socialized, programmed, or brainwashed, depending on your point of view) to relate to men.

In her 1991 review of feminist literature on humor, Regina Barreca claimed that women who came of age in the 1950s or earlier generally grew up believing that good girls were supposed to be more quietly passive and receptive than boys. It was all right for them to smile and giggle at jokes, according to Barreca, but if a girl insisted on telling jokes and laughing uproariously, then she was in danger of being considered bad or "loose," probably someone who smoked and drank too much, chewed with her mouth open and fooled around too easily with boys. Of course, although some of it still persists, this simplistic distinction between good girls and bad girls is no longer widely accepted. Over the past quarter century, we have grown accustomed to seeing women in traditional male occupations, including stand-up comedians. Yet we are also accustomed to seeing frequent news stories about the various forms of harassment and discrimination women often encounter in such positions. In general, therefore, it is still true that if women deviate too far from the old good girl standards, they are likely to face some type of criticism or rejection.

Another perspective on gender humor is provided by the results of a survey concerning differences between the types of humor preferred by men and women. The main findings were that both men and women tend to dislike jokes about religion, but in social situations, men are much more inclined than women to tell jokes about other people. Women, however, indicated preferences that are in line with some of the observations previously mentioned. They enjoy jokes about themselves to a significantly greater extent than men and view such jokes as a useful means of self-disclosure, a way of telling people about themselves. Typical examples include this line by comedian Wendy Liebman: "I've been on so many blind dates, I should get a free dog." Here is another, from Rita Rudner: "I want to have children but one of my friends told me she was in labor for 36 hours. I don't even want to do anything that feels good for 36 hours."

Nancy Walker's analysis of women's humor emphasizes that such jokes also stand as examples of incongruity theory, except that for women, the incongruity is between traditional sexist behavior standards and their ability to satisfy them. In line with Walker's observation is the fact that women comedians often use routines designed to ridicule sexist stereotypes. This type of incongruity humor was carried to a very successful extreme by Roseanne Barr. She began her career doing stand-up routines disparaging her role as a "normal" housewife. Thus, on housecleaning:

> "The day I worry about cleaning my house is the day Sears comes out with a riding vacuum cleaner."

> And on childrearing: "When my husband comes home at night, if those kids are still alive, hey, I've done my job."

The critic Sian Mile called Roseanne Barr's stand-up and sitcom work "chainsaw humor," because it directly attacks the traditional roles imposed on women and does so in a way that spares neither men nor women. In one of Roseanne's lines about being unattractive and overweight, for example, she cut right to the bone, saying, "If you're fat, shut up and live with it! If you're thin, fuck you!"

As with all ethnic humor, the types of jokes men and women use to ridicule each other are likely to either be directly hostile (grossly obscene and insulting) or involve the more subtle tactics of irony (shrewdly amusing observations about male and female social behaviors). The following direct aggression jokes are brutally simple and not terribly funny:

"What's the difference between a dog and a fox? About five drinks."

"Why do women have two holes close together? In case you miss."

"What do you call a gadget you screw on the bed to get a fur coat and feed the kids? A husband."

"How many men does it take to wallpaper a room? It depends on how thin you slice them."

The folklore scholar Alan Dundes described an unusual collection of both aggressive and more subtle gender jokes targeting males and females that circulated widely during the early 1980s. The authors were anonymous, but it is assumed that radical feminists were responsible for the document, titled *97 Reasons Why Cucumbers Are Better Than Men.* Among the more directly aggressive reasons were:

"Cucumbers stay hard for a week."

"Cucumbers won't tell you a vasectomy will ruin it for him."

"Cucumbers don't leave whisker burns, fall asleep on your chest or drool on your pillow."

"You only eat cucumbers when you feel like it."

The relatively more subtle, ironic comments included:

"A cucumber will always respect you in the morning."

"A cucumber won't pout if you have a headache."

"A cucumber won't drag you to a John Wayne film festival."

Not long after discovering the cucumber jokes, Dundes received a listing of male responses, titled *The Reasons Why Sheep Are Better Than Women.* The directly aggressive assertions included:

"A sheep will never tell you the ceiling needs to be painted while you're screwing."

"Sheep don't mind doing it in a pickup truck."

"You'll never catch your sheep masturbating to a picture of Tom Cruise."

Some of the more ironic social behavior lines were:

"Sheep won't ask you if you're gay the first time you can't get it up the second time."

"A sheep won't care if you keep your fish bait in the refrigerator."

"Sheep don't get moody once a month."

Finally, it should be noted that some types of gender humor are not particularly aimed at disparaging either men or women, but instead suggest the amusing nature of differences between their outlooks on life. A good example is the story told about President Calvin Coolidge and his wife. While visiting a farm they saw a bull mount four cows one right after the other. Mrs. Coolidge said to her husband, "Look, what masculine strength." He replied, "But look, how many partners!" In other jokes, too, it is hard to tell whether the point is to ridicule either men or women or both. Thus, after having many arguments with her, a young man breaks up with his girlfriend, and asks God:

"Why did you have to make women so beautiful?"
God replies, "So that you would be attracted to them."
"But why did you make them so dumb?"
"So that they would be attracted to guys like you."

Humor scholars generally suggest two reasons why women's humor tends to be different—more subtle and ironic—from men's. Most often cited is the tradition of male domination that has led women to be cautious about expressing humor. There is a great deal of evidence for this in many nineteenth-century novels and plays, where the heroines cleverly disguise their wit lest they be perceived as too smart by their boyfriends or husbands. Examples of such more or less covert forms of women's humor are also present in the novels, films, and theater productions of the twentieth century. The second reason emphasizes that women typically have greater verbal skills than men, are more sensitive to the emotional significance of social and sexual relationships, and are more inclined to discuss their subtle implications. Because most men are not interested or attuned to such discussions and may even find them threatening, they often dismiss them with jokes like, "Sheep won't talk about the Myth of Vaginal Orgasm at your office Christmas party."

More specifically, the four distinctive characteristics of women's humor identified by Regina Barreca include, first, their tendency to dislike slapstick humor and practical jokes where individuals are injured or victimized. Seeing someone slip on a banana peel, get a pie in the face, or suffer some other humiliation is not considered particularly funny. Slapstick humor apparently triggers laughter in men because it evokes their feelings of superiority, whereas in women, it evokes feelings of sympathy. Second, women are more inclined to enjoy humor aimed at ridiculing the pretensions of people in powerful positions. Their jokes tend to be directed upward, against high-status people who seem insensitive to the needs of others, rather than downward. It is rare, for example, to find women telling dialect jokes making fun of immigrants or minorities. Third, women are more inclined to use irony in remarks that appear to be positive, such as when they tell a boyfriend how strong he is because he can crush a beer can with one hand. Fourth, women are more likely than men to use self-critical humor as a means of gaining acceptance and approval. This is a conspicuous feature of the routines employed by women doing stand-up comedy, as well as those performing in TV sitcoms. Two of the best-known sitcom examples still showing in reruns are *I Love Lucy* and *The Mary Tyler Moore Show*. The comedy themes in both of these shows typically centered on embarrassing or awkward situations that the stars would get themselves into. The self-critical themes that have become practically obligatory for women doing stand-up almost always concern their attractiveness to men. A classic self-critical joke of this type was told by Joan Rivers:

> "When I was little, I had to beg a boy to play doctor with me.
> He finally agreed, and sent me a bill."

Other familiar themes include failures to stay on a diet, embarrassment when buying a bathing suit, and incompetence at cooking and housecleaning. But as in most cases of current ethnic humor, the self-critical themes are primarily brought up in order to ridicule the stereotypes they are based upon.

Contemporary feminist comedians owe part of their success to adopting a more openly aggressive masculine style. No longer likely to be rejected by audiences for ridiculing men, but applauded for it, they often focus their monologues on male arrogance and insensitivity. Some examples cited by Barreca include the following lines by comedians Elayne Boosler and Carol Liefer.

Boosler on abortion: "These guys say they're against abortion because birth is a miracle. Popcorn is a miracle, too, if you don't know how it's done."

Liefer on her ex-husband: "It was a mixed marriage, I'm human, he was Klingon."

And one of the most definitive remarks along this line was contributed by Gloria Steinem:

"Some of us are becoming the men we wanted to marry."

But such feminist humor was a long time coming. The women comedians who first gained national reputations during the 1930s, 1940s, and 1950s did so by presenting themselves as relatively meek helpmates to their husbands or boyfriends. Thus, on the Fred Allen radio program, his female partner Portland Hoffa primarily acted out the stereotype of a dumb blond. Gracie Allen had a similar role with George Burns, while Mary Livingston played the wise-cracking girlfriend of Jack Benny. In the parlance of show business, these women were all "second bananas" or foils for the dominant male comedians. One outstanding exception in the 1930s and 1940s, however, was the buxom blond actress Mae West, who became famous for her sophisticated, self-possessed dialogues with men:

Man: "How did you get that jewel?"
Mae: "From a patron of the arts."
Man: "Weren't you nervous getting such a precious jewel?"
Mae: "I was calm, and collected."
Man: "My goodness, it certainly is a lovely stone."
Mae: "Goodness had nothing to do with it."

During the 1950s, women like Carol Channing, Judy Holiday, and Judy Canova emerged as independent stage and film performers, yet unlike Mae West, they were still required to act silly or dumb while delivering ironic humor lines.

This pattern started to change in the 1960s when Phyllis Diller developed a stand-up act that in part ridiculed her husband, whom she referred to as "Fang" in such one-liners as:

"Fang decided that blonds have more fun so he bleached his hair and asked me for a divorce."

"My mother told me how to cure Fang's hiccoughs. Hold his head under water."

"Fang brought home a dozen flowers—three bottles of Four Roses."

But she also did self-critical humor:

"When I got my first job I thought a filing system had something to do with fingernails."

"I'm looking for a perfume to overpower men—I'm sick of karate."

In addition to being a pioneer—one of the first stand-up performers to break through the 1950s prejudice against assertive women comedians—Phyllis Diller was also unique because she was thirty-seven years old and the mother of five children when she began her comedy career at a San Francisco nightclub in 1955. When interviewed by Larry Wilde for his 1968 book about comedians, she explained that she had started by performing a mixture of songs and jokes at local community groups. It was only after polishing her nightclub act for a few years that she developed her comic "voice" or stage persona, as a relatively tough, alienated housewife. Roseanne Barr would later adopt a similar stage presence with a much more aggressive style. Diller also said that at the start of her career in the late 1950s she had to cope with a great deal of resistance from male professionals and audiences who thought women had no business trying to do stand-up comedy. It was considered to be unfeminine, and even a threat to the social status of men. Oddly enough, however, and perhaps for exactly these reasons, Diller claimed that her earliest fans were gay men.

The prejudice against women comedians that Diller encountered was merely the tip of a major gender-bias iceberg. Long before their recent gains in social power, it was widely believed that women were simply incapable of performing comedy effectively. In their valuable 1986 book *Women in Comedy*, Linda Martin and Kerry Segrave noted that during the 1920s, pseudo-scientific articles based on Darwin's theory of evolution proclaimed that men had a superior sense of humor because of the quicker reflexes they had inherited from centuries of hunting. The idea that it was biologically unnatural for women to have a strong sense of humor also followed from the notion that it was mainly unattractive, ungainly women—the "rejects"—who frequently told jokes and made witty remarks. A popular cliche of the time, "Men don't make passes at girls who wear glasses," neatly epitomized this general attitude. More surprising is that even in 1962, when Diller, Carol Burnett, and a handful of other women comedians were already making their mark in TV, a woman writing in *Mademoiselle* claimed that they were obviously unattractive, had to work too hard at getting laughs, and were clearly inferior to male performers.

But as Martin and Segrave discovered, such biases against women co-medians had not always been widely accepted. Martin and Segrave identified fourteen women who had successful careers during the period from 1860 to 1920 in traveling variety shows, vaudeville, and the Broadway theater, per-forming as comic singers, dancers, and actors. The first of the major women comedians was Lotta Crabtree, who at the age of twelve in 1860 was already supporting her whole family with a successful song-and-dance comedy act in San Francisco. By 1870, she was touring the country with her own variety show. A few of the other major comedy stars of the 1880s and 1890s included Trixie Friganza, Marie Dressler, and Eva Tanguay, all of whom performed songs, dances, jokes, and comedy skits. In 1914, Marie Dressler went on to begin a successful career in silent films by starring in Mack Sennett's first full-length comedy, *Tillie's Punctured Romance*. She also claimed to have arranged a part in this movie for the then-unknown Charlie Chaplin.

The whole situation for women in comedy began changing in the 1920s and 1930s when there was a public reaction against assertive female behavior. With a few exceptions, such as Mae West and Fanny Brice, women perform-ers were reduced to the role of second bananas, acting like frivolous dummies or silly housewives, the role Lucille Ball perfected in her TV sitcom. One woman who bucked the trend in the 1920s and 1930s by doing aggressive dirty jokes in her nightclub act was Belle Barth. But she never became widely known, probably because the public was not ready for material like her line that the hardest thing for a woman to do on the wedding night of her second marriage is to scream, "It hurts!" The reasons for the reactions against assertive women comedians, which lasted into the 1960s, are not clear. Martin and Segrave spec-ulate that following World War I, when many women had taken jobs outside the home, men may have felt the need to reinforce their traditional dominance. It is also likely that the efforts of women suffragettes, who were pushing hard to obtain the right to vote, created a general backlash against outspoken women. Eleanor Roosevelt, for example, was widely criticized and ridiculed for her social activism during the 1930s and 1940s.

By the 1970s, however, talent was triumphing over prejudice. At least partly because of Phyllis Diller's success in the 1960s, as well as the growing women's liberation movement, a number of strong women stand-up and sit-com performers like Joan Rivers, Bea Arthur, Carol Burnett, and Lily Tomlin were gaining large, enthusiastic audiences. During the 1980s, the final turn toward public acceptance of aggressive feminist humor occurred with the ar-rival of Rita Rudner, Paula Poundstone, Ellen DeGeneres, Whoopi Goldberg, and later, Roseanne Barr and Margaret Cho. In sum, if we date the contem-porary rise of self-assertive women in comedy from the start of Phyllis Diller's career, it has taken nearly fifty years for women comedians to attain the same level of acceptance as men and to give as good as they get when it comes to the male and female stereotypes underlying gender humor.

This brief summary is accurate insofar as it concerns mainstream white comedians, but it fails to do justice to the remarkable career of the black woman comedian known as Moms Mabley. Mabley was already performing before large black audiences in New York in 1927. Born Loretta Aiken in 1897 in North Carolina, she began doing a song-and-dance comedy act on the black vaudeville circuit at the age of sixteen. Wearing ill-fitting old clothes and oversized shoes, she adopted the comedy persona of a shrewd old-timer who, like Richard Pryor's Mudbone, would make amusing comments about human behavior. Over the next dozen years or so, she became known as a consistently reliable crowd pleaser, developing routines that often centered on ridicule of older black males who tried to dominate women. In this context, she became famous for the line "An old man can't do nothin' for me except to bring me a message from a young man." Moms Mabley was widely known among African Americans but only gained national recognition as segregation broke down and she began appearing on TV specials and talk shows in the late 1960s. During this time, the first of her comedy recordings sold over a million copies. Before her death in 1975, she also performed in films, made additional comedy albums, and finally enjoyed the wider recognition that segregation had prevented during most of her life.

No discussion of gender humor would be complete without consideration of the classic sexist joke targets: mothers-in-law, dumb blonds, Jewish Mothers, and Jewish American Princesses. Jokes about these four groups thus focus on specific categories of women rather than women in general, and although some of the jokes in this area are no longer current, in the past they have all been standard equipment for male comedians. The reasons for this vary, but one thing these four categories of women have in common is familiar, well-understood stereotypes. Mothers-in-law are exemplary. They were traditionally stereotyped as nosy intruders into the lives of married, especially newly married, couples. While it was mainly men who complained about them, women also had their complaints. The portfolio of mother-in-law jokes told by women comedians usually emphasize the ways men were spoiled by their mothers and now expect their wives to serve and pick up after them. Male comedians focus more on the critical attitudes of their mothers-in-law, who think they are not good enough for their daughters, or do not earn enough money. The male jokes are often directly aggressive, as in this one about the farmer whose mule kicked his mother-in-law to death. At her funeral, the minister notices a group of men surrounding the farmer and asks him if they were expressing their sympathies. "No," says the farmer, "they were just wanting to know if they could borrow the mule."

There are more than enough mother-in-law stereotypes to go around, and since they evoke a familiar range of experiences (what married couple cannot tell stories about interfering mothers-in-law?), they have provided reliable themes for comedy. But such humor is less popular now than it was in the past. Fewer young couples today have to live with their mothers-in-law as they did during the economic depression of the 1930s and the post–World War II housing shortage. Mothers-in-law are also not what they used to be. With the rise of feminism and growing presence of women in business, government, and industry, middle-aged women today have more to do than poke into the lives of their married children. And perhaps because of all the traditional jokes, it is not unusual to hear them say things like, "I don't want to act like a mother-in-law," even when they are. Then too, manners have changed. Any woman acting like a classic interfering mother-in-law today runs a high risk of being summarily told to mind her own business.

Jokes about dumb blonds, or more accurately, attractive dumb blonds, apparently can be traced back to stereotypes created by vaudeville and burlesque performers. Many of them found that they could improve their comedy, dance, or magic acts by including buxom women assistants. Dressed in skimpy costumes and often wearing blond wigs, their job was to act sexy and stupid. The stereotype is also probably based on the false notion that beauty and brains do not go together. This idea would surely appeal to many people who might feel inferior to attractive blonds and therefore try to compensate by thinking of them as dumb. Among women who do not meet Barbie Doll standards of attractiveness, dumb blond jokes are bound to be a hit. In any case, such jokes have been a staple of gender humor and are virtually interchangeable with stupid Polish jokes.

Jewish Mother and Jewish American Princess jokes mainly originated among Jews themselves, yet they are more about particular types of women than about Jews as such, and they do not have a strong flavor of anti-Semitism. Consequently, they really have more to do with gender than ethnicity. While the mother and princess jokes are closely related, the mother jokes have priority. They first began circulating in the 1960s, based on stereotypes described in a 1964 book titled *How to Be a Jewish Mother*. It presented satirical discussions of themes about making sacrifices for children, encouraging children to overeat, and making children feel guilty for disappointing their mothers. A clever example of the guilt theme is the joke about the difference between a Jewish mother and an Italian mother. The Italian tells her son, "If you don't eat all the food on your plate I'll kill you." The Jewish mother says, "If you don't eat all the food on your plate I'll kill myself."

Jewish Mother stereotypes have been traced to the nineteenth-century East European ghetto communities, but they gained wider popularity in America among the children of immigrants anxious to provide better lives for their families. As these children and later generations of children became assimilated to American culture, they began using ironic humor to cope with the demanding behavior of their overprotective, ambitious parents. While this was true of most immigrant groups, it was particularly intense among the children of East European Jewish women who followed a culture tradition emphasizing close ties between mother and child. In keeping with traditional sexist values, boys typically received more attention than girls. They were supposed to work hard to satisfy their mother's aspirations for material success and social status by becoming doctors, dentists, or lawyers; certified public accountants and college professors were acceptable alternatives. So there is the joke about a Jewish woman out walking with her two little boys. A passerby stops and says, "What beautiful children. How old are they?" She replies, "The doctor is seven and the lawyer is five." Another example asks, why does a Jewish boy become a CPA? "Because he can't stand the sight of blood and he stutters."

Jewish girls, on the other hand, were merely supposed to grow up to marry successful Jewish boys. Oddly enough, this bias in favor of boys can be understood as the basis for Jewish American Princess (JAP) stereotypes. The logic here is that since Jewish mothers felt guilty about identifying more closely with their sons, they would compensate by overindulging their daughters. As a result, these daughters, whose chief mission in life was to marry well, became selfishly preoccupied with their sense of entitlement, their appearance, and the material benefits associated with an affluent marriage. According to the stereotype, their egocentric, money-player attitudes did not leave much room for the drudgery of housework or the spontaneous pleasures of sex. These elements of the stereotype showed up in the princess jokes that were popular in the 1970s and 1980s:

> "How does a JAP call her family to dinner? 'Get in the car, kids.'"

> "What is a JAP's favorite position? Facing Bloomingdale's."

> "What is a JAP's idea of perfect sex? Simultaneous headaches."

> "Why do JAP's like Chinese food? Because Won Ton spelled backwards is Not Now."

Alan Dundes suggested that such jokes became popular among both Jewish and gentile men in the 1980s because they reflected male anxieties about the increasing assertiveness of all women. That is, the JAP stereotype was seen as relevant to the behavior tendencies of all ambitious, independent women, Jewish or otherwise. Dundes argued that the same thing may be true of Jewish Mother jokes: any American woman who identifies too closely with her children can be seen as a Jewish Mother.

The final category of gender humor concerns homosexual men and women, who certainly qualify as an oppressed minority group in our society. There is no shortage of jokes and slurs ridiculing them as "queers," "faggots," "fruits," "pansies," "fairies," and so on. In some respects, the slurs and jokes targeting gay and lesbian individuals appear more intense than those aimed at ethnic minorities. The psychology underlying this situation is well known. Many people, particularly teenagers and young adults, are insecure about their sexual identity. Since they experience considerable anxiety about this, they are easily threatened by the presence of homosexuals, and are therefore more inclined to attack them with aggressive humor, sometimes including physical violence. So we have jokes like the following one-liners:

"What's the definition of a lesbian? Just another darn woman trying to do a man's job."

"What do you call a gay in a wheelchair? Rolaids."

"What's the difference between a gay rodeo and a straight one? At a straight one they yell 'Ride that sucker!'"

There are plenty of others like this, most of them in even worse taste. In some instances, ethnicity is added:

"Did you hear about the Polish lesbian? She loved men."

"Is it better to be born black or gay? Black, because you don't have to tell your parents."

The prejudice against homosexuals is more severe than that leveled against other minorities because in addition to being linked with sexual anxieties, it is endorsed by some religious leaders who justify it by citing passages from the Bible. Nevertheless, homophobia is declining, and this may be partly due to the defensive humor developed by gays and lesbians. As with other minorities, such in-group humor originally served the purpose of promoting group cohesion and coping with stress. Yet as both gay and straight ridicule of homophobia has become more popular, prejudice against homosexuals has become less socially acceptable. Also noteworthy is that until quite recently, when such popular women comedians as Ellen DeGeneres and Margaret Cho came out as lesbians, homosexual humor was mainly performed by gay men. This fits the pattern noted earlier that men are more likely to initiate humor and find it easier to become comedians than women. Another interesting aspect of homosexual humor is that it typically is not focused on heavy-handed disparagement of heterosexuals. One reason for this may be that homosexuals all have heterosexual parents, and they accordingly do not have strong feelings of hostility. Where such ridicule occurs, it is fairly gentle:

> "Two gay men are shopping. When they see a married couple engaged in a bitter argument, one turns to the other saying, 'See, I told you mixed marriages never work.'"

Most gay jokes, however, are clearly aimed at showing the arbitrary nature of homophobia. For example:

> "A cab driver picks up a nun, and while driving tells her that he has always fantasized about having a nun give him a blowjob. The nun says she is willing to do this, providing that he is single and a Catholic. He says he is, she does it, and afterward the driver thanks her for a wonderful experience, but then confesses that he is married and Jewish. The nun replies, 'That's OK, my name is Bruce and I'm on my way to a costume party.'"

The defensive point here suggests that sexuality is relative, not absolute, and more in the mind than the body. Another defensive gay joke is one about a priest who has been hearing confessions all day and needs to take a break. He gets his new assistant to take over, explaining that the next person waiting to confess is an elderly woman who never has much to say and should just be given ten Hail Mary's. But the woman confesses that she has recently been doing oral sex. Uncertain what to do, the assistant whispers to a passing altar boy, "What does Father Mike give for oral sex?" The alter boy responds: "A coke and two candy bars."

A recent one-liner by David Letterman gives a different twist to the same theme: "The priest shortage is so bad that today in Brooklyn an altar boy had to grope himself." Both of the foregoing jokes appeal to incongruities designed to ridicule sexual hypocrisy, whereas the following relates to social hypocrisy:

> "A gay man phones his Jewish Mother to say that he has met a wonderful girl and is getting married. Furthermore, she is Jewish, and her father is a doctor. Overjoyed, his mother asks, 'What's her name?' The man replies, 'Monica Lewinsky.' After a long silence, his mother says, 'So what happened to the nice Catholic boy you were dating last year?'"

Another variety of defensive gay humor is the list of "good reasons to be gay":

> "You're the only one at your high school reunion who looks a lot better now than you did when you graduated."

"You don't care who Julia Roberts is sleeping with."

"You know how to program your VCR."

"You'll never have to hear your mother complain about your wife."

Before leaving the topic of gay humor, it deserves emphasis that in recent years homophobia has been declining not only because some admired athletes and celebrities have "come out of the closet" but also because of the way negative gay and lesbian stereotypes have been undermined in popular TV dramas, sitcoms, and films. A prime example several years ago was the film titled *The Birdcage*, with Robin Williams as the main gay character and Gene Hackman as the homophobic "straight." The movie contained a good deal of in-group gay comedy but also strong ridicule of homophobia. As will be argued more specifically in the following chapter, it seems that just as humor ridiculing other types of prejudice has made it less socially acceptable, the same thing is beginning to occur with homophobia.

In general, it seems obvious that gender humor will always be with us— it works too well as a surefire basis for comedy to ever be lost or curtailed. The classic themes based on male versus female attitudes toward sex, power, and relationships are bound to remain perennial favorites. Yet with the increasing success of women comedians, the range and content of gender humor is bound to expand in new directions. This is an easy prediction to make, because as the relative status of men and women in our society continues to change, the humor will certainly follow. Gay and lesbian comedians, for example, are gaining wider visibility. Ellen DeGeneres has shown that the public will readily respond to jokes about her lesbian orientation, and there is at least one transvestite comedian, Eddie Izzard, who has successfully exploited the comic aspects of his unusual situation. But then, humor never stands still. The following chapter considers how historical events and the emerging new breed of comedians are transforming the nature of ethnic humor.

8

The "New Breed" of Comedians and Transformation of Ethnicity

> People of humor are always in some degree people of genius.
> —*Samuel Taylor Coleridge*

The transformation of ethnicity and the humor associated with it means, simply, that you cannot punch up your jokes by just saying "kike," "wop," or "nigger" anymore and count on getting a laugh. The new breed of comedians who began making their mark in the 1980s and 1990s know this. Most are well aware of the fact that audiences have come to expect a good deal more from racial, ethnic, and gender humor than familiar slurs and stereotypes. Joseph Boskin was apparently catching on to this, too, when he titled his 1987 book chapter about Jewish and African American humor "Beyond Kvetching and Jiving." Even those performers who use their obvious ethnic origins as a means of creating tension in their audiences have for the most part realized that slurs and stereotypes now serve primarily as background furniture. To be sure, the new generation of comedians—Margaret Cho, Bernie Mac, Paul Rodriguez, Chris Rock, and Jerry Seinfeld, as well as some of the veterans like Eddie Murphy, Whoopi Goldberg, Billy Crystal, and Robin Williams—still follow the paths opened up by Lenny Bruce and Richard Pryor. They use the free association shpritzing technique, and they create ethnic characters in their routines. But much of their humor has become a more complex affair in which stereotypes are not only subverted but also played off against each other.

Chris Rock, for example, has a routine in which he ridicules middle-class white boys who listen to black rap musicians and try to identify with them. In the same act he accuses black women who neglect their children of being responsible for raising the gang bangers who in a few more years will try to rob him. When the white actor-comedian Jim Carrey began performing with the Wayans brothers on *In Living Color*, one of his funnier bits was a parody of white rappers who try to appropriate the black hip-hop style but do not quite succeed. According to the African American author Leon Wynter, the slang expression for such wannabes who try to appropriate the speech, body language, and clothing styles of African Americans is "wiggas," for "white niggas." The mere existence of a term like "wiggas" already says much about recent trends in our society.

Ongoing changes and developments in ethnic humor were also unmistakable in popular sitcoms of the 1990s like *Seinfeld, Fresh Prince of Bel Air, Family Matters*, and many others. Those who keep track of mainstream TV offerings have noted that the presence of Jews, African Americans, Hispanics, and other ethnic minorities as stars in sitcoms, and many of the other programs shown on network and cable TV, has been the most conspicuous trend in mass entertainment over the past decade. Todd Boyd elaborates on one aspect of this trend in his 2003 book, *Young, Black, Rich, and Famous*. He discusses how black basketball stars with their hip-hop personal styles have become virtual icons of popular culture in America. The same general trend can be seen in movies, and a number of the most successful recent TV shows feature gays and lesbians.

Clearly, this trend is something new in American society. Along with demographic studies showing that white males will soon be a minority in America, the increasing visibility of racial and ethnic groups marks a profound change in our culture. To be sure, there are some minority scholars such as Robin R. Means Coleman who are critical of this trend. In his 1998 study of black sitcoms, Means Coleman points out that many of them were still offering stereotype humor and imagery reminiscent of the racist *Amos 'n' Andy* programs. He correctly identified certain sitcoms as merely providing updated versions of Sambos performing in the tradition of minstrelsy, while police dramas offered a number of threatening Zeb Coon characters. In short, Means Coleman finds quite a few rotten apples in the media barrel. He fails to consider, however, that the sheer volume of ethnic programming ensures some degree of creative diversity. In his book *American Skin*, Leon Wynter sees the media scene as indicating the "erosion of white privilege" in America. He argues persuasively that the increasing presence of African Americans and Hispanics across the whole spectrum of society shows that we are becoming a "transracial" culture. I would add to this argument that the success of stand-up comedians who perform ethnic humor is partly responsible.

One need look no further than to the careers of people like Chris Rock, Whoopi Goldberg, Eddie Murphy, and Jerry Seinfeld to find justification for this assertion. Other minority figures, such as Colin Powell, Tiger Woods, and

Oprah Winfrey, have become prominent household names in America. But another perspective supporting the argument that we are becoming a transracial culture is directly observable in stand-up comedy, in the outstanding example of Robin Williams.

Prior to his later success acting in films, Williams had become one of the most successful mainstream comedians in America. He is particularly significant in the present context because he stands as a contradiction of widely accepted views about ethnic humor performers. Thus, despite having grown up in a well-off white gentile family, he seems to have perfectly assimilated the styles and much of the substance of African American and Jewish humor. How he came to do this is discussed in a later chapter on the making of comedians. The critical point here is that he represents the synthesis of minority ethnic humor traditions into a form that has become definitive of American humor in general. His one-man comedy concerts contain an essentially seamless blend of the elements previously identified as characteristic of Jewish and African American humor. Typically, he entices audiences to join him in a conversation with himself (very Jewish), over antiestablishment or outsider themes (very African), that he carries out in such a rapid fire, stream of consciousness (shpritzing) fashion that some of his funniest lines are occasionally lost in the flow. Like the idol of his youth, Jonathan Winters, Williams can immediately improvise humor over anything from a toothbrush to a pizza to nuclear war. He also uses a wide range of techniques, ranging from ironic, free association commentaries to comic scenarios acted out in a mix of different voices or dialects. Thus, one of his best-known routines begins as a parody of Doctor Ruth, the Jewish sex therapist, and segues into his impression of what he imagines a streetwise African American sex therapist named Doctor Ruf would sound like when responding to women seeking advice. In another routine with overtones of self-criticism, he attributes a separate personality to his penis, and proceeds to carry out an elaborate argument with it, before moving on to ridicule men for their preoccupation with women's nipples.

No observer can fail to be impressed by Williams' creativity and ingenuity; what is less obvious is that by running together so many of the themes, techniques, and stereotypes that have been associated with ethnic humor in the past, he succeeds in transcending it. The ethnicity is quickly overwhelmed and reduced to background by the manic pace of the humor. We barely have time to recognize a stereotype before Williams pushes it in a new direction or confounds it with another.

Among prominent comedians today, it is probably Chris Rock who most closely approximates elements of the style perfected by Williams, although Rock works at a slower pace, delivers punch lines more emphatically, and sometimes repeats them lest he get too far ahead of the audience. Like Richard Pryor and Eddie Murphy, Rock tends to be explicitly racial in his initial approach to audiences, but the racial approach is soon left behind as he focuses on more general human themes. This comic style or pattern observable in the work of Williams and Rock can be seen in the performances of other contemporary comedians as well, whether they be African American, Hispanic, Jewish, or Asian American. Unwittingly perhaps, but in line with other changes in our society, their performances have contributed a good deal toward the breakdown of former ethnic tensions and prejudices. This is not to suggest that all such tensions have been eliminated. It is rather that recent decades of stand-up ethnic comedy have shown that ethnic tensions can hardly be maintained in the face of humor. Our top comedians have succeeded in pulling many of the sharpest teeth from the bite of slurs and stereotypes by ridiculing them. In the process, they have made ethnicity if not fashionable, then at least much more interesting to the general public than ever before. Philosophers of science might call this nothing less than "a paradigm shift": a major change in the way that humor and ethnicity can be understood.

A good argument can also be made that at least part of the shift toward humor informed by the Jewish and African American traditions of irony is that the general situation of Americans in the world has become increasingly ironic. In the past, we did not have to worry about stepping on sensitive toes when throwing our international weight around. Now, we are still seen as the most powerful nation but are at the same time the one most criticized around the world. The ironic paradox here is that our apparent wealth and power put us in the position of a stigmatized minority. If we use our power to try to change things anywhere in the world, we are bound to be accused of being bullies (stereotype of the Ugly American, or shoot-from-the-hip cowboy); if we fail to use it, we are accused of being indifferent to the needs and sufferings of others (stereotype of a complacent Uncle Sam, only concerned with his own comfort). There is even a third alternative: if we only use our power when we can be supported by a number of allies, we are accused of being a timid, insecure giant (stereotype of the Big Man fearful of offending others). The irony of our situation therefore appears inescapable, and we see it being played out around the world almost every day. Some Americans in Europe and Asia now say they try to pass as Canadian, and while many Muslims, Palestinians, and others say they do not hate individual Americans, there are some who applauded the 9/11 attacks.

Of course, we have more than enough of our own domestic self-criticism and distrust of authority to justify the ironic humor offered by contemporary comedians. Our politics alone provides a consistent source of raw material with gender and ethnic overtones, whether it be the sexual adventures of our former president with a Jewish intern or the spectacle of Californians recalling their elected governor in favor of a film star with an Austrian accent. It is hardly an exaggeration to suggest that anyone who does not keep up with current events by watching news programs can do so by watching talk show comedians and *Saturday Night Live.*

The bottom line here is that as our society and status in the world have been changing, the forms and content of our humor have also been changing. Thus, while the basic psychological mechanisms remain in place—people will always laugh at pie-in-the-face slapstick and enjoy surprising incongruities and the release of tension—the themes and language of humor are continually moving in new directions. The most conspicuous of these new directions has already been described as the trend toward ethnicity in our mass media, but there are other new directions such as the breakdown of traditional rules and customs governing what can be joked about in public. Fifty years ago, for example, comedians like Bob Hope, Jack Benny, and Red Skelton would never have used ironic material referring to a president's sex life. They were very cautious about anything to do with religion and always took every opportunity to show their patriotism. The flag, mom, and apple pie were sacred cows. They were cautious about ethnicity as well, although gender was fair game as long as it was "clean" and limited to jokes about women drivers, nosy mothers-in-law, and ladies' hats. On one occasion Bob Hope crossed the line of social acceptability. He was severely criticized for telling a double meaning joke on the radio that would hardly be blinked at today. It was a bit about meeting a girlfriend in front of a pawnshop. In those days, everyone knew that hanging above the entrance to pawnshops there was an ornament consisting of three globes, roughly the size of softballs. In one of his monologues, Hope used a line that went something like, "My girlfriend and I went to a pawnshop and she kissed me under the balls." It was considered scandalous and Hope made a public apology.

Today, of course, the only general rule about comedy seems to be "anything goes." This is apparently true for sex, gender, religion, politics, race, ethnicity, and obscene language, but there are still some topics that are beyond the pale of acceptability. Neither stand-up comedians nor those who circulate raunchy sexist and racist jokes on the Internet seem willing to risk humor—ethnic or otherwise—touching on the destruction of the World Trade Center or on American soldiers in Iraq. The emotional baggage associated with 9/11 still lies too heavily on most Americans. Our post-9/11 efforts to gain security from terrorism have produced a new range of humor possibilities, however, especially with respect to air travel. The old familiar cluster of airline jokes concerning lost baggage, bad food, and late or canceled flights has now given way to routines about little old ladies being subjected to strip searches, pilots locked in behind armored doors, and all of us needing clean socks for when we remove our shoes for inspection. (How is getting on a plane like entering a Muslim Temple? You first have to take off your shoes.) As we are subjected to increasingly tight, sometimes absurd security checks, we are bound to see more jokes about them. We already have jokes about joking, comic routines ridiculing the rules prohibiting people from joking while being inspected by security personnel. There is also a whole new range of ethnic humor themes concerning Muslims or anyone who looks as if they might be from the Near East. Some African American comedians get laughs pointing out that white airline passengers are now more willing to sit next to a young black male than to someone who looks like an Arab.

World historical events like 9/11, and lesser domestic scandals as well, have also expanded the language of ethnic humor. Additions to the comic vocabulary of punch lines now include a new stock of phrases such as "racial profiling," "pedophile priests," "collateral damage," and "weapons of mass destruction (WMDs)," some of which carry explicit or implicit ethnic implications. Certain names have entered the vocabulary of comedy either because they sound funny (Arnold Schwarzenegger) or because they conjure up amusing imagery (Bill, Hillary, and Monica). Then there is "Dubya," the diminutive for George W. Bush, as well as the terms "Bushies" and "neocons" (neoconservatives) applied to his circle of supporters. The language of humor has also benefited from computer technology, which has given us phrases like "chat rooms" and "porn sites," new words like "blog"—short for weblog, whereby some people maintain a public record of their lives on a Web page— not to mention new meanings for old words, like "virus" and "spam." Some computer-oriented one-liners and jokes have emerged, such as the one about the fellow who says, "In order to spend more time with my children I'm using their faces as icons" and the one about the woman at a cosmetics counter who explains to the clerk that she would like to get a perfume that smells like a computer in order to try attracting her husband.

At this point, it is only possible to sketch some of the more obvious ways that our whole culture has recently been changing out from under us and the effects this is having on our humor. But it is not necessary to wait until social historians get around to doing the heavy lifting to see how the impact of 9/11, along with other domestic and international events, has begun to influence ethnic humor. On the surface, it shows up in the themes and language of jokes and stand-up routines. Below the surface, there are good reasons to argue that 9/11 has had a more fundamental impact on the general meaning of race and ethnicity. Traditional differences between most ethnic groups are fading because terrorist attacks make no such distinctions. All of us are in the same boat, equally and impartially threatened. The wide visibility of minorities and women in the military and security services who are, in effect, protecting our boat also works against traditional prejudices. So it is arguable that at least with respect to the acceptance of racial-ethnic diversity, some good may have blown in on the ill winds of 9/11.

In this connection, one of the few iron laws of social behavior is that when any group of people, no matter how diverse, is facing a collective life-threatening situation, they invariably come together and set aside their differences. This was true of people in cities that were heavily bombed during World War II, and it occurred in New York City during and after the World Trade Center attack. The one exception has been Muslims and others with a Near Eastern background. Even though some were also victims of the attack, there was an immediate reaction against them. Yet historians say that anti-Muslim feelings following 9/11 were not nearly as intense as anti-Japanese reactions following the attack on Pearl Harbor. Unlike the situation after Pearl Harbor, when many Japanese Americans were placed in internment camps, prominent authorities from the president on down have spoken out against anti-Muslim prejudice.

The critical issue here is that recent events associated with terrorism have altered the general social climate. There is now widespread anxiety about security that has never existed before, and the effect has been to emphasize what all Americans have in common. A number of social commentators have already noted this change. Writing in the January 2003 issue of *Harpers*, for example, Thomas de Zengotita suggested that familiar ethnic and social class issues dividing Americans in the past are receding. Instead, there is a new concern with fundamental human values that apply to all of us. The Summer 2003 electricity blackout in New York, in which people pulled together and managed to cope effectively, has been cited as clear evidence of the new social climate.

If most of the issues discussed up to this point are approximately correct and there is, in fact, a decline in the significance of ethnicity in our society, then it follows that the way people respond to ethnic humor must also be changing. But how? Does it mean that such humor is disappearing? No. On the contrary, we have more of it now than ever before despite political correctness campaigns to stamp it out. Alternatively, does it mean that the familiar stereotypes used in jokes and stand-up routines are going away? Again, no. If anything, comedians appear freer than ever to throw them around in more complex, inventive ways than in the past. So what can be changing? The answer seems to be public sophistication, and it can be summed up as follows:

We laugh at ethnic humor based on stereotypes today precisely because we know they are essentially false yet contain enough residual grains of truth to raise the tension necessary for laughter.

This is a pretty strong assertion that may immediately upset a number of people, particularly those over the age of fifty who are still sensitive to any jokes based on racial-ethnic stereotypes. Worse yet, it cannot be defended with references to objective surveys or the opinions of other humor scholars, although there may be some who would agree. The assertion is not entirely arbitrary, however, because it follows from how I have seen hundreds of students react to ethnic humor in my classes over the past few years, and it shows up as well in other situations. These reactions appear unmistakably based on the prevalent "psychology of cool" that is part of our culture of irony. Among young people today, it has become a hallmark of sophistication, of a cool, superior attitude, to show that one can see through stereotypes and rise above them to enjoy the release of tension that a funny ethnic joke or comedy routine can provide. If the humor works, moreover, it does not matter whether it is your own or someone else's group being ridiculed. In fact, it is often even cooler to relish or wink at the stereotypes applied to your own group. This general attitude may even extend to ethnic slurs, at least insofar as admired TV or film characters are concerned. When James Bond, for example, is trapped by his enemies and disparaged as a limey sonuvabitch, he only smiles tolerantly before coming up with a cool, superior response. The film heroes played by Eddie Murphy or Samuel L. Jackson typically do the same when disparaged with racial slurs. Of course, this cool reaction to slurs and stereotypes is by no means present in all situations. It clearly applies, however, in comedy venues where performers are able to present their acts in ways that encourage audiences to adopt a superior posture toward raunchy insult humor.

In many respects, therefore, it is arguable that in situations where people are primed to expect humor they seem to become fairly immune to slurs and stereotypes. But this requires a certain level of maturity. I began to see this showing up consistently among students in my humor classes. When writing papers about their personal experiences with ethnic humor, they frequently mentioned going through three or four stages. Regardless of whether they were white, black, Hispanic, Jewish, or of any other group, they said that as children they were occasionally upset but mainly puzzled by jokes or slurs ridiculing either their own group or other minorities. (They did not understand the ridicule because they did not know what it meant.) By age eleven or twelve, and on into the early teens, some of them found such material to be disturbing, but most of them said they quickly learned to roll with the punches and respond in kind. Later on, after exposure to diverse groups and varieties of humor while attending college or serving in the military, they developed a more sophisticated perspective, recognizing that although stereotypes are unfair and usually false, they can still provide enjoyable occasions for humor. Most of them are not bothered by the idea that this may seem like an amoral contradiction. They simply react to racial-ethnic jokes and comedy routines according to their playful intent, taking their cues from the context of the situation and the attitude of the performer.

Unfortunately, there are always borderline or ambiguous instances where matters of intent can be difficult to judge and people of goodwill might honestly disagree. There have been serious arguments about stereotype humor among African Americans, Jews, Hispanics, and others in which some complain that any negative stereotype about their group, regardless of its context, is intrinsically harmful. Thus African Americans criticize TV sitcoms and films that contain representations of the Sambo and Mammy stereotypes, Hispanics complain about hot-tempered, macho-man images, and Jews resent being shown as crooked lawyers or businessmen. Some Italian Americans, for example, have singled out the prize-winning HBO series *The Sopranos* and movies like *The Godfather* as reinforcing Mafia gangster stereotypes, and since these productions usually portray at least one Jew, Latino, or African American collaborating with the gangsters, they can be taken as broad-spectrum insults to ethnic sensitivities. But none of this has hurt their popularity with the public, including most of those with relevant ethnic roots. Worse yet, according to the critics, many ethnic youth seem to take a perverse pride in these outlaw images. A *New York Times* story (3/7/04) reported that when the National Association of Italian Americans issued a public protest against *The Sopranos,* an executive in the organization grudgingly admitted that his son loved the program.

Conflict over the significance of racial-ethnic stereotyping for the sake of humor, as well as for straight dramatic effects, has been particularly intense within the African American community. In his book about how blacks are shown in films and sitcoms, Robin R. Means Coleman comes down firmly on the side of those who consider most of these representations to be racist. In the same book, however, he also notes that many black performers and producers and some scholars like himself do not agree. They have argued that the critics should "lighten up" and accept the fact that stereotypes will probably always be with us and that there is no great harm, and perhaps there is even some value, in having fun with them. Ultimately, their argument falls back on the issue of intent: as long as the intent of a performance is to amuse rather than seriously insult or disparage, they feel comfortable with it. Yet because intent is always open to interpretation, conflicts of this sort appear unresolvable. What seems harmlessly amusing to many may be seen by others as merely a sugar-coated expression of racism that is especially pernicious because it has the deceptive appearance of being "all in fun."

So in general, there are strong arguments available to both sides in this conflict, and it extends well beyond the area of racial-ethnic humor. When Martin Scorsese made his film *The Last Temptation of Christ*, he was severely criticized by many Christians for showing Jesus to be capable of sexual feelings, but praised by others for showing his humanity. At the present writing, the same thing is happening to Mel Gibson. His film about the crucifixion of Jesus has provoked criticism by Jews worried that it may encourage anti-Semitism, whereas other Jews in Hollywood are defending his work. In the final analysis, whether the issue is humor or the life of Jesus, psychologists know that individual differences in personality and social adjustment incline people to take one side or the other. Some see dangers or evil intentions where in fact there are few or none, and others fail to see dangers even when they are clearly present. As pointed out repeatedly in prior chapters, though, there is no objective evidence showing that racial-ethnic humor can be construed as seriously evil.

On the contrary, it is not difficult to see the more or less benign ways in which such humor is playing out in our society. As this humor deals more and more freely with stereotypes, it is becoming more complex and ironic, using ethnic cliches as the basis for setting up amusing incongruities and contradictions. A good example is the recent film *My Big Fat Greek Wedding*. The title alone implies a disparaging theme, and almost all of the humor in the film is based on simplistic stereotypes about Greek Americans, ranging from excessive pride in their heritage to their patriarchal family structure. Yet the film has been a great success. There has been no outcry against it in the Greek American community. Rather than feeling offended, Greek Americans seem to enjoy it as an exaggerated but good-humored representation of their close-knit family traditions. Its popularity among the wider public probably follows from the fact that most Americans have an ethnic family background similar in some degree to that shown in the film.

All in all, therefore, it seems reasonable to conclude that although specific instances of racial-ethnic humor may deserve criticism along the lines emphasized by Means Coleman and some other critics, the contemporary forms of such humor and the new generation of comedians performing it have all but destroyed its value as a vehicle for prejudice. As noted at the beginning of this chapter, race and ethnicity no longer carry the same weight they have had in the past. Our population steadily grows more diverse, intermarriage between people from different racial-ethnic groups is increasingly common, and the threat of terrorism draws people together regardless of their background. Further evidence for this conclusion can be seen in the following chapter, which concerns the development of professional comedians.

9

Becoming a Comedian: Ethnicity Helps but Is Not Enough

> The comedian confronts the audience with his or her personality and wins celebration—the highest form of acceptance—or is scorned and rebuffed as a pitiable outsider.
>
> —*David Marc*

It will not come as news to most scholars that we occasionally fail to recognize important issues because they are right under our noses, so obvious that they are taken for granted and ignored. In this case, it is the fact that every human group, from families to tribes to whole societies, has one or more members who provide most of the humor, and everyone in the group usually knows who they are. They typically begin to stand out to their families and peers during childhood. By the time they are in second or third grade, children might not agree on their selections of class clowns, but their teachers typically know who the natural comedians are. In any family with more than one child it is usually clear which of them has a greater tendency to generate humor and enjoy "making fun." These are the kids who will likely grow up to be the wisecracking jokers offering comic relief to their classmates, work-site colleagues, or any group they happen to be in.

This all-too-obvious point is important, first, because it provides good commonsense evidence for the view that humor must be recognized as a profoundly significant and largely inborn human capacity. It not only serves to promote the good feelings and comradeship necessary for the smooth functioning of families and other groups, including children, but also helps people to maintain a sense of dignity and self-esteem in all sorts of stressful, even life-threatening situations. Right up until her death from cancer, for example, it was widely reported that the comedian Gilda Radner was able to set her friends, family, and caretakers at ease with comic remarks about her condition. Another, less obvious implication of the signs of comic talent that show up during childhood is the indication that comedians are born, not made; that when it comes to humor, heredity is probably more important than environment. It seems clear from what we know about the personality attributes required for an individual to become an effective class clown, let alone to achieve even moderate success as a professional comedy performer, that certain inborn, genetically linked abilities and behavior tendencies are necessary.

This follows from the fact that at a minimum, all effective comedians need excellent verbal skills, a high level of practical social intelligence and sensitivity, the capacity for rapid information processing, and quick cognitive reflexes. These attributes do not grow on trees, and are not for sale at Wal-Marts. Noteworthy too is that many of the most famous comedians, from Chaplin through Laurel and Hardy, Eddie Murphy, and Chevy Chase, also show remarkable physical agility in their performances. Yet practical, effective intelligence is the most essential attribute. This is not to say that all comedians would have scored high on conventional intelligence tests or received good grades in school. Many would not bother to make the effort, and others might not have the required formal knowledge. What they *would* show, however, is the quick thinking and sense of timing necessary to come up with the appropriate wisecrack, joke, or gesture at the right moment to get a laugh. Some of this can be learned, of course, but just as in sports and music, learning will not get someone very far if they have not been born with the appropriate cognitive and neural equipment.

Yet there are also good commonsense arguments for the importance of environmental learning. These begin with the fact that while a number of children may be endowed with the right equipment for comedy, few of them become class clowns, and fewer still aspire to become comedians when they grow up. Children can gain social status, self-esteem, and attention in other ways besides making peers and adults laugh, and most try to do so by excelling at sports, schoolwork, or hobbies, or even by becoming class bullies rather than clowns. The clown role is inherently risky. Children who pursue it may get attention, but if they are not fairly cautious about their behavior, they are likely to be considered silly fools—jerks who refuse to take schoolwork, sports, or other things seriously, and a pain in the neck to those who do. Parents and siblings who may generally enjoy a child's humor may get angry when it seems out of place or gets too personal. Few things are more irritating to parents than when a clever child mimics or ridicules their behavior. Despite all these discouraging circumstances, some children will always begin to employ humor as their primary social passport, their typical mode of relating with others, because they are spontaneously good at it and gain a satisfying rush of pleasure from their ability to make people laugh.

Most of the information available about the childhood situations of successful comedians (nobody bothers to discuss the failures) indicates one of two general patterns. The first and most frequent—especially among the older, traditional performers who started in vaudeville or burlesque—is that they grew up in relatively poor minority families. In the past these were mainly Jewish, Irish, and Italian; more recently they were African American, and today they are frequently Hispanic and Asian. For children, especially boys, growing up in rough minority neighborhoods, the primary ways for them to gain acceptance and respect are through sports, street fighting, or petty crime. Being good at schoolwork does not rate very high on the street. Of course, there are always some exceptions, but those who are not tough or strong or cunning enough to succeed at these activities can usually gain respect by ingratiating themselves with those who are. Humor provides one of the most effective ways to do this. Anyone with a quick enough wit to readily amuse their friends, relatives, and higher status peers will always have a place at their table. As the lyrics of a show business song express it, "Make em laugh, tell em jokes, and you'll always stop with top folks."

The class clown or family fun maker is more or less in the same position as the medieval court jester who lived by his wits and prospered so long as he could entertain his patron. If he or she can bring it off, the role is virtually made to order for the clever but awkward or undersized minority child growing up in harsh circumstances. Such children have at least one distinct advantage in their favor. As described in earlier chapters, it is that racial-ethnic minorities typically place a high value on humor to cope with their daily hardships. So the minority child or teenager who shows a talent for humor is more likely to be rewarded than one from a mainstream, middle-class family. And while the minority culture assures budding comedians of greater acceptance, it also provides an established tradition of humor—role models, folk stories, and the stereotypes associated with prejudice—that they can draw upon. Most of the Jewish comedians who began in vaudeville benefited in this way, and so have most of the prominent African American, Hispanic, and Asian comedians who came along later. Both Eddie Murphy and Billy Crystal, for example, have shown home movies taken of themselves when they were children doing imitations and parodies for their relatives at family gatherings. We have already noted how Richard Pryor turned to humor at an early age. It is no accident, therefore, that the majority of our major comedians are from minority ethnic groups. In a study first published in 1976, for example, Howard Polio and John Edgerly reported that out of their sample of forty-two well-known comedians, only sixteen were white Protestants. There is a very differ-

ent developmental pattern, however, that can be seen among successful comedians who grew up in relatively benign middle- or upper-middle-class circumstances.

It is often loneliness that turns privileged children toward comedy.
Lonely children are the ones most likely to invent imaginary companions or
identify with TV characters they begin to imitate. Left to their own devices,
they may create their own fantasy world populated with characters they act
out themselves. This was the case with Robin Williams, who grew up in an
affluent Detroit suburb and turned his playroom into a personal theater
where he would act out several roles simultaneously. He is said to have done
this sort of thing later on, in some of his early nightclub routines, when he
would sometimes leave the stage and heckle his own act from the audience.
Andy Kaufman, who grew up in a prosperous Long Island suburb, is another
good example. As a child, he too was described as a loner who spent much of
his time imitating TV characters and pretending to perform their acts. By the
age of ten he was already entertaining at parties for younger children. During Gilda Radner's childhood, her well-off family spent the winter months in
Florida every year, which meant that her friendships were always being dis-
rupted. She compensated with food, became a lonely, overweight "fatty"
picked on by other children, and found relief by mimicking the characters she
saw on TV. In her autobiography, she also mentions learning to use self-
disparaging, witty remarks as a way of warding off nasty comments about her
appearance.

Loneliness is not the only reason why middle-class children may move
toward comedy. There are many ways for a child or teenager to be bitten by
the performance bug and experience the high that comes from getting laughs.
In some cases it is simply a matter of exposure to the show business environment or to a performer who becomes a role model. Steve Martin grew up
comfortably in California and had his first experience performing when as a
young teenager he worked in Disneyland wearing a cartoon character cos-
tume and entertaining tourists on their way to various attractions. By age
eighteen, while attending junior college, he was performing part time at
Knotts Berry Farm. Billy Crystal's father was a music producer for a record
company. As a child and teenager, Crystal was accordingly exposed to show
business gossip, spent time with many of the musicians who visited at his
home, and began his career by mimicking celebrity performers. Eddie Murphy claims that as a youngster his idealized role model was Richard Pryor. He
more or less stole some of Pryor's routines and at the age of sixteen began
performing them in Long Island clubs.

In general, it seems clear that heredity and environment are both important factors in the making of comedians. Inherited personality qualities

and abilities are a necessary precondition for success, but events in the individual's environment may either facilitate or block his or her development toward a comedy career. This generalization, and some of the specific points mentioned earlier, is confirmed by formal studies of the lives of comedians. An outstanding example concerns the famous comedy writer-producer-director Norman Lear, who provided a detailed account of his career to the humor scholars William Fry and Melanie Allen. In their 1975 book they explain that he grew up in a poor Jewish family in New York City. His parents frequently had bitter arguments, and as a child he began doing silly things in order to make them laugh. He picked this up in part from his witty, good-humored grandmother, who took care of him for a few years and became something of a role model. Later, in high school, he wrote a humor column for the school paper, and then, after military service, an uncle with show business connections helped him start selling jokes to a New York newspaper columnist. Eventually, after moving to Los Angeles, he was able to meet with the comedian Danny Thomas by pretending to be a journalist from New York, and was able to sell Thomas a skit for his TV show. The skit was a success, and on the strength of this Lear began working regularly as a TV comedy writer. Although it only concerns a single successful individual, this brief description of how Norman Lear got started is in line with more extensive material on the early experiences of comedians published by the psychologists Seymour and Rhoda Fisher in 1981.

The Fishers interviewed thirty-five male and eight female comedians and found that, like Lear, most of them first began using humor as a means of coping with unhappy family situations. Their mothers typically were described as not providing much in the way of support or affection. Woody Allen, for example, has been quoted as saying that his mother slapped him every day of his life. So they tended to relate more closely with their fathers, or with other adult males if no father was present. This orientation toward fathers or father figures when it comes to humor is not surprising. Research on family dynamics indicates that fathers are more likely than mothers to be tolerant or encouraging of nervy, wisecracking kids. Many of the comedians studied by the Fishers also recalled that as children, they were surprised and happy to discover that they could entertain their parents and get the attention they craved from their mothers by doing or saying silly things. To some extent, all children learn that cute, amusing behaviors generate positive reactions from their parents, but for the comedians, this became an important family adjustment technique. They learned at a very young age that affection could be earned through humor. The majority of them later brought their humor to school and acknowledged being class clowns, as well as indifferent students, who were often punished by their teachers for cutting up in class.

They would skip going to school whenever they could get away with it. Woody Allen's biographer quotes him as saying that he never did his homework, thought of school as boring and ugly, and frequently just did not go. George Carlin, like Lenny Bruce and Richard Pryor, dropped out of high school and joined the military. We have already discussed this pattern of alienation from school in connection with Jack Benny, and biographies of Charlie Chaplin, Bert Lahr, Groucho Marx, Jimmy Durante, and others all confirm it. In sum, it is no exaggeration to say that as children most of the older comedians hated school, viewed it as a kind of prison, and typically developed a rebellious, critical attitude toward the social values represented by school.

This attitude is particularly conspicuous in the personal lives of those comedians who have based their careers on routines specifically aimed at ridicule of conventional, middle-class norms and behaviors. Thus, Lenny Bruce, Richard Pryor, and George Carlin could no more tolerate military discipline than school discipline. They all received bad conduct discharges, later became addicted to hard drugs, and were known to occasionally not show up or to walk out on shows they were contracted to perform. In contrast to these more or less outlaw comedians, are many others, mostly younger performers, who also did not fit in very well at school but never rebelled against it to the point of quitting. Margaret Cho, for example, managed to complete high school despite being a poor student who was picked on for her appearance and Korean ancestry, and she was already getting into drugs and alcohol as a teenager. Chris Rock experienced racist abuse at the mainly white high school he attended in Brooklyn, but his mother was a schoolteacher who kept him at it long enough to graduate. As one of the few Jews growing up among Mormons in a Salt Lake City neighborhood, Roseanne Barr recalls being singled out as the "designated heathen." Nevertheless, she did well at school.

Contrary to popular beliefs, the idea that blacks, Jews, and other minority comedians turned to humor specifically as a means of dealing with prejudice during their childhood or adolescence does not hold up. Caryn Elaine Johnson, better known as Whoopi Goldberg, grew up in a low income housing project in New York City, attended public schools where she did well, claims to have had no problems with racism, and only dropped out of high school in order to pursue her acting career. Among her generation of performers there is a majority like Billy Crystal, Eddie Murphy, and Lily Tomlin, who began as class clowns but probably were not alienated from education because schools had become less rigidly authoritarian by the time they came along. In fact, many of these comedians clearly benefited from school situations and college programs that provided opportunities for them to perform. Jim Carrey had a seventh grade teacher who allowed him to have fifteen minutes at the end of each school day to entertain his classmates. Gilda Radner majored in theater at the University of Michigan before quitting to take a job performing as a clown on a children's TV show. Steve Martin was a theater student at UCLA when he began doing routines at local comedy clubs. Eddie Murphy did stand-up comedy in his high school talent shows, as well as local nightclubs, before briefly attending college and joining the cast of *Saturday Night Live.* Billy Crystal followed a similar path. Lily Tomlin began doing comedy in coffee houses while a student at Wayne State University. Jerry Seinfeld only began performing in clubs after graduating from Queens College in New York. Robin Williams attended college in California before studying drama at Juilliard and then starting his stand-up career.

When it comes to the effects of schooling and education, therefore, what emerges is a mixed bag of evidence. The generations of comedians who came of age in the 1970s and 1980s did much better at school than most of those who came before them, but even in the earlier generation of those who started in the 1950s there were exceptions. Mort Sahl, for example, was a contemporary of Lenny Bruce but grew up in a middle-class Jewish family and graduated from the University of Southern California. He was occasionally attending graduate school when a girlfriend, impressed by his ability to come up with witty comments about politics and current events, encouraged him to try doing this on a local nightclub stage. In 1955 he quickly caught on at the Hungry i in San Francisco with a style of intellectual humor that frequently referred to philosophy and history and was focused on ridicule of the conservative Eisenhower administration. Humor scholars point out that Lenny Bruce copied Sahl's informal, philosophical style of stand-up comedy but took it in different directions. In any case, Sahl is thought to be the first comedian to perform one-man comedy concerts at universities, and he clearly paved the way for George Carlin, whose intellectual style also made him very popular with college audiences.

The life histories that are available emphasize another general point that applies to the careers of virtually all comedy writers and performers, namely, that success does not come easy. Even those who have the appropriate abilities or talent for comedy, and grow up in conditions that encourage them to develop it, find that it is a difficult, often painful path to follow. To make any sort of career out of it requires much more than just a good sense of humor. In fact, the humor scholars Lawrence La Fave, Jay Haddad, and William Maesen have argued in an important 1976 article that there is no such thing as a "sense of humor" and refer to the idea as a "myopic illusion." While they acknowledge that some people seem to crack jokes more frequently and laugh more easily than others, they maintain that such behavior can be traced to many factors besides a general sense of humor. People may use jokes and laughter as a defense mechanism, as a way of warding off anxiety in social situations, or as an indirect expression of aggression. The common notion that people who are willing to laugh at themselves a lot are demonstrating a good sense of humor is also dismissed by these authors. They suggest that such people may just use self-critical jokes as a way of gaining attention. Consequently, whether or not one agrees with this analysis, to think that comedians succeed mainly on account of their good sense of humor is to miss the point of the hard work involved.

In *The Last Laugh: The World of Standup Comics*, author Phil Berger provides a show business "insider" view of the ups and downs experienced by young comedians as they struggle to establish their professional style and identity. It is a challenging, frequently discouraging trial and error process. Many of them begin by trying to perform like an admired role model. Eddie Murphy identified with Richard Pryor, and Robin Williams with Jonathan Winters. Others, like Gilda Radner and Billy Crystal, got started by mimicking a broad range of characters, and still others, such as Whoopi Goldberg, only moved into comedy after starting out as drama students. Robin Williams did all of these things. But regardless of how they begin, in order to become successful all comedians have to find their own unique voice or stage presence. Thus Richard Pryor found that as a performer, he was most effective by presenting himself as a ghetto "brother," a voice from the streets at the low end of society. This succeeded because of his brilliant use of body language and dialect as well as his ironic narratives. By contrast, Steve Martin's standup style was that of an obviously zany but well-educated, middle-class character eager to show off his eccentric humor and occasional "wild and crazy" guy routines. At the height of his career, Lenny Bruce came on as an Old Testament prophet using obscene rhetoric to criticize the people for their sins, whereas Robin Williams performs in the style of a spontaneous free spirit, at one moment acting as a bright, mischievous child, and at another as a wise philosopher or visitor from outer space. Woody Allen, of course, has been the eternally insecure and ineffectual New York Jew, and Jackie Mason does comedy as the fast-talking, in-your-face Brooklyn Jew.

Phil Berger maintains that in many cases—Billy Crystal, Steve Martin, Robin Williams, and others—the managers or agents of young comedians served as coaches who were able to identify the qualities their clients should emphasize or discard in their acts. Coaching helped Billy Crystal, for example, who initially relied too heavily on his parodies of celebrities and TV cartoon characters. Robin Williams had to be toned down because he had such a rapid-fire delivery that audiences could not always follow his funniest material. Woody Allen began as a comedy writer and was fearful of performing before an audience until a manager convinced him that his anxiety could be used to comic effect. In short, no matter how gifted they may be, comedians invariably must be willing to work hard on polishing their performances, either through their own trial and error or by taking pointers from experienced managers or other performers. In her 1989 autobiography, Roseanne Barr gave an excellent account of what many comedians go through as they learn their craft.

During her childhood growing up in one of the few Jewish families in Salt Lake City, she first gained an awareness of comedy from her father, who would call her to the TV whenever a comedian was on. And she explained that her grandmother was the perfect model of an independent woman, who was never intimidated by men, anti-Semitic prejudice, or anything else. A bright student and great reader who wanted to become a writer, as a young adult Roseanne was already the mother of two children. While living in Denver and doing her housework, she usually listened to the Alan Berg radio call-in show. Particularly appealing was that Berg, like her grandmother, was a Jew who never took any nonsense from his callers and had a confrontational style of humor. Her very first move toward show business occurred when she phoned in some comments to Alan Berg, heard herself on the radio, and more importantly, was congratulated by other people who heard her. Not long afterward she began working as a greeter and barmaid in a restaurant, where male customers would often make offensive remarks about her full-breasted figure. At first embarrassed by this, after a while she finally struck back. When a guy she was serving insisted on calling her honey, she impulsively responded: "Don't call me honey, you fuckin' pig," and instead of getting angry, he laughed out loud.

She quickly discovered that a tough-talking, wisecracking style was enjoyed by most customers, who showed their approval by leaving her bigger tips. Many of them became regular fans who brought their friends along to the bar. Often when standing on the raised platform behind the bar swapping lines with customers, she said that it felt as if she were on stage, and she loved it. Her local fans and friends soon started urging her to literally go on stage at a local comedy club. After preparing material for almost a year, she finally went on during an amateur night and was a success. The next time out she flopped, and she spent the next few months in this hit-or-miss fashion, doing a mainly spontaneous act at small nightclubs. During this period, she met a number of other comedians, including one, Dianne Ford, who gave her some important advice about how to improve her act.

One of her main problems was inconsistency. Like many talented amateurs, Roseanne enjoyed making frequent changes in her routine and would often improvise while on stage. Ford explained that she needed to tape her act, identify the material that was going over effectively, stick with it, and polish her presentation—the gestures, timing, voice tones, and points of emphasis. She also urged Roseanne to pay more attention to her clothing, hair-style, and makeup. The advice added up to a short course in professionalism that Roseanne took to heart, and after another period of trial and error she began appearing in better clubs. At this point, however, she was still doing journeyman comedy bits and jokes about any topics that came to hand. It took some time until she found the comic persona or professional image that became the basis for her later success. This occurred during a conversation with her sister when they were reminiscing together about the way their mother always used to read magazine articles about how to become a perfect housewife. They recalled that one of these articles contained the phrase "do-mestic goddess," and both of them suddenly recognized that most of Roseanne's best material could be organized under this heading. By present-ing herself as a tongue-in-cheek domestic goddess, ridiculing the absurd de-mands made upon homemakers to be ideal mothers, wives, cooks, maids, and sex objects, she could develop a uniquely personal comic style. It worked al-most immediately. She was quickly headlining in Kansas City and other major venues, then in TV specials, and the rest, as they say, is history.

Roseanne's story highlights the more or less standard challenges that co-medians face as they are getting started, particularly the point that while tal-ent is necessary, it is not a sufficient condition to assure success. It also takes serious, self-critical effort and personal discipline. This can be a major stum-bling block for young comedians. Unlike Roseanne and Phyllis Diller before her, who both developed a sense of responsibility during their experiences of marriage and childrearing prior to their move into comedy, young people who start in comedy as teenagers have a hard time handling the emotional ups and downs. One night a hit, the next, a flop; the same routine that succeeds with one audience fails with another. And as in all professions, but even more often in show business, opportunities for advancement often depend on connec-tions. Having a well-connected agent or skillful publicist can determine whether or not a performer, no matter how talented, can gain access to an appropriate venue. In addition to these sources of anxiety, there are also the loneliness and depression that many performers experience when they take their act "on the road." The memoirs of comedians and musicians, both of whom often spend months working for a few days or a week in one town after another, invariably describe the hardships of living out of their suitcases, miss-ing their friends and families, and having little to look forward to every night after their show except a sterile motel room. These conditions go a long way toward explaining why so many young performers begin using drugs and al-cohol, both of which are readily available in the nightclubs where they usu-ally start out. As they gain some success, hanging out with "groupies" may be added to the drugs and alcohol mix. Margaret Cho, one of the first breakthrough Asian American comedians, experienced these problems while in her teens and barely beyond them.

She grew up in a rough part of San Francisco in the 1970s, where her Korean parents owned a bookstore. Her childhood was marked by many of the same unhappy conditions seen among other ethnic comedians: quarreling parents, schoolmates who ridiculed her Korean first name Moran by calling her moron, and racial slurs. As a teenager, humor became her defense against all this and she became very good at it. At age sixteen she began performing in a local comedy club doing routines in a style copied from Richard Pryor. Because many of her early fans and friends were gay men, she started calling herself a "fag hag." After winning a comedy contest and appearing in a show with Jerry Seinfeld, her career took off. By the time she was twenty-six, she received an award as the best female comedian of the year, and starred in an Asian American sitcom called *All American Girl*. But the sitcom work did not go well. She was pressured to change her style and lose weight. When the show was canceled her heavy drinking, use of drugs, and efforts to lose weight combined to cause kidney failure and a period of depression severe enough to make her contemplate suicide. It took almost five years until she recovered to restart her career by writing and performing a successful, one-woman theater piece.

Although Margaret Cho was able to bounce back, too many other young comedians sink beneath the weight of drugs, alcohol, and their disorderly lifestyle. Margaret claims to have often lived only on food from vending machines when she was first on the road. We never hear of most of those who fall by the wayside while trying to succeed as comedians. Some flirt with disaster even when successful. Robin Williams, for example, has publicly acknowledged that he and his good friend John Belushi were both heavily into drugs when they were already starring in films and TV. It was the death of Belushi from an overdose that led Williams to reassess his lifestyle and finally throw off his drug habit. This evidence from comedians who were at the top of their game should be enough to convince anyone that success is, in itself, no guarantee of well being. In fact, for many performers, attaining high status only means that if they slip up in any way, they have further to fall and more to lose. Psychotherapists refer to this situation as the "wrecked by success" syndrome. It is apparently quite common among those who are unusually successful at an early age.

Apart from the childhood patterns and career issues that comedians themselves have described, another useful perspective on the "making of comedians" can be found in accounts describing the show business environment. Phil Berger and George Carlin, for example, have both pointed out that the TV "cable revolution" was largely responsible for the rapid growth of stand-up comedy. Once a performer is chosen to appear on a cable special, he or she is virtually assured of a near-instantaneous national reputation. The typical sequence leading up to this begins when the individual gains attention for their success in comedy clubs. Invitations to be on talk shows, which notoriously depend upon the wheeling and dealing of agents, managers, and producers, then may follow, and if all goes well, a cable special will be arranged. Where comedy is concerned, the cable revolution began in 1975.

According to George Carlin, this was a time when the HBO channel was having a hard time attracting subscribers. Producers decided to take a chance on broadcasting a comedy concert by an up-and-coming young comedian named Robert Klein. The risk to HBO was minimal because compared with other forms of programming, a comedy concert is a bargain. There is no need for expensive sets and camera work, and there is only the one performer, who cannot demand a big paycheck if he or she is relatively unknown. When Klein's show turned out to be an unexpected hit, the HBO executives realized they had struck gold. They decided to make comedy concerts a regular feature of their programming, but in order to do so, they had to showcase a steady stream of talented new comedians. There were plenty to choose from, including George Carlin himself, and part of their appeal was due to their violation of prior TV censorship regulations. Because HBO was a subscription channel, the comedians were free to use obscene language, racial-ethnic slurs, and explicit sexual material. The result was wide circulation of previously forbidden material that has had a significant effect on contemporary comedy. Any aspiring young comedian can now hardly avoid learning the uses of slurs and obscenities. Because many of these free-wheeling comedy concerts have been broadcast in other parts of the world, foreign audiences sometimes believe that the obscene language is normal. Eddie Murphy claims that he occasionally has been greeted by some of his enthusiastic foreign fans who innocently praise him as a "wonderful motherfucker."

Surveys and research studies provide yet another perspective on the ways that comedy careers may develop. Comedians usually become typecast or categorized based upon their typical performance style and material. This was established in a 1976 study by Howard Polio and John Edgerly, who found that people generally perceive comedians as either sarcastic/aggressive or whimsical/clownish. Although many of the comedians who fit these categories in the 1970s are no longer with us, the categories themselves remain appropriate. Most comedians fit easily into one or the other, and while some are able to work in both, they can be "typed" according to their general tendencies. The sarcastic aggressive type is perfectly represented by Don Rickles, a veteran master of personal and frequently insulting racial-ethnic humor. Roseanne Barr could easily match him at this when ridiculing sexism, and

Margaret Cho would not be far behind. Eddie Murphy's stand-up routines were notorious for their sarcastic/aggressive themes concerning gays, lesbians, whites, and almost everybody else. He even performed a scathing parody of Mr. Rogers on *Saturday Night Live* that is considered to be a classic of its type. Paula Poundstone and Chris Rock usually do sarcastic/aggressive humor, and George Carlin is also known for this style when he does routines ridiculing American foreign policy, the antiabortion movement, or just the kinds of people he dislikes. But Carlin can also be whimsical when discussing the amusing contradictions he sees in everyday life.

In the past, Red Skelton and Jerry Lewis were definitive of the whimsical/clownish style. Their performances often included amusing impressions of children (Skelton was known for his "mean little kid" routine), as well as the silliness, pratfalls, and funny faces associated with clowns. Carol Burnett and Billy Crystal could do this as well, but for pure whimsy with little or no clowning, few comedians today can match Bill Cosby. Whether telling long anecdotes about the children he grew up with or the problems parents encounter with their teenagers, he stands as the master of this form. Carol Liefer and Ellen DeGeneres both do feminist humor in a relatively whimsical style, but it is more difficult to categorize women comedians because the assertiveness necessary for them to perform their acts can easily be confused with aggression. Robin Williams apparently has no difficulty cycling through variations of all of these categories in a single performance. Yet for the most part, his ability to improvise bizarre situations and characters marks him as more whimsical/clownish than aggressive/sarcastic. The same seems to be true of Whoopi Goldberg's stand-up routines.

Two additional findings from the research by Polio and Edgerly were first, that people who enjoy comedy generally think whimsical/clownish comedians are more likeable but less powerful than those who are sarcastic/aggressive. The latter run the risk of appearing too intimidating, and this may explain why many contemporary comedians try to employ elements of both styles, even if one or the other predominates. A second, related finding was that audiences made up of people who did not know each other were more uncomfortable and less likely to laugh when listening to sarcastic/aggressive humor. Laughter at such material comes more easily when people in the audience are friends, presumably because they feel more secure.

These findings raise interesting and largely unexplored questions about how audience characteristics may or may not mesh with a performer's style. Experienced comedians say that when going on stage they quickly gain a sense of the audience's temperament and can tell if the crowd they are facing is warm and receptive or cold and skeptical. For the performer, it is like going on a first date: there is either an immediate sense of connection with the au-

dience or indifference and a feeling of rejection. All of the familiar demographic differences that might be present in the audience, such as their age,
gender, education, social class, ethnicity, and regional background potentially
come into play here. One reason why comedians like to perform at colleges
and universities is because they know they will have a relatively homogenous
young adult audience that is likely to enjoy material ridiculing conservative
politicians, sexism, fundamentalist religion, and grades. (George W. Bush even
got a round of applause from a university audience when he confessed to having been a C student.) But most of the time, comedians have little to go on
except their intuitive impressions of how audiences in, say, Milwaukee, Wisconsin, might respond to their material as compared to those in Atlanta,
Georgia. This is more of a problem for beginning comedians who enter different venues as an unknown quantity than it is for headliners, who have reputations, fans, and established styles that precede them. When established
comedians do their one-man or one-woman concerts on nationwide TV, the
"market demographics," as they say, are well known. HBO audiences, for example, are mostly older teenagers, young adult urban professionals, and more
male than female. In any case, when established major stars like Billy Crystal,
Chris Rock, or Whoopi Goldberg come on stage, they know that almost anything they do, from tripping on the floor to reading a newspaper headline
aloud, is guaranteed to get laughs. Their mere presence, gestures, and tone of
voice are enough.

Aside from those stars who reach a point where they can virtually do
no wrong on stage, comedians who focus primarily on racial-ethnic jokes and
comedy routines that deliberately ridicule certain groups obviously have a sar-
castic/aggressive style and require no further discussion. But there is a substantial range of stereotype humor that is sarcastic and disparaging, yet also
touched with whimsy, in which some performers become identified with a
minority group character they have created. In the past, such routines have
involved blatant ridicule. During the the 1970s, Bill Dana took on the persona of "Jose Jiminez," a poor, foolish immigrant who spoke English with a
heavy Latino accent. Dana usually played Jose as the butt of stupid jokes, but
sometimes included a good deal of whimsy, when Jose's peasant shrewdness
would allow him to get the better of upper-class Anglos. After considerable
national success with this character and frequent appearances on network talk
shows, Dana finally gave it up and retired, as more and more people found
his "stupid Hispanic" act offensive. Flip Wilson, one of the first black comedians to have his own successful TV variety show in the 1970s, would regularly appear in drag as "Geraldine," a bossy, conceited, black woman character
he invented. Overbearing and overweight, Geraldine nevertheless had the redeeming feature of representing feminist attitudes in humorous confronta-

tions with men. In doing this character, Flip Wilson was following in the footsteps of Milton Berle, who frequently appeared in drag on his popular TV variety show of the 1950s.

The creation of stereotyped ethnic characters has been a perennial comic technique. Gilda Radner became well known for this by playing Rosann Rosannadanna, a pushy, fast talking Italian American on *Saturday Night Live*. Richard Pryor and Lily Tomlin both created a brilliant cast of comic characters. Tomlin was particularly successful with her invention of Ernestine, a smug, wisecracking telephone operator. The technique goes back to the days of vaudeville, when some comedians would impersonate Jewish, Irish, Italian, or German immigrants speaking in laughable broken English, and even further back to the minstrel shows where whites performed parodies of blacks. A more elaborate and ingenious variation on this technique was employed by Whoopi Goldberg in her classic HBO concert. She created and acted out several different stereotyped characters including a black male drug addict, a Jamaican house maid, a California valley girl, and a little black girl who wanted to be white. She developed each character in such a way that after starting out laughing at their stereotyped language and behaviors, the audience ended up sympathizing with them. It was a remarkable performance because Goldberg was able to move the audience from ridicule to empathy by dramatizing the positive human qualities of her characters.

When comedians invent characters for the sake of humor or, for that matter, use mimicry in order to ridicule well-known celebrities and politicians, they are demonstrating a type of humor technique analyzed in detail by the theorist A. A. Berger. In his book on the anatomy of humor, he claims that the theme or content of the comic parody—whether it concerns blacks, Jews, or a president—is less important than the way the central character is presented. According to Berger, there are four specific components necessary for a successful presentation: *identity, logic, language,* and *action.* All of them are important sources of the humor and should fit stereotypes familiar to the audience. *Identity* refers to the central character. He or she must be readily identifiable as representing a particular ethnic group like Bill Dana's Jose and Flip Wilson's Geraldine, or, in the case of well-known celebrities, have a personal style that lends itself to parody (Rosie O'Donnell's parody of Madonna; Billy Crystal's parody of Desi Arnaz).

Once the character's identity has been established, *logic* follows, that is, the logic of the comic situation, which usually involves some sort of obvious incongruity. A good example was Bill Dana's routine in which he had Jose Jiminez being recruited to become an astronaut, or Woody Allen's piece about when a Jewish intellectual tries to rob a bank, he ends up arguing with the teller over the grammar in his holdup note. The central character's *language* must be in accord with and must help to define his identity. This usually involves use of an exaggerated accent or dialect. Finally, there is the *action*, dealing with physical behavior. This can range from gestures and facial expressions to pratfalls, farts, or punches in the nose. Andy Kaufman employed the principles of logic, language, and action when he assumed the identity of "Lotka," an East European immigrant cab driver he created for a TV sitcom, and it is easy to see Eddie Murphy using these principles in his *Beverly Hills Cop* movies. As Berger indicates, however, for the most part audiences remain happily unaware of these techniques when performers integrate them smoothly as part of their act.

No matter how well all the techniques of humor are used, failure awaits the comedian who cannot employ them with an effective sense of timing. All performers and students of comedy agree that timing—the spacing between lines or gestures, the time allowed for an audience to react during the build-up to a punch line, is what makes the difference between mediocrity and success. Most comedians start out with an intuitive sense of timing, or they would probably never try going on stage in the first place. Nevertheless, it is one thing to sit around with friends and tell a few jokes effectively, although some of us cannot even do that very well, and quite another to stand up and do this in front of a group of indifferent or skeptical strangers. Nor is this problem limited to comedians. I have seen more than one mature graduate student, and a few professors as well, freeze up or get lost in their presentation when required to "perform" before strangers at a professional conference. But while academics can usually take refuge in their notes and slides or mumble their way through, comedians are out there in the spotlight living or dying by their wits alone. All of us have probably had the experience of our wits deserting us in the face of stress or anxiety. So if it takes considerable experience before teachers can become comfortable lecturing to a captive audience of students, imagine how much more experience, and sheer nerve, it must take before stand-up comedians can give a polished, properly timed performance to a group of strangers. It is no wonder that many young comedians feel that they need a few drinks, or something stronger, prior to doing their acts.

The important thing to appreciate is that timing, including the smooth coordination of verbal and physical action, is the first thing to go south in the face of anxiety. Good timing requires what military psychologists have called situation awareness, the ability to stay cool and keep track of what is going on in complex, stressful situations. In the military, this is learned through extensive training, yet even there it sometimes fails in high-stress situations. Comedians only have on-the-job training and whatever benefit they can gain from rehearsing. As comedians gain experience, however, their timing seems to become part of their general style. The sarcastic/aggressive style of an Eddie

Murphy or Don Rickles generally goes with rapid-fire timing, whereas whimsical material is delivered in the slower, drawn-out fashion that is typical of a Bill Cosby performance. In the annals of comedy, however, the acknowledged grand master of timing was Jack Benny. Benny is famous for a minimal routine in a radio skit where he is accosted by a holdup man who demands, "Your money or your life." This is followed by a long silence. The holdup man impatiently repeats his demand, and there is another long silence, finally broken when Benny replies in an angry tone of voice, "I'm thinking it over!" Some successful comedians, like Robin Williams and George Carlin, who do both sarcastic/aggressive and whimsical routines, are able to mix and match their timing to suit the material at hand.

Poor timing is a frequent problem for aspiring comedians who may have well-rehearsed, funny lines but become too anxious to get them out when on stage. They rush the build-up to the punch line and deliver it before the audience is set to receive it. Experienced comedians can be seen using props or gestures to avoid this problem. In a recent HBO show Robin Williams paused every few minutes to drink from bottles of mineral water. Alan King, Groucho Marx, George Burns, and others of their generation would come on stage with a cigar, pausing between lines to take a puff, flick the ash, or simply contemplate the cigar for a moment after completing a line. Phyllis Diller would gesture with a long cigarette holder. Bill Cosby frequently takes a moment to grimace or make a face in order to emphasize a line. Noteworthy too is the way Chris Rock will stride and sometimes scuttle back and forth across the stage, coordinating the rhythm of his delivery with his back-and-forth movements. Some of the best comedy effects involve using a pause to "top the topper." This is achieved when a performer gets a good laugh from a punch line, waits until the laughter subsides, and then hits the audience with an even funnier elaboration of the punch line. Many comedians will also create brief pauses in their act by laughing at their own jokes, joining in for a moment when the audience is laughing and in this way opening up a little space before their next bit. But this can be a dangerous habit if it is not done with careful attention to audience reactions. Inexperienced performers fail to realize that too much laughter on their part gives the impression that they are straining to get a sign of appreciation from the audience.

By far one of the worst things new comedians are likely to do is try to "save" a joke that fails by backing up to explain it, or by offering an excuse: "Hey folks, they loved this joke last night in Philadelphia!" Equally off-putting are self-critical asides when a joke does not work: "Oh well, I knew I shouldn't have got out bed this morning"; or, "My mother told me there would be nights like this." Beginners who do not learn to avoid these things do not last long. For those who do, timing remains as a major challenge.

The necessity for effective comic timing is confirmed by analyses of how people comprehend humor. The cognitive effort required has been described as a decoding process in research by Howard Giles. The first step in the process is *arousal*. Comedians can get nowhere if they are not able to stimulate some interest and attention in their audience. The most reliable way of accomplishing this is by establishing some sort of incongruity. It can take the form of an introductory line, as when someone like Margaret Cho begins by saying she hopes her parents are not watching the show. Why? Because they thought she was home minding the store. Or it can be accomplished by simply coming on stage wearing a funny hat, earmuffs, or carrying a prop that arouses audience curiosity. In some of his early stand-up performances, Steve Martin would enter wearing a gadget that made it look as if he had an arrow stuck through his head. And of course, any kind of opening line concerning sex or gender differences usually works: "Marriage is really hard on a girl; like my husband has a dick that wakes up every morning ten minutes before he does." (Pause, look toward your crotch, etc.) Regardless of what the incongruity may be, the fact that it is working will be indicated when the audience begins to smile or chuckle in anticipation. This assures that they have reached the second phase of the cognitive process: *perceiving*, or comprehending the elements of the incongruity that is being developed. So if there are two elements, as in, "What's the difference between a Rottweiler and a Jewish Mother?" it will be clear from the audience response that they know the type of dog and the Jewish Mother stereotype. Third, the audience must *evaluate* the way the incongruity is resolved—"Eventually, the Rottweiler lets go"—in order to conclude whether or not they think it is funny. Finally, the decoding process will end in either laughter or disappointment. All of this can happen in a few seconds, of course, but the point is that even then, the process takes time, and experienced comedians know that the timing of their presentation must be adjusted to fit both the nature of their material and the nature of their audience. This is particularly important where racial-ethnic humor is concerned. If an audience is not familiar with the stereotype being evoked, say, about the controlling tendencies of Jewish Mothers, then the comedian must take the time to build this information into the routine.

Much more could be said about the techniques of humor that can make or break a comedian. The principles of timing and examples of subtle variations in the use of language, logic, identity, and action that may depend upon whether the material is aggressive or whimsical, or a mixture of both, could easily fill a separate book. Indeed, there are such books that serve as how-to-do-it manuals for aspiring comedians. The aim of the present discussion has merely been to highlight some of the major skills that must be mastered, as well as the stress and uncertainties that must be faced, in other words, to appreciate what comedians are up against and how they learn to cope. When we see good comedians in performance, or summarize how their careers have developed, much of the hard work that has gone into their art is not apparent. It does not show, and most of us do not want it to show; we just want to be entertained. Some of my students have occasionally been reluctant to discuss the techniques of comedy, lest this interfere with their ability to enjoy it. They do not put it this way, but what it amounts to is, "I don't want to risk losing my pleasure by contaminating my feelings with knowledge." My usual response is to say they have nothing to fear, that the more they know about how performers are able to do their magic and make us laugh, the more they will enjoy and appreciate the art. This admittedly intellectual viewpoint is not appreciated by everyone, including many comedians. Comedians, like other artists and many athletes, tend to be superstitious about their work and uncomfortable about analyzing how they do it. If they have "the gift," they are fearful of losing it if they examine it too closely. There is, in fact, some truth to the idea that "thinking too much can ruin your game," so perhaps it is best to leave close analysis to critics and college professors.

Yet another question that comes up in discussions about the making of comedians more or less relates to their "unmaking," the way so many prominent performers have moved beyond their original careers in stand-up to become TV and movie stars. This movement from live comedy began long before TV, when vaudeville stars like Marie Dressler, W. C. Fields, and Charlie Chaplin were hired to appear in silent movies. Their success brought them so much money and recognition that they could no longer afford to do anything else. The same thing happens among contemporary comedians as they move from nightclubs to TV and films. Only now many of the most successful like Steve Martin, Whoopi Goldberg, and Robin Williams move still further away from comedy as they appear in straight dramatic film roles.

Although there are no formal studies dealing with the question of how it is possible for our top comedians to transform themselves so readily into major TV and film stars, at least three factors are involved. First, and probably most important, is the extensive range of experience that the comedians bring to their acting work. Many of them, like Whoopi Goldberg and Robin Williams, have had dramatic training prior to their comedy careers, and all of them have had on-the-job training in the performance skills noted earlier: timing, the use of body language, the ability to role play or mimic a broad range of characters, and not least, experience dealing with the stress and anxiety associated with stand-up work. Accordingly, since they already know how to create comic effects, they are very well prepared to create dramatic effects. In fact, most acting coaches and theater professionals say that comedy is the most difficult form of acting, so those who have mastered this have a significant head start on drama. Comedians are also quick studies. Their general attributes mentioned at the beginning of this chapter—excellent verbal skills, practical intelligence, and quick cognitive reflexes—would obviously facilitate learning the tasks necessary for acting in TV and movies. In some respects it is arguable that most comedians have been intuitive actors from the time they were children and teenagers. Finally, there are the conditions of TV and film acting as compared with stand-up comedy. The stand-up performer works without any supportive structure or framework, whereas actors have a script, a director, substantial rehearsal time, and usually the opportunity to repeat a scene several times if need be. It is the difference between working with and without a safety net. So it appears much easier for comedians to try acting than for actors to try doing stand-up comedy.

About the only thing most comedians complain of when working in movies is the loss of freedom. In exchange for the sense of security, not to mention big money, that comes with TV and movie work, they lose the freedom, spontaneity, and high excitement of going on stage alone to take on the challenge of making an audience laugh. For any good stand-up performer, the necessity of working with other members of a cast, and trying to satisfy an opinionated director, must be a serious source of frustration. This is surely why some, like Robin Williams, who become Hollywood stars claim that they still look forward to doing occasional live stand-up shows.

There is no simple way to sum up all the issues considered in this chapter. If they do not offer a detailed, cradle-to-the-grave review of everything that goes into the making of comedians, the main points discussed should at least provide a good perspective on what it takes for performers to succeed. Whether viewed from the standpoint of developmental psychology, illustrative life experiences, or the skills and techniques that must be learned, it should be apparent that making a career in comedy is no picnic. All authorities on the subject agree that it is difficult to create or perform humor effectively and gain recognition, because it involves both inspiration and a high level of craftsmanship, let alone the help of a good manager or agent and just being in the right place at the right time. Many successful comedy writers and performers may not be fully aware of all the issues examined here, but they would be failures if they did not have an implicit understanding of them. The following chapter shifts gears to focus on the larger social implications and meanings of ethnic humor—just the thing that most professional comedians prefer to avoid because they usually have neither the time nor the inclination to philosophize about their art.

10

In Defense of Ethnic Humor and Its Role in Our Multicultural Society

There is more logic in humor than in anything else. Because, you see, humor is truth.

—Victor Borge

The absolute truth is the thing that makes people laugh.

—Carl Reiner

There is a good deal to be said for the idea that all humor always has a certain logic and connection with truth, and that some truths may be so painful to acknowledge openly that they can only be expressed when presented as humor. But let us begin again with the obvious: anyone who has ever nearly fallen out of their chair laughing from watching Richard Pryor, Robin Williams, Whoopi Goldberg, or other masters of racial, ethnic, and gender humor doing their acts should know that it needs no defense. Its primary meaning is simply "the gift of laughter." This is precisely the view of Christie Davies, who has spent a distinguished scholarly career studying the subject. As noted in the earlier chapter on theory, Davies consistently argues that those who view ethnic humor as contributing to prejudice are missing the point. They are misled by the presence of disparaging stereotypes. Such humor does, of course, largely hold up identifiable groups to ridicule. But if people were primarily concerned with expressing hostility, there are plenty of ways to do this without going to the trouble of inventing jokes. Consequently, Davies contends that ethnic humor is simply a form of social play that people everywhere find intrinsically amusing. My own studies as well as others that have been cited confirm this point. If we laugh at a disparaging ethnic joke, it does not necessarily mean that we dislike or wish to insult the group it concerns; it is rather testimony to the power of humor over moralistic good manners. When women enjoy jokes ridiculing men and men chuckle over jokes about women, this is less indicative of serious prejudice than of our recognition that, for better or worse, there are some painfully amusing differences between men and women. One of the jokes used recently on Garrison Keillor's *Prairie Home Companion* radio show provides a good example of this point:

> "If the Three Wise Men going to Bethlehem had been women, they would have asked for directions, arrived on time, cleaned the stable, made a good meal, and brought practical gifts for the baby."

The same thing seems to be true about other varieties of ethnic humor. Thus it has never been demonstrated that Americans who laugh at jokes about blonds, Poles, and Jewish Mothers really believe all blonds are dumb, Polish Americans are dirty and stupid, and Jewish Mothers are too possessive. This claim is at least partially supported by the fact that in situations where ethnic groups are in deadly conflict or have traditions of mutual hatred, they do not always create jokes to ridicule each other. Current examples might include the Protestants and Catholics in Northern Ireland and the Israelis and Palestinians. I had confirmation of this recently in correspondence with a colleague in Israel who said there were few if any ethnic jokes aimed at ridicule of Palestinians. Whether this means there is little hatred of Palestinians or that the hatred runs so deep as to preclude joking about it remains an open question. What it does indicate is that in and of itself, racial-ethnic humor should not be automatically taken as a sign of group conflict or hatred. Finally, there is no consistent evidence showing that people who are the butt of ethnic jokes always take them seriously enough to feel hurt or abused. Most minority students in my classes, for example, have said that humor at the expense of their own group is only disturbing if they see it as deliberately malicious or meant as a personal insult.

The humor scholar Harvey Mindess has gone further, commenting that politically correct efforts to censor or prohibit stereotype humor may be a mistake, because when such humor is shared across ethnic groups, it may facilitate an authentic form of mutual sympathy. An illustration of what Mindess suggests could be seen in a recent concert performance by *The Latin Kings of Comedy*. One of them did a routine explaining how much he admired Native Americans who were finally getting even with whites by taking their money in casinos. But he thought they might be discriminating against Mexicans because their slot machines do not accept food stamps. This was received with enthusiastic applause by the largely Mexican American audience.

It is noteworthy, too, that in suggesting a positive social value for such humor, Mindess differs from Davies, who claims it has neither positive nor negative social significance.

Although Davies and Mindess, as well as Randall Kennedy, Leon Wynter, and others, defend racial-ethnic humor against accusations that it fosters prejudice, some social scientists disagree. A. A. Berger, for example, takes an intermediate position in his 1993 book, *An Anatomy of Humor.* Summing up his conclusions in a way that almost lends itself to the construction of a Jewish joke, Berger says, in effect, that on the one hand, because it provides entertainment and allows people to safely ventilate aggressive feelings, ethnic humor is quite benign. But on the other hand, since it may encourage people to stigmatize minorities with negative stereotypes, it can be harmful. This may appear to be a rather easy way of avoiding the problem because it covers all the bases, yet by emphasizing that the meaning of ethnic humor depends on its context, Berger's view can be taken as a perfectly reasonable assertion that no all-embracing positive or negative judgment is possible.

Another perspective in line with Berger's can be seen in the work of Alan Dundes. Based on his studies of folklore, Dundes maintains that ethnic humor grows out of the stereotypes present in the traditions of all human groups. The roots of these stereotypes lie in the self-serving myths and shared memories fundamental to folklore everywhere. Intrinsic features of such lore are images and attitudes that are passed on from one generation to another and lend themselves to ridicule of outsiders. Moreover, just as folklore resists change, since it has the quality of a natural, universal phenomenon—does any substantial human group not have a folk tradition specifying its origins, history, and superiority to other groups?—the stereotypes contained in folklore also resist change. This implies that regardless of how we feel about it, some types of racial-ethnic humor will always be with us so long as folklore itself remains with us. And it suggests what may be the strongest argument that can be made in defense of such humor: *it plays with stereotypes and exploits them, but it does not create them.* Writers and comedians are not guilty of inventing the stereotypes or the slurs and obscenities that often accompany them. Instead, they only force us to confront these elements of folklore and popular culture in the context of humor.

Consequently, most of us who have closely examined it see racial-ethnic humor mainly as a playful form of entertainment that can have significant social benefits. Can it be a damaging source of prejudice if employed in a deliberately aggressive, reckless fashion? Yes, but then almost all forms of entertaining human activities, playing sports, driving cars, even eating—you can choke to death on a chicken bone—can also be damaging if carried out in a reckless fashion. Why then do so many people, including many social scientists who have never studied or done research on ethnic humor, consider such humor to be harmful? Among the general public, as indicated at the start of this book, it is mainly a matter of appearances. Any time a group is made to seem laughable or ridiculous, it can be taken as an expression of hostility. But if the majority of the public actually thought it was seriously harmful, then like hard drugs and child pornography, it would be banned. The African American scholar Randall Kennedy has even argued that it would be wrong to outlaw the N-word, because such a remedy could have worse legal consequences than the problem it was supposed to cure. Many people in the social sciences, however, hold to a critique of ethnic humor based upon widely accepted behaviorist theories of learning.

Their argument follows from the idea that the most basic forms of learning in animals, from worms on up to chimpanzees and humans, occurs through processes of classical and operant conditioning, that is, according to the principles of association or reinforcement. When it is extended to the problem of ethnic humor, the argument goes that two things happen if someone laughs at a joke containing a negative stereotype. First, there is an association formed between the stereotype and the group it ridicules, and second, the laughter acts as a reward reinforcing the association. This is not a one-shot affair, however; it requires a good deal of repetition before someone will become conditioned to automatically apply the stereotype to the targeted group. While the logic here is seductive, behavior researchers know that not even the rats and pigeons conditioned in laboratory studies always respond as predicted. Yet the argument derived from learning theory, and never put to any experimental test with real people and real jokes, is that when we laugh at a racial-ethnic joke or comedy routine, then whether we are aware of it or not, we are being conditioned to accept the negative stereotype. The more we are exposed to such humor, the more we are likely to accept the negative stereotypes involved.

A somewhat more sophisticated line of argument appeals to the principle of imitation. Derived from work in the field known as social learning theory, this criticism of ethnic humor is especially persuasive when applied to children. There is no doubt that children are particularly susceptible to learning both through conditioning and the imitation of rewarded behaviors. What parent has not been upset when their child comes home repeating an obscenity or ethnic slur he or she has picked up in the schoolyard because other children thought it was funny? Given this common experience, and the opinions of social scientists familiar with the behaviorist learning theories, it is no wonder that many people morally opposed to prejudice see ethnic humor as a blight on our society. But can it be banned or eliminated? The answer is obviously no. Even in Hitler's Germany and Stalin's Soviet Union, where people could be imprisoned or worse if caught telling jokes ridiculing the Nazis or Communists, such jokes continued to circulate. So much the less would it be possible to prohibit ethnic humor in our society. The fallback argument is that it should at least be banned from TV, but that is also not likely, because the market rules: as long as substantial audiences enjoy it, it will be programmed. A more powerful counterargument is that most of the racial-ethnic humor presented on TV is designed to undercut prejudice rather than support it.

This counterargument is also relevant to the fear that children can be contaminated with prejudice when exposed to such humor. If children are allowed to freely watch TV, they will certainly learn that many different racial-ethnic groups and stereotypes exist, but since most of what they may see shows negative stereotypes to be foolish and unfair, children will also learn not to take them seriously. The basis for this argument against the social learning and conditioning theories is cognitive theory, which stipulates that higher order thought processes can override attitudes acquired through imitation and conditioning. If this were not true, women would still not be allowed to vote, and we would still have segregation in the military. Among countless studies concerning the effects of TV on children, I have never heard of any studies that show TV encourages children to become prejudiced toward minorities. Even the retrograde Amos 'n' Andy type of "minstrelsy" considered harmful by some commentators appears trivial compared with the social pressures and childrearing practices known to be the fundamental sources of prejudice.

In the end, however, it may be best to acknowledge that the question of whether or not racial-ethnic humor fosters prejudice can never be resolved in ways that will satisfy everyone. There are too many different forms and varieties of such humor, and too many different perspectives that people bring to it. At the time this book was written, for example, an Associated Press news story by Deborah Kong appeared under the title *Race Humor Still a Balancing Act*. Kong describes a handful of recent cases in which some minority individuals have claimed to be offended by stereotypes presented in the context of humor. In one instance, a Chinese American took offense at a TV skit where an Asian martial arts expert attacked a stereotyped Asian businessman. In another, a Sikh group complained about a movie scene that had a character wearing a turban who was jokingly called Osama Bin Laden, and in yet another, a few Hispanics claimed to be insulted by a Mexican American cartoonist who draws disreputable-looking Mexican characters in his syndicated *La Cucaracha* comic strip. When interviewed about these complaints, the TV and movie producers apologized, saying they never thought anyone would take their humor seriously, whereas the cartoonist was quoted as saying that in humor, "anything goes." The reporter also solicited opinions from a few comedians, who admitted that some of their racial-ethnic routines occasionally offend a few people, but they essentially agreed with the cartoonist. The comedian Bill Maher added that there is an implicit double standard governing racial-ethnic humor: whites have to be careful about any references to people of color, but it is always open season for ridicule of mainstream whites.

For what it is worth, I generally agree with Christie Davies that ethnic humor is largely a matter of play. But unlike Davies, my study of the relevant research and trends in the development of humor in America over the past half century indicates that ethnic humor has become an important force against prejudice. This opinion is also based on observations of how hundreds of diverse students in my classes have responded to stereotype humor. All of them immediately grasp the sword and shield metaphor: the idea that as an expression of aggression, such humor can cut both ways, rather than mainly at minorities. If this seems obvious to them, it is because they have all been exposed to the routines of major stand-up comedians. Having grown up watching TV sitcoms, they are also familiar with the racial-ethnic identities of many of their favorite performers because of the traditional stereotypes these performers either ridicule or exaggerate for the sake of satire. The students, and much of the larger public as well, clearly appreciate the incongruities following from racial, religious, and gender differences, do not take them seriously, and enjoy clever ridicule and parodies of familiar stereotypes. Thus, contrary to Davies, who may not keep up with trends in American sitcoms and films, particularly the way stand-up comedians have succeeded in using the sword of comedy to undercut the significance of stereotypes, it seems clear to me that such humor operates against the social acceptability of prejudice.

But there is more to my argument than just the change in standards of social acceptability. Stand-up comedians have also changed the way many people perceive racial-ethnic humor by shifting the focus from prejudice to amused irony, or often, in the case of minorities, to pride. This might be called the Charlie Chaplin Effect, whereby the impoverished little guy maintains his dignity and pride against all obstacles, and often gets the better of rich and powerful adversaries. The stand-up comedian who acknowledges all the stereotypes disparaging his or her minority group, holds them up to ridicule, and then turns the tables by puncturing the pretensions of better off groups is doing much the same thing as Chaplin, that is, asserting pride in the face of prejudice, and in the process imposing a critical perspective on the mainstream audience.

This is where the shield aspect of the metaphor comes directly into play, because it is clear that minority individuals who identify with comedians from their group enjoy seeing them both acknowledge and defy disparaging stereotypes. Witnessing such humor provides a defensive shield against prejudice by encouraging an enhanced sense of self-esteem. More specifically, when it is plain that the minority performer, whether it be Chris Rock, Paul Rodriguez, Margaret Cho, or another, is able to openly confront stereotypes about their group and use humor to rise above them, this paves the way for minority viewers to do the same. Basically, such comedians are presenting a valuable model of how members of their group can employ humor to ward off any feelings of inferiority due to prejudice. In other words, this is not merely a show of how to laugh off demeaning stereotypes. You do not have to be a scholar to see that much of the time comedians are literally performing a critical deconstruction of stereotypes by revealing their intrinsic contradictions. Accordingly, comedians offer an informal, liberating intellectual experience along with the entertainment. When viewed from this standpoint, it is not unreasonable to recognize successful performers of racial-ethnic humor as minor culture heroes.

We usually reserve the phrase "culture hero" for people like Martin Luther King Jr. or Sigmund Freud, individuals who by means of their creative and sometimes hazardous efforts have changed the way we look at or behave in the world. It may seem absurd, therefore, to suggest that even the best of our comedians deserve this level of recognition. Yet insofar as they succeed in transforming stereotypes to objects of ridicule, they do, indeed, help to change the way people look at the world. The best examples, as described earlier, are Lenny Bruce and Richard Pryor, both of whom broke through the prevailing standards of middle-class good taste when using hard edged, "dirty" routines in order to attack hypocritical social norms. Whether intentionally or not, their personal lives were sacrificed to this end. In certain respects, too, Bruce, Pryor, and other innovative comedians such as Dick Gregory and George Carlin can be seen as following in the biblical tradition of the "holy fool," the individual who deliberately acts out absurd, self-sacrificing and humiliating behaviors as a form of testimony to the mysterious ways of God, as compared to the ways of men.

The sociologist Peter Berger described this metaphysical connection between religious spirituality and comedy in his book *Redeeming Laughter.* Berger explains that those who became "fools for Christ's sake," mainly during the Middle Ages, were men and women who wished to imitate Jesus by renouncing their worldly goods and identities. They wandered from place to place as strange outsiders testifying to the powers of God with their bodies and their seemingly irrational behaviors. The point of this was to show that practical, rational self-interest is merely a human invention encouraging people toward the sin of pride. Berger also notes that the holy fools were primarily acting on the basis of a passage from the New Testament, First Corinthians, in which the apostle Paul claims to be speaking as a fool and urges other Christians to do the same. Paul elaborates on what this means by saying:

> "God chose what is foolish in the world to shame the wise, God chose what is weak in the world to shame the strong, God chose what is low and despised in the world . . . so that no human being might boast in the presence of God."

One could hardly create a more un-American statement. More important in the present context, however, are some of the striking similarities between the holy fools and aspiring comedians today. Comedians too become wanderers from one venue to another, are usually impoverished, are considered by many of their families and friends to be a little crazy, and often seem to have an irrational grudge against mainstream society. They also tend to use what seems "foolish and weak in the world" to ridicule the rich and powerful. And the parallel extends a bit further. Some of the holy fools were eventually thought to be saintly and were given a special status in their societies. The same thing is true of some of our more successful comedians who acquire a privileged star status in our society. Although the claim of similarities between these very different groups may be stretching things a bit too far since our comedians are usually not inspired by religious values, they are, nevertheless, willing to run the risks of public humiliation when they challenge established social, political, and sexual attitudes with jokes and parodies.

Apart from the controversial careers of Lenny Bruce and Richard Pryor, however, and at the opposite end of the comedy spectrum, one ethnic performer stands out today as a noncontroversial, indeed, eminently acceptable culture hero. Is there anyone in America today who would not like to spend an hour or two with Bill Cosby? He has, in many ways, done for the field of comedy what Jackie Robinson did for baseball: almost singlehandedly shown that racist attitudes preventing African Americans from full participation in our culture belong in the trash heap of history. Cosby is particularly interesting in this context because as a black man, his ethnicity is clear, yet unlike all the other comedians—black, white, Hispanic, or Asian—mentioned previously, he has always refused to use racial-ethnic stereotypes or obscene language in his stand-up and sitcom work, and he has not hesitated to publicly criticize other comedians who do. Simply by his presence, moreover, he has done as much as if not more than most others to undermine ethnic stereotypes. In many ways, and apparently by virtue of his personal style and presentation of self, his unique talent lies in his ability to charm or enchant audiences to the point where they ignore his racial identity. To put it another way, like Jackie Robinson, his race is overshadowed and rendered irrelevant by the quality of his performance. Thus, when considered in terms of the struggle against racism, Cosby represents African Americans who "take the high road," by refusing to confront mainstream audiences with blatant, down-and-dirty material.

Yet it is precisely because of his remarkable status in mainstream society that some African American intellectuals and most of the urban, hip-hop youth are critical of Cosby or indifferent to him. Perhaps it is testimony to the perversity of human nature that he has been targeted with the "Oreo cookie" criticism, that he is black on the outside but white on the inside. Why? Because he speaks in conventional English (no black slang expressions or intonations), dresses according to middle-class standards, and rarely mentions specific African American themes or attitudes in his performances. There is also the more subtle, comfortably moralistic aspect of Cosby's style and public persona that disturbs some of his intellectual critics. That is, the voice speaking out from his amiable, father figure image is a traditional one, admonishing young people to do the right thing: get an education, keep clean, work hard, and aim for a piece of the American Dream. These points show up in many of his stand-up routines about the silly behaviors of teenagers and the problems they pose for their parents, and was an important feature of his family sitcom. Part of his style is undoubtedly due to his age, but not entirely. As compared with Woody Allen, for example, who is about the same age, Cosby's image is that of a good-humored but respectable, demanding father, while Allen appears as a pleasantly neurotic, permissive, and slightly dotty uncle. So, not to put too fine a point on it, Cosby just seems too middle-class white, and therefore not acceptable as a valid representative of many African Americans. This view is particularly prevalent among the youth, some of whom insist on "acting black" as a point of pride, and see those who do not as betraying their culture heritage. Other older blacks who have achieved great success and acceptance in mainstream white society—Harry Belafonte, Sammy Davis Jr., Sidney Poitier—have been criticized along the same lines as Cosby. All of them became prominent in the 1950s and early 1960s when the struggle against racism was focused on integration, assimilation, and the achievement of a color-blind society. To some extent, this is still true, but what is different today is the increasing public awareness that integration does not require ignoring, or leveling out, all cultural differences between racial-ethnic groups. In American society today, the ideal of equality now includes respect for diversity that has overshadowed the goal of total assimilation. This can be seen in the way humor is presented by most of the younger African American comedians. At the other extreme from Cosby are black performers such as Bernie Mac, Martin Lawrence, Chris Rock, and Eddie Murphy when he was doing stand-up, who have followed the path established by Richard Pryor and have been criticized for acting too black, too much like the stereotype of black street hustlers or ghetto gangsters.

This sort of double bind, in which performers can be damned if they act out stereotypes, even if only for the sake of satire, and damned if they do not, is not limited to African Americans. The actor and comedian Cheech Marin has been criticized by Hispanics for some of his humor about low-status Latinos, whereas the Hispanic actor Jimmy Smits has occasionally been criticized by some Hispanics for acting too white. Among Asians, Margaret Cho has been accused of catering to stereotypes about Korean Americans. In the early 1960s, Lenny Bruce was hated by some Jews for being a troublemaker who apparently delighted in exaggerating the pushy, smart-aleck Jewish stereotype. Jackie Mason was seen as acting too Jewish, and Rodney Danger-field was criticized for not acknowledging he was Jewish.

As a general rule, it appears that every racial-ethnic group is divided in this fashion. Those who have gained success and acceptance in mainstream society are resented by those who have not and are often criticized for having outgrown or shuffled off their ethnic identity. On the other hand, those who parade and exploit their group identity are seen as opportunists acting out negative stereotypes to advance their careers. This internal division can be a serious problem, but at the same time it provides good material for in-group humor. So blacks have jokes among themselves about those who straighten their hair or lighten their skin to look more white, and also jokes about those who try to exaggerate their blackness by wearing dashikis and dark glasses in order to "mau-mau Mr. Charlie" (intimidate whites). Jews joke about those who convert to Christianity and have surgery on their noses, and at the opposite extreme about the ultraorthodox who consider themselves superior to everyone else. Among Hispanics, there is something of a humor pecking order, such that Cuban Americans ridicule Puerto Rican and Mexican Americans for their lack of skills or laziness, while Mexicans and Puerto Ricans joke about the Cubans as manipulative snobs. All of these groups, of course, also have jokes about their own greenhorns.

What do all these apparent contradictions mean? I am convinced that it is a matter of social class. The more closely one examines the various patterns of humor both within minority groups and between minority and majority groups, the more they appear to reflect social class differences. In fact, although there are no traditional social class standards in North America as there are in Europe, the two practical criteria that divide people in America are money and education. Unlike the firmly established class boundaries in Europe, where family traditions and connections may still count for more than money and education, in America these standards are about all we have, and they easily lend themselves to behaviors that may contradict or outweigh ethnicity. So it is not unusual for well-off, well-educated Hispanic, Asian, and African American professionals to find that they have more in common with each other and with well-off, educated whites, than with poor, uneducated members of their own group. The same is generally true among minority working-class people, who are quick to criticize members of their own group who do not share their values.

There is no better example of the class consciousness found in most ethnic groups than my own Jewish mother, who could well have served as a model for all of the jokes. She arrived in America as a young teenager, was a true believer in the melting pot ideal, and was passionately devoted to middle-class values. As far as she was concerned, any Jewish greenhorn who failed to work hard, make money, get an education (if only by attending night school), and adopt American ways deserved to be called a kike. On the other hand, she referred to one of my uncles who got rich by working with racketeers in the garment center as nothing but a gangster. None of this was a matter of anti-Semitism; she only wanted all Jews to live up to her standards. So if I arrived home from school with a bad report card, or bruises and a bloody nose from a street fight, then after the usual spanking she would accuse me of ruining her life by acting worse than a kike; I had acted like a "goyische" (gentile), good-for-nothing bum! I was, of course, later forgiven everything when she learned that my Ph.D. allowed her to call me doctor.

The general point about class consciousness, however, is that one's professional status, income, and education in America are likely to be a more important determinant of attitudes and values than one's racial-ethnic identity. Minority group loyalties may remain, but they are typically reduced to a few cultural traditions such as the food, music, and dancing that occur at weddings and the customs followed at funerals. It is not an inflexible rule, but as people achieve higher levels of success in our society, their group identity becomes less definitive of their self-concepts, and the result is some degree of group "dis-identification," occasionally softened by donations to a relevant good cause. This social process is what accounts for the conflicting and contradictory patterns of humor found within various minority groups, where it is largely a matter of ridicule exchanged between the haves and have-nots. Because the have-nots may be on their way to becoming haves, while the haves may still maintain a sense of connection with those less fortunate than themselves, the tensions resulting from this situation offer rich possibilities for humor. To make matters even more complex, when confronted with serious slurs or insults by outsiders, all members of the group, whether rich or poor, tend to pull together and respond in kind. This sort of cohesion can also be seen in benign situations, such as when a minority comedian does a routine ridiculing the pretensions of mainstream whites and everyone in the minority audience, regardless of their apparent social class, joins in the laughter. But here again, things are not so simple, because mainstream whites in the audience will also join in the laughter. Thus, as already noted in several other contexts, if ethnic humor is presented in situations where there is no clear intention to seriously disparage or insult the targeted group, the humor overrides the ethnicity.

Ultimately, the meaning of racial-ethnic humor will always lie in the eye of the beholder. The very fact that racial-ethnic humor is based on the tensions associated with stereotypes is enough to guarantee that some people will find it offensive while others who may be prejudiced will find it comforting. And yet, not only such humor but all comedy depends on a mixture of ambiguity and tension and usually has an aggressive edge to it that some will find threatening. As discussed in several different contexts throughout this book, there can be no humor without some degree of tension or anxiety. Even the simple child's game of peekaboo is nothing if not a deliberately playful encounter with anxiety: what will be out there when the child opens his or her eyes, or the child's mother uncovers her face? In the same vein, there is always some implicit anxiety aroused when adults hear comedians joke about the stereotypes applied to various minority groups: what will be the punch line? In both cases, the anxiety will dissolve into healthy laughter if all goes well, but if it does not, the child may become frightened, and the adults may become angry. So it is by no means absurd to suggest that exposure to some degree of anxiety is the price we pay for humor. LOL !!

Most of us willingly pay this price because of the benefits we gain: not only the laughter, but also the liberating experience of "critical distance" that humor allows us to maintain in the face of our uncertain condition in the world. Insofar as our condition is bound to our group identity, a sense of critical distance provides the means for us to accept it, and at the same time, rise above it—to not allow ourselves to be narrowly defined or limited by a rigid or fanatical attachment to our group. More specifically, when we can enjoy good-natured stereotype humor about ourselves as well as others, this implies that we recognize the fact that no group is perfect, not even our own, and that we need not take stereotypes too seriously, whether they concern ourselves or others.

Clearly, this formal, redemptive aspect of racial-ethnic humor is not apparent to people, black, white, Jewish, or of any other group, who are caught up in laughter at a performance by Whoopi Goldberg, Chris Rock, Jerry Seinfeld, or Margaret Cho. Yet the wide popularity of such comedians, along with the proliferating stereotype humor present in films and TV sitcoms, is an unmistakable sign of its significance in our multicultural society. We are, after all, held together in American society by shared values that transcend our wide range of group differences, and few things provide such strong evidence for this as our rich stock of ironic humor. The fact that we can not only tolerate our differences but also play with them, even at the risk of occasionally offending each other, ought to be recognized as more a matter of pride and creativity than of prejudice.

Bibliography

Adams, P. 1998. *Gesundheit!: Bringing good health to you, the medical system and society through physician service, complementary therapies, humor and joy.* Rochester, VT: Healing Arts Press.

Allen, I. L. 1983. *The language of ethnic conflict: Social organization and lexical culture.* New York: Columbia University Press.

Ariniello, L. 2001. Humor, laughter and the brain. *Brain Briefings.* 12/01 issue. Society for Neuroscience, 1–2.

Barreca, R. 1991. *They used to call me Snow White . . . but I drifted: Women's strategic use of humor.* New York: Viking Penguin.

Baxter, J. 1998. *Woody Allen: A biography.* London: HarperCollins.

Benny, M. L., and H. Marks with M. Borie. 1978. *Jack Benny.* New York: Doubleday.

Berger, P. 1975. *The last laugh: The world of stand-up comics.* New York: Morrow.

Berger, A. A. 1993. *An anatomy of humor.* New Brunswick, NJ: Transaction Publishers.

Berger, P. L. 1997. *Redeeming laughter: The comic dimension of human experience.* New York: Walter De Gruyter.

Bier, J. 1988. The problem of the Polish joke in derogatory American humor. *Humor: International Journal of Humor Research* 1 (2): 135–41.

Boskin, J. 1979. *Humor and social change in twentieth century America.* Boston: Boston Public Library.

Boskin, J. 1987. Beyond kvetching and jiving: The thrust of Jewish and Black folk humor. In S. B. Cohen (ed.), *Jewish wry: Essays on Jewish humor.* Bloomington: Indiana University Press, 53–79.

Boyd, T. 2003. *Young, black, rich, and famous.* New York: Doubleday.

Bruce, L. 1967. *How to talk dirty and influence people: An autobiography.* Chicago and New York: Playboy Press and Pocket Books.

Bryson, B. 1990. *Mother tongue: English and how it got that way.* New York: William Morrow.

Cann, A., and L. G. Calhoun. 2001. Perceived personality associations with differences in sense of humor: Stereotypes of hypothetical others with high or low senses of humor. *Humor: International Journal of Humor Research* 14 (2): 117–30.

Chapman, A. J., and H. C. Foot, eds. 1996. *Humor and laughter: Theory, research and applications.* New Brunswick, NJ: Transaction Publishers.

Cohen, J., ed. 1967. *The essential Lenny Bruce.* New York: Ballantine Books.

Cohen, S. B., ed. 1987. *Jewish wry: Essays on Jewish humor.* Bloomington: Indiana University Press.

Cohen, T. 1999. *Jokes: Philosophical thoughts on joking matters.* Chicago: University of Chicago Press.

Coleman, R.R.M. 1998. *African American viewers and the black situation comedy: Situating racial humor.* New York: Garland Publishing.

Collins, R., and D. M. Skover. 2002. *The trials of Lenny Bruce, the fall and rise of an American icon.* New York: Sourcebooks.

Davies, C. 1990. *Ethnic humor around the world.* Bloomington: Indiana University Press.

Davies, C. 1991. Ethnic humor, hostility, and aggression: A reply to Elliot Oring. *Humor: International Journal of Humor Research* 4 (3–4): 415–22.

Davies, C. 1998. *Jokes and their relation to society.* New York: Mouton de Gruyter.

Davies, C. 1999. Change and continuity in one of Europe's oldest comic ethnic scripts. *Humor: International Journal of Humor Research* 12 (1): 1–31.

Davies, C. 2002. *The mirth of nations.* New Brunswick, NJ: Transaction Publishers.

Derks, P. 1996. Twenty years of research on humor: A view from the edge. In A. Chapman and H. Foot (eds.), *Humor and laughter: Theory, research and applications.* New Brunswick, NJ: Transaction Publishers, vii–xxvi.

de Zengotita, T. 1996. Celebrity, irony and you. *The Nation,* Dec. 2, 15–18.

Dorinson, J., and J. Boskin. 1988. Racial and ethnic humor. In L. Mintz (ed.), *Humor in America: A research guide to genres and topics.* Westport, CT: Greenwood Press, 163–94.

Dresner, Z. 1988. Women's humor. In L. Mintz (ed.), *Humor in America: A research guide to genres and topics.* Westport, CT: Greenwood Press, 137–62.

Dundes, A. 1987. *Cracking jokes: Studies of sick humor cycles and stereotypes.* Berkeley, CA: Ten Speed Press.

Epstein, L. J. 2001. *The haunted smile: The story of Jewish comedians in America.* New York: Public Affairs.

Erasmus, D. 1979 translation by C. Miller. *In praise of folly.* New Haven: Yale University Press.

Fine, G. A. 1983. Sociological approaches to the study of humor. In P. McGhee and J. Goldstein (eds.), *Handbook of humor research.* New York: Springer, 159–81.

Finney, G., ed. 1994. *Look who's laughing: Gender and comedy.* Langhorne, PA: Gordon and Breach Science Publishers.

Fisher, S., and R. L. Fisher. 1981. *Pretend the world is funny and forever: A psychological analysis of comedians, clowns and actors.* Hillsdale, NJ: Lawrence Erlbaum Associates.

Ford, T. E., and M. A. Ferguson. 2004. Social consequences of disparagement humor:

A prejudiced norm theory. *Personality and Social Psychology Review* 8 (1): 79–94.

Foxx, R., and N. Miller. 1977. *The Redd Foxx encyclopedia of black humor.* Pasadena, CA: Ward Ritchie Press.

Fraiberg, A. 1994. Between the laughter: Bridging feminist studies through women's stand-up comedy. In G. Finney (ed.), *Look who's laughing: Gender and comedy.* Langhorne, PA: Gordon and Breach Science Publishers, 315–34.

Franklin, J. 1979. *Joe Franklin's encyclopedia of comedians.* Secaucus, NJ: The Citadel Press.

Freud, S. 1959. Humor. In J. Strachey (ed.), *Collected papers of Sigmund Freud, vol. 5.* New York: Basic Books, 215–21.

Freud, S. 1963, first published 1905. *Jokes and their relation to the unconscious.* New York: W. W. Norton.

Fry, W. F., and M. Allen. 1975. *Make em laugh: Life studies of comedy writers.* Palo Alto, CA: Science and Behavior Books.

Galloway, G., and A. Cropley. 1999. Benefits of humor for mental health: Empirical findings and directions for further research. *Humor: International Journal of Humor Research* 12 (3): 301–14.

Giles, H., R. W. Bourhis, N. J. Gadfield, G. J. Davies, and A. P. Davies. 1996, first published 1976. Cognitive aspects of humor in social interaction: A model and some linguistic data. In A. J. Chapman and H. C. Foot (eds.), *Humor and laughter: Theory, research and applications.* New Brunswick, NJ: Transaction Publishers, 139–52.

Ginger, R. 1974. Ethnic jokes. In *Ray Ginger's jokebook about American history.* New York: New Viewpoints, 29–43.

Glanz, R. 1973. *The Jew in early American wit and graphic humor.* New York: KTAV Publishing House.

Goldman, A. 1971. *Ladies and gentlemen—Lenny Bruce!!* New York: Random House.

Gregory, D. 1964. *Nigger.* New York: E. P. Dutton.

Hampes, W. P. 1999. The relationship between humor and trust. *Humor: International Journal of Humor Research* 12 (3): 253–59.

Heilman, R. B. 1978. *The ways of the world: Comedy and society.* Seattle: University of Washington Press.

Holland, N. 1982. *Laughing: A psychology of humor.* Ithaca, NY: Cornell University Press.

Horowitz, S. 1997. *Queens of comedy.* Philadelphia: Gordon and Breach.

Hughes, L. 1957. *Simple stakes a claim.* New York: Rinehart.

Hughes, L., ed. 1966. *The book of Negro humor.* New York: Dodd, Mead.

Husband, C. 1977. The mass media and the functions of ethnic humor in a racist society. In A. Chapman and H. Foot (eds.), *It's a funny thing, humor.* London: Pergamon, 267–72.

Janeway, E. 1975. *Between myth and morning: Women awakening.* New York: William Morrow.

Jones, J. M., and H. V. Liverpool. 1996, first published 1976. Calypso humor in

Trinidad. In A. J. Chapman and H. C. Foot (eds.), *Humor and laughter: Theory, research and applications.* New Brunswick, NJ: Transaction Publishers, 259–86.

Juni, S., B. Katz, and M. Hamburger. 1996. Identification with aggression vs. turning against the self: An empirical study of turn-of-the-century European Jewish humor. *Current Psychology* 14 (4): 313–28.

Kantha, S. S. 1999. Sexual humor on Freud as expressed in limericks. *Humor: International Journal of Humor Research* 12 (3): 289–99.

Kaufman, S. J. 2001. *Modern hatreds: The symbolic politics of ethnic war.* Ithaca, NY: Cornell University Press.

Keith-Spiegel, P. 1972. Early conceptions of humor: Varieties and issues. In J. Goldstein and P. McGhee (eds.), *The psychology of humor.* New York: Academic Press.

Kelley, W. D. 1888. In T. A. Rice (ed.), *Reminiscences of Abraham Lincoln by distinguished men of his time.* New York: The North American Review, 286–87.

Kennedy, R. 2002. *Nigger: The strange career of a troublesome word.* New York: Pantheon Books.

Klages, M. 1992. What to do with Helen Keller jokes. In R. Barreca (ed.), *New perspectives on women and comedy.* Philadelphia: Gordon and Breach Science Publishers, 13–22.

Kofsky, F. 1974. *Lenny Bruce: The comedian as social critic and secular moralist.* New York: Monad Press and Pathfinder Press.

Koller, M. R. 1988. *Humor and society: Explorations in the sociology of humor.* Houston: Cap and Gown.

Kong, D. 2003. Race humor still a balancing act. *CBS News.com.* Sept. 22, 14:41:37.

La Fave, L. 1977. Ethnic humor: From paradoxes towards principles. In A. J. Chapman and H. C. Foot (eds.), *It's a funny thing, humor.* London: Pergamon, 237–60.

La Fave, L., J. Haddad, and W. Maesen. 1996, first published 1976. Superiority, enhanced self-esteem, and perceived incongruity humor theory. In A. J. Chapman and H. C. Foot (eds.), *Humor and laughter: Theory, research and applications.* New Brunswick, NJ: Transaction Publishers, 78–91.

La Fave, L., and R. Mannell. 1976. Does ethnic humor serve prejudice? *Journal of Communication* 26 (3): 116–23.

Lee, J. Y. 2000. *Defining New Yorker humor.* Jackson: University of Mississippi Press.

Lefcourt, H. M. 1996. Perspective-taking humor and authoritarianism as predictors of anthropocentrism. *Humor: International Journal of Humor Research* 9 (1): 57–71.

Lefcourt, H. M. 2001. *Humor: The psychology of living buoyantly.* New York: Kluwer Academic/Plenum Publishers.

Lehman, K. M., K. L. Burke, R. Martin, J. Sultan, and D. R. Czech. 2001. A reformulation of the moderating effects of productive humor. *Humor: International Journal of Humor Research* 14 (2): 131–61.

Leveen, L. 1996. Only when I laugh: Textual dynamics of ethnic humor. *Melus* 21 (4): 29–55.

Levine, L. W. 1977. Black laughter. In *Black culture and black consciousness.* New York: Oxford University Press, 298–366.

Lincoln, K. 1993. *Ind'n humor: Bicultural play in native America.* New York: Oxford University Press.

Lipman, S. 1991. *Laughter in hell: The use of humor during the Holocaust.* Northvale, NJ: Jason Aronson.

Livingstone, M., and H. Marks with M. Borie. 1978. *Jack Benny.* Garden City, NY: Doubleday.

Lowe, J. 1986. Theories of ethnic humor: How to enter, laughing. *American Quarterly* 38 (3): 439–59.

Martin, L., and K. Seagrave. 1986. *Women in comedy: Funny ladies from the turn of the century to the present.* Seacacus, NJ: Citadel Trade.

Martin, R. A., and N. A. Kuiper. 1999. Daily occurrence of laughter: Relationships with age, gender and Type A personality. *Humor: International Journal of Humor Research* 12 (4): 355–84.

McGhee, P. E., and N. S. Duffey. 1983. Children's appreciation of humor victimizing different racial-ethnic groups. *Journal of Cross-Cultural Psychology* 14 (1): 29–40.

Mile, S. 1992. Roseanne Barr: Canned laughter—containing the subject. In R. Barreca (ed.), *New perspectives on women and comedy.* Philadelphia: Gordon and Breach Science Publishers, 24–38.

Miller, L. 2002. This is a headline for an essay about meta. *The New York Times Magazine*, Nov. 17, 22–28.

Mindess, H. 2001. Ethnic humor in America: A comparison of six major groups. Paper presented at the annual conference of the International Society for Humor Studies at the University of Maryland, July 6.

Mintz, L. E. 1996. Humor and ethnic stereotypes in vaudeville and burlesque. *Melus* 21 (4): 19–28.

Mintz, L. E. 1977. Jewish humor: A continuum of sources, motives and functions. *American Humor*, 4–22.

Mintz, L. E., ed. 1998. *Humor in America: A research guide to genres and topics.* Westport, CT: Greenwood Press.

Morreal, J. 1983. *Taking laughter seriously.* Albany: SUNY Press.

Mulkay, M. 1988. *On humor.* New York: Basil Blackwell.

Nachman, G. 2003. *Seriously funny: The rebel comedians of the 1950s and 1960s.* New York: Pantheon Books.

Nezlek, J. B., and P. Derks. 2001. Use of humor as a coping mechanism, psychological adjustment, and social interaction. *Humor: International Journal of Humor Research* 14 (4): 395–413.

Nilsen, D. L. F. 1993. *Humor scholarship: A research bibliography.* Westport, CT: Greenwood Press.

Nilsen, D.L.F., and A. P. Nilsen. 2000. *Encyclopedia of 20th century American humor.* Westport, CT: Greenwood Press.

Olson, J. M., G. R. Maio, and K. L. Hobden. 1999. The (null) effects of disparagement humor on stereotypes and attitudes. *Humor: International Journal of Humor Research* 12 (2): 195–219.

Olson, S. K. 1988. Standup comedy. In L. E. Mintz (ed.), *Humor in America: A research guide to genres and topics.* Westport, CT: Greenwood Press, 109–36.

Oring, E. 1992. *Jokes and their relations.* Lexington: University Press of Kentucky.

Oring, E. 2003. *Engaging humor.* Urbana: University of Illinois Press.

Oshima, K. 2000. Ethnic jokes and social function in Hawaii. *Humor: International Journal of Humor Research* 13 (1): 41–57.

Osofsky, G. 1969. *Puttin' on ole massa: The slave narratives of Henry Bibb, William Wells Brown, and Solomon Northrup.* New York: Harper and Row.

Pinsker, S. 1987. Lenny Bruce: Shpritzing the Goyim/shocking the Jews. In S. B. Cohen (ed.), *Jewish wry: Essays on Jewish humor.* Bloomington: Indiana University Press, 89–104.

Polio, H. R., and J. W. Edgerly. 1976. Comedians and comic style. In A. J. Chapman and H. C. Foot (eds.), *Humor and laughter: Theory, research and applications.* New Brunswick, NJ: Transaction Publishers, 215–42.

Provine, R. 2000. *Laughter.* New York: Penguin Putnam.

Pryor, R., with T. Gold. 1995. *Pryor convictions and other life sentences.* New York: Pantheon Books.

Roback, A. A. 1944. *Dictionary of international slurs.* Cambridge, MA: Science Art Publishers.

Schutz, C. E. 1989. The sociability of ethnic jokes. *Humor: International Journal of Humor Research* 2 (2): 165–77.

Spaulding, H. 1972. *Encyclopedia of black folklore and humor.* Middle Village, NY: Jonathan David Publishers.

Stengel, M. 2002. For Seinfeld in *Comedian*, stand-up is deadly serious business. *Time*, Nov. 4, 75–76.

Tate, G. 2003. *Everything but the burden: What white people are taking from black culture.* New York: Harlem Moon, Broadway Books.

Toll, R. 1974. *Blacking up: The minstrel show in 19th century America.* New York: Oxford University Press.

Turnbull, C. M. 1972. *The mountain people.* New York: Touchstone.

Unger, L. S. 1996. The potential for using humor in global advertising. *Humor: International Journal of Humor Research* 9 (2): 143–68.

Walker, N. 1988. *A very serious thing: Women's humor and American culture.* Minneapolis: University of Minnesota Press.

Watkins, M. 1994. *On the real side: A history of African American comedy.* New York: Simon and Schuster.

Welles, G. 1911. *Diary of Gideon Welles, vol. 1.* Boston and New York: Houghton Mifflin, 519–20.

Wilde, L. 1968. *The great comedians.* Secaucus, NJ: The Citadel Press.

Wilde, L. 1978. *The complete book of ethnic humor*. Los Angeles: Corwin Books.

Wynter, L. E. 2002. *American skin: Pop culture, big business, and the end of white America*. New York: Crown Publishers.

Yacowar, M. 1981. *Method in madness: The comic art of Mel Brooks*. New York: St. Martin's Press.

Zilberg, N. 1995. In-group humor of immigrants from the former Soviet Union to Israel. *Israeli Social Science Research* 10 (1): 1–22.

Ziv, A. 1984. *Personality and sense of humor*. New York: Springer Publishing.

Ziv, A. 1988. *National styles of humor*. Westport, CT: Greenwood Press.

Ziv, A. 1998. *Jewish humor*. New Brunswick, NJ: Transaction Publishers.

Index

Japanese Americans, 125
Japanese stereotypes, 54–55
Jefferson, Thomas, 5
Jeffersons, The, 97
Jewish American Princesses (JAPs), 101–2, 113–15
Jewish humor: "Americanization" of, 89; in-group, 37, 76, 87, 158; Lenny Bruce and, 71–80; levels of meaning in, 89–90; root, 82–90, 98–99; self-critical, 89–90, 99; women and, 113–14
Jewish Mother stereotype, 113–15
Jews: definitions of, 4–5; dominant role of in comedy, 65–80; Eastern European, 83, 85, 113–14; ethnic slurs on, 32, 47–49; oppression of, 82–83; prejudice and, 66–67; stereotyping of, 84–87, 127
Jim Crow Rice, 92
Johnson, Caryn Elaine. *See* Goldberg, Whoopi
Jokers, 40
Jokes: about joking, 124; airline, 123–24; computer, 124; "conditional," 18; Irish, 34; most frequent themes of, 20; Polish, 33–34; redneck, 61; rural, 34; shared, and group cohesion, 40–41, 159–60; stupid, 32–34. *See also* African American humor; Ethnic humor; Gender humor; Jewish humor
Jokes and Their Relation to the Unconscious (Freud), 19
Jones, James, 62
"Jose Jiminez" (character), 142–43
Juba, 92

Kantha, Sachi Sri: *Sexual Humor on Freud as Expressed in Limericks,* 22
Kaufman, Andy, 132, 144
Keaton, Buster, 15
Keillor, Garrison, 55, 150
Keith, Benjamin, 85–86

Keith-Spiegel, Patricia, 14–15
Kennedy, Randall, 53, 152; *Nigger,* 48
Kersands, Billy, 94
Kierkegaard, Soren, 16
"Kike," origins of, 48–49
"Kikes on bikes," 53
King, Alan, 5, 145
Kinky Friedman and the Jewboys, 52
Kirby, George, 96
Klein, Robert, 140
Kofsky, Frank, 78
Koller, Marvin, 38
Komoidia, 7
Kong, Deborah, *Race Humor Still a Balancing Act,* 153
Koyemci, 7
Kronenberger, Louis, 1
Kubelsky, Meyer, 87

La Cucaracha (comic strip), 153
La Fave, Lawrence, 135
Lahr, Bert, 134
Lake Wobegon, 55
Lane, Juba, 93
Last, Laugh, The (Berger), 136
Last Temptation of Christ, The, 128
Latin Kings of Comedy, The, 150
Laugh-In, 68
Laughing gas, 14
Laughter: babies and, 15; causes of, 13–23; nervous, 19; as reflexive, spontaneous response, 21; tickling and, 14
Laughter in Hell (Lipman), 37
Laurel and Hardy, 130
Lawrence, Martin, 158
Lear, Norman, 133
Learning: behaviorist and social theories of, 152; cognitive theory and, 153
Lee, Judith, *Defining New York Humor,* 10
Lee, Spike, 99
Lefcourt, Herbert, 24
Lehrer, Tom, 71
Letterman, David, 116

ship, 53; African Americans and, 32, 47–48, 52; cool reaction to, 126; defined, 46; within groups, 45–46; HBO and, 140; homosexuals and, 115; Italian Americans and, 49; Jews and, 32, 47–49; on mainstream values, 33; origins and psychology of, 45–54; ridicule of, 80; turned into positive statements, 52–53; white Americans and, 33, 49

Smits, Jimmy, 158
Social change and humor, 66–67
Social class differences, 158–60
Social context of humor, 39–42
Social learning theory, 152
Social status and humor, 16, 41, 104; women and, 108
Social testing and humor, 40
Socrates, 7–8
Sopranos, The, 127
Stand-up comedy: rapid growth of, 139–40. *See also* Comedians
Steinem, Gloria, 109
Step'n Fetchit stereotype, 99
Stereotypes: African American, 91–94, 99, 120, 127–28; in America, 58–62; of Americans, 122–23; Australian, 57; behaviorist theory and, 152; benign, 54–55, 128; conflict over significance of, 120, 127–28; cool reaction to, 126; critical deconstruction of, 155; defined, 54; double-bind pattern of, 94; ethnic characters and, 142–44; female, 103, 109, 112–15; French, 57–58; Hispanic, 127; international, 55–56; Israeli, 58; Italian, 58; Japanese, 54–55; Jewish, 84–87, 101–2, 127; Minnesota, 55, 61; racism and, 127–28; regional, 56; ridicule of, 80, 96–97, 105, 108, 122, 154; roots of, 151; stereotypes about, 56–57; vaudeville and, 86. *See also* Ethnic humor
Structure of ethnic humor, 37–38, 56
Study of humor: difficulty of, 3–4; im-

portance of, 8–10; sociological focus to, 39–42

Stupid jokes, 32–34
Success and comedians, 135–39, 148; "wrecked by" syndrome, 139
Suffering and humor, 2–3
Sullivan, John Florence. *See* Allen, Fred
Summers, Shirley Feldman, 26
Superiority theory, 15–16, 35, 50, 84, 103, 108
Supreme Court, ruling on obscene language, 52
Surprise theory, 17
Sword and shield metaphor, 1–2, 154–55

Taking Laughter Seriously (Morreal), 22–23
Tanguay, Eva, 111
Techniques, comic, 143–47
Tension: breakdown of by comedians, 122; and humor, 6, 19–20, 38, 50, 160; passive aggressive behavior and, 83
That Nigger's Crazy, 78
Theories about humor, 13–23; ambivalence, 17–18; cognitive, 18–19; early efforts, 14; incongruity, 16–17, 22, 105, 146; John Morreal and, 22–23; psychoanalytic, 19–22; release and relief, 19–20, 38, 50, 83; superiority, 15–16, 50, 84, 108; surprise, 17, 22; triumph, 15
Tickling, 14
Tillie's Punctured Romance, 111
Timing of comedians, 144–46
Tomlin, Lily, 111, 134–35, 143
"Top the topper" technique, 145
"Transcendence" and Jewish humor, 89–90
Transformation of ethnicity, 79–80, 119–28; Robin Williams and, 121
Transracial culture, 120–21

About the Author

LEON RAPPOPORT is Professor Emeritus of Psychology at Kansas State University. A prolific author of many research articles, review essays, and book chapters, he has also published books on personality, decision making, psychohistory, and the Holocaust. His current work in humor is based on several years spent researching and teaching classes about the significance of ethnic, racial, and gender humor at Kansas State University.